CICERO

OTHER TITLES FROM BLOOMSBURY

Reading Cicero: Genre and Performance in Late Republican Rome,
C. E. W. Steel
978-0-7156-3279-6

Cicero and Rome, David Taylor
978-1-8539-9506-4

Cicero and the End of the Roman Republic, Thomas Wiedemann
978-1-8539-9193-6

Cicero: A Portrait, Elizabeth Rawson
978-0-8629-2051-7

Cicero
Politics and Persuasion in Ancient Rome

Kathryn Tempest

Bloomsbury Academic
An imprint of Bloomsbury Publishing Plc

B L O O M S B U R Y
LONDON · OXFORD · NEW YORK · NEW DELHI · SYDNEY

Bloomsbury Academic

An imprint of Bloomsbury Publishing Plc

50 Bedford Square   1385 Broadway
London   New York
WC1B 3DP   NY 10018
UK   USA

www.bloomsbury.com

Bloomsbury is a registered trade mark of Bloomsbury Publishing Plc

First published in 2011 by the Continuum International Publishing Group Ltd
This edition published by Bloomsbury Academic, 2014
Reprinted 2016 (twice)

British Library Cataloguing-in-Publication Data
A catalogue record for this book is available from the British Library.

ISBN: PB: 978-1-4725-3056-1
ePub: 978-1-4411-3226-0
ePDF: 978-1-4411-5482-8

Library of Congress Cataloging-in-Publication Data
Tempest, Kathryn, author.
Cicero : politics and persuasion in ancient Rome / Kathryn Tempest.
pages cm
Includes bibliographical references and index.
Originally published: London ; New York : Continuum, 2011.
ISBN 978-1-4725-3056-1 (pbk.) – ISBN 978-1-84725-246-3 (hardback) – ISBN
978-1-4411-3226-0 (epub) – ISBN 978-1-4411-5482-8 (epdf)
1. Cicero, Marcus Tullius. 2. Statesmen–Rome–Biography. 3. Rome–History-
-Republic, 265-30 B.C. I. Title.
DG260.C5T46 2014
937'.05092–dc23
2013039567

Typeset by Pindar NZ, Auckland, New Zealand
Printed and bound in Great Britain

Contents

Maps and Illustrations

MAPS

ILLUSTRATIONS

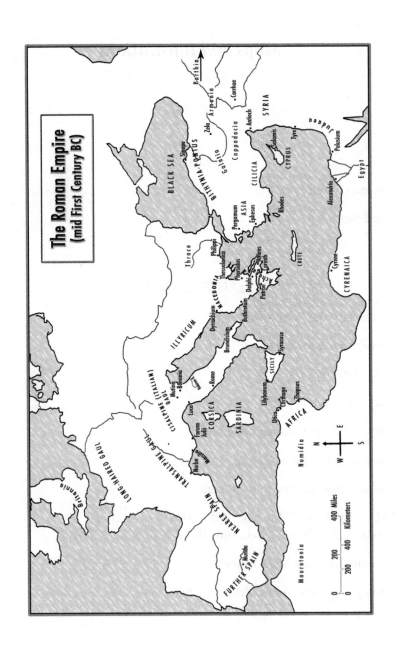

The Roman Empire
(mid First Century BC)

Italy &
Sicily

PROVINCE OF
CISALPINE GAUL

VIA AURELIA

Mutina
Bononia

VIA AEMILIA

ILLYRICUM

Luca Pistoria
Pisae Faesulae Ariminum
Arno R.

Arretium

ETRURIA

PICENUM

Tiber R.

VIA FLAMINIA

Ameria

Corfinium

Rome Tiber
Tusculum
Frascati
Alba
Antium
Astura

LATIUM

Arpinum

SAMNIUM

ADRIATIC SEA

Formiae
Suessa
Cumae
Baiae
Puteoli
Misenum
Naples

Capua

CAMPANIA

Pompeii

VIA APPIA

Brundisium

TYRRHENIAN SEA

LUCANIA

Tarentum

CALABRIA

Key
Cicero's known villas are
shown in *italics*.

Vibo

BRUTTIUM

Lilybaeum Mt. Eryx

Messana

Rhegium

PROVINCE OF
SICILY

IONIAN
SEA

Leontini
Syracuse

0 20 40 60 80 100   English Miles
0 20 40 60 80 100   Roman Miles

Chronologies

The following chronologies list both the principal dates and major events in Roman history as well as the more specific details of Cicero's life. Cicero's main works are given in italics and are listed by either their date of delivery (for speeches) or composition (for major works or compositions). Where known, the results of forensic trials are given in brackets, based with only minor deviations on the evidence presented by Powell and Paterson (2004, 416–22). All dates are BC unless otherwise stated.

GENERAL CHRONOLOGY

753	Traditional date for the foundation of Rome by Romulus.
753–510	Period of the Kings, ending in the expulsion of Tarquinius Superbus.
510–264	Early Republic: including the struggle of the orders between patrician and plebeian families (494–440); Roman expansion in Italy (340–264).
264–133	Middle Republic: including the first Punic war and the acquisition of Rome's first overseas provinces (264–241); the second Punic war and Hannibal's invasion of Italy (218–202); the third Punic war, ending in the destruction of Carthage and the fall of Corinth (149–146).
133–31	Late Republic.

CHRONOLOGY OF THE LATE REPUBLIC
AND CICERO'S LIFE

133	Tribunate and death of Tiberius Gracchus.
123–122	Gaius Gracchus holds the tribunate twice and is murdered.
107	Marius elected consul.
106	Cicero born (3 January); Pompey born (29 September).
104–100	Marius holds five successive consulships.
102	(or perhaps 104) Cicero's brother Quintus born.
100	(or perhaps 102) Caesar born (13 July); a year of unrest and riots at Rome, including the murder of the tribune Saturninus.
90s	Cicero educated at Rome in the house of Lucius Licinius Crassus; later continues his studies with Scaevola the augur (?91).
91–88	Social war; Cicero serves under Gnaeus Pompeius (89) and Sulla (88); Italians win Roman citizenship.
88	Sulla first marches on Rome.
87–86	Marius and Cinna occupy Rome (87); Marius' seventh consulship and death (86); domination of Cinna (until 84).
87–83	Sulla in the East; first war against Mithridates.
?86	Cicero composes a rhetorical treatise, *On Invention*.
83–81	Second war against Mithridates.
82	Sulla marches on Rome for a second time and is made dictator (82–81); proscriptions (82 to 1 June 81).
81	Sulla's reforms, including establishment of seven permanent criminal law courts with senatorial juries; senate strengthened (numbers increased to 600); rights of the tribunes dramatically curtailed. Cicero delivers his first surviving oration in a civil trial, *For Quinctius* (result unknown, probably unsuccessful).
80	Cicero's first appearance in a criminal trial: *For Roscius of Ameria* (successful).
79–77	Cicero marries Terentia (exact date uncertain) and travels abroad; travels to Athens for six months and then studies with Apollonius Molo.
78	Sulla dies.
?78	Cicero's daughter Tullia born.
75	Cicero (aged 30) becomes quaestor in western Sicily; henceforward a member of the senate.
73–71	Spartacus' slave revolt; Verres governor of Sicily.

70   Joint consulship of Pompey and Crassus; restoration of the
       tribunate.
       Prosecution of Verres and the *Verrine Orations*, including the
       *Divinatio Against Caecilius, First Hearing (Actio Prima) Against
       Verres* and the *Second Hearing (Actio Secunda) Against Verres*
       (all successful); staffing of the juries transformed and split
       between senators, equestrians and treasurers.

69   Cicero (aged 36) becomes plebeian aedile; defends first
       senatorial client in *For Fonteius* (probably successful).

68   The extant *Letters to Atticus* begin.

67   The Gabinian law gives Pompey an extraordinary command
       against the pirates.

66   Cicero (aged 39) becomes praetor in charge of the extortion
       court; delivers his first political oration, *On the Command
       of Pompey (On the Manilian Law)*, which gives Pompey the
       command over Mithridates. Continues his forensic activity
       with the speech *For Cluentius* (almost certainly successful).

65   Cicero's son Marcus born; Cicero speaks *For Cornelius*
       (successful) and *On the Egyptian Kingdom* (only fragments
       survive).

64   Cicero's campaign for the consulship; attacks Catiline and
       Antonius in *Speech whilst a Candidate (In the White Toga)*.

63   Cicero (aged 42) obtains the consulship; the Catilinarian
       conspiracy and the execution of five of the conspirators
       (5 December); during the year Cicero delivers speeches *On the
       Agrarian Law*; *For Gaius Rabirius on a Charge of Treason* (trial
       abandoned); *Against Catiline*; *For Murena* (successful).

62   Catiline defeated and killed; further trials of alleged
       conspirators, including Cicero's defence *For Sulla* (successful);
       Clodius' intrusion of the *Bona Dea* festival; Pompey returns
       from the East. Cicero's *Letters to Friends* begin; they cover the
       period from January 62 to July 43.

61   Cicero provides testimony against Clodius in the *Bona Dea*
       trial; Clodius acquitted.

61–58 Quintus governing Asia, Cicero's *Letters to his Brother Quintus*
       begin, and continue through to 54 BC.

60   Cicero writes a poem *On His Consulship* and publishes a
       collection of the speeches he delivered in 63.

59	Domination of Rome by Pompey, Crassus and Caesar (the so-called 'first triumvirate') begins; Clodius adopted into a plebeian family.
58	Clodius' tribunate and the exile of Cicero.
58–57	Cicero's exile and return (4 September). He delivers speeches *On His Return to the Senate*; *On His Return to the People* and *On His House* (successful).
56	Cicero speaks *For Sestius* (successful) and ferociously cross-examines the witness in a speech *Against Vatinius*; also delivers a defence speech *For Caelius* (successful). Conference at Luca; Cicero forced to submit to the triumvirs.
55	Cicero begins philosophical and rhetorical works: *On the Orator* (finished 55); On *the Republic* (published 51); *On the Laws* (circulated posthumously).
54–53	Cicero unwillingly takes on several cases, including the defences of Vatinius and Gabinius. Weakening of triumviral alliance: death of Julia (54); death of Crassus at Carrhae (53); Cicero elected onto board of augurs (53/52).
54–52	Quintus legate to Caesar in Gaul.
52	Clodius killed by Milo (18 January) and Cicero's defence *For Milo* (unsuccessful). Further trials of men involved in the gangs of Milo and Clodius take place, including Cicero's second, and last ever, prosecution of T. Munatius Plancus Bursa (successful).
51–50	Cicero governor of Cilicia, accompanied by his son Marcus, the two Quinti and freedman Tiro.
49	Outbreak of civil war between Caesar and Pompey. Many leading senators evacuate from Rome; Pompey crosses to Greece (17 March); Caesar visits Cicero (28 March); Cicero crosses to Greece (7 June) where he serves under Pompey but is taken ill.
48	Pompey defeated at Pharsalus (9 August) and later murdered in Egypt (28 September); Cicero returns to Italy and forced to wait at Brundisium.
47	Cicero pardoned by Caesar (September) and allowed to return to Rome.

46   Cicero and Terentia divorced; Tullia and Dolabella divorced;
      Cicero has an ongoing quarrel with the Quinti. Pompeians
      defeated at battle of Thapsus (Cato commits suicide); Cicero
      delivers speeches and works for the recall of Pompeians,
      including *For Marcellus* and *For Ligarius* (successful) before
      resuming his philosophical and rhetorical works: *Brutus*,
      Stoic Paradoxes; *Cato*; *The Orator*; *Classification (Divisions) of
      Oratory*.

45   Final Pompeians defeated at Munda in Spain (17 March).
      Death of Tullia, shortly after the birth of her son (1 April) who
      also died. Cicero composes *Consolation*; *Hortensius*; *Academic
      Questions*; *On Ends*; *Tusculan Disputations*.

44   Assassination of Julius Caesar (15 March); Octavian named
      as his heir; Cicero leaves Rome (June) and continues writing:
      On the Nature of the Gods; *On Divination*; *On Fate*; *On Old
      Age*; *On Glory*; *On Friendship*; and later, the *Topics*. Antony
      attacks Cicero in the senate (1 September) and Cicero replies
      (2 September: the *First Philippic*): their enmity begins and
      Cicero leaves Rome until November. In the meantime, he
      composes the *Second Philippic* and *On Duties*. On his return
      to Rome, Cicero delivers the *Third Philippic* and the *Fourth
      Philippic* (20 December).

43   Consulship of Hirtius and Pansa and the outbreak of civil war.
      Cicero delivers the remaining extant *Philippics* (the *Fifth* to the
      Fourteenth), with the result that Antony is declared a public
      enemy (26 April). Cicero's *Letters to Marcus Brutus* are all dated
      between March/April and July 43. Octavian occupies Rome
      and assumes the consulship (August); formation of the 'second
      triumvirate' (November); proscriptions; Cicero murdered
      (7 December).

42   Battle of Philippi; deaths of Brutus, Cassius and the remaining
      republican forces (except Sextus Pompeius).

39   Sextus Pompeius pacified (later killed in 35); Marcus Cicero
      the Younger pardoned by the triumvirs.

31   Battle of Actium.

30   Consulship of Marcus Tullius Cicero (the Younger); deaths of
      Antony and Cleopatra.

27   Octavian 'restores' the Republic and assumes the name
      Augustus.

AD 14   Death of Augustus.

Acknowledgements

I am grateful to many people for their patience, support and encouragement during the completion of this work. Stephanie Gomm, Charlotte Behr, Gesine Manuwald, Jonathan Powell, Antonio Cartolano, Raj Sehgal, Rosemary Barrow and Ryan Timoney all generously read and commented on various chapters, in large or small chunks. I should like to thank Paul Pritchett-Brown for his huge assistance in editing the maps and illustrations, and Hannah Swithinbank for the photographs of Rome used in this book. I am indebted, as always, to friends and colleagues who also work on Cicero, especially to Jonathan Powell, Henriette van der Blom, Gesine Manuwald and Lynn Fotheringham, whose conversations and guidance have helped shape the way I think about his works. In addition, the regular Cicero awaydays, organized by colleagues at Glasgow, Edinburgh, St Andrew's and Newcastle, have been a great source of inspiration over the years.

The present book is distantly based on lectures I have given both to students at Roehampton University as well as to audiences at various schools, colleges, INSET days and schoolteacher conferences. In particular, I have been motivated and encouraged by the regular invitations to present at the ARLT (Association for Latin Teaching) Summer School and the feedback I have received there. I am grateful to all of these for the chance to test my material on fresh ears, and for the stimulus of having to present my research on Cicero in an entertaining and succinct manner. And in this connection, I also owe a huge debt of gratitude to Michael Greenwood, both for his invitation to write this book and for his encouragement throughout its completion.

Finally, I must single out a group of people whose support of all kinds has made this work possible: Mary and Derek Tempest, Vicki Craig, and Stephanie Gomm – to all of whom this book is dedicated.

To Mum, Dad, Vicki and Stephanie

Prologue

A Master of Words and a Patriot

MARCUS TULLIUS CICERO (106–43 BC)

A portrait bust of Cicero in later life.

On 7 December 43 BC, Marcus Tullius Cicero – Rome's greatest orator, leading politician and defender of the Roman Republic – was hunted down and murdered on the orders of a man he had staunchly opposed: Marcus Antonius (better known as Mark Antony). Cicero's death was inevitable and he knew it; resolved at first to hide, then to escape, he finally faced it head on. He was making his way along a shady woodland path near his coastal villa at Formiae when he heard his assassins approaching. He was intending to board ship and leave Italy, maybe forever, but he ordered his slaves to stop and put down the litter – the sedan chair – on which they were carrying him. And when his murderers finally caught up with him, Cicero clasped his chin with his left hand and stretched out his neck for them to slit his throat. As proof of the deed, they cut off his head and his hands, and now Cicero's ghastly remains made an undignified journey back to Rome.

According to the historian Cassius Dio, Mark Antony took a morbid delight in looking at the heads of men he had slain. But Cicero's head was more precious than most. Even Mark Antony's wife, Fulvia, was famously supposed to have spat and cursed at it, before taking the head into her lap. There, she ripped out Cicero's tongue and stabbed it time and time again with a pin taken from her hair. Afterwards, on Mark Antony's orders, Cicero's head and hands were carried into the forum of Rome, where they were nailed to the *rostra* – the speaker's platform – for all to see in the thriving hub of Rome's market-place.[1]

It is a sign of the turbulent times in which he lived that Cicero was not the first, or last, Roman to be brutally murdered and decapitated. Even so, the story that spread about Cicero's courageous stance in the last moments of his life made him at once heroic, brave and exemplary. However, these are not words that were at the time, or have been since, used of the rest of Cicero's life. His death has been viewed almost unanimously – by ancient and modern historians alike – as Cicero's finest hour, yet judgements on the rest of his achievements have varied extensively. Let us begin by examining the cause and nature of these mixed reactions.

JUDGING CICERO

Many years after the death of Cicero, Augustus Caesar went to see one of his grandsons. The boy was holding a book of Cicero's in his hands. He was terrified and he tried to hide it in his cloak. Seeing this, Caesar took the book, stood there and read a great part of it. Then he handed the book back to his grandson and said: 'He was a master of words, my child, a master of words and a patriot.'[2]

In this way, the Greek historian Plutarch draws his account of Cicero's life to a close: he puts into the mouth of the Emperor Augustus (who had acquiesced in Cicero's murder), the flattering and fitting memorial to Cicero that he died as a master of words and a patriot. But history has remembered Cicero as much more than this. From successful statesman to political failure, from philosopher to poet, and as a man of letters and a scholar, reactions to Cicero have been as diverse as the angles from which we can approach his life and times; the sources documenting his life provide us with an exceptional glimpse into the thoughts and actions of a man who lived in an age that can be deceptively similar, but which was essentially very different, to the times of those who study him.

It has often been said that we know more about Cicero than about any other ancient Roman, thanks largely to the number of his own publications. During the sixty-three years of his life, Cicero delivered a great number of speeches: fifty-eight of these can still be read today but, according to the last count, we know of at least eighty-eight further speeches that have either been lost or which he did not publish. Cicero was also a copious letter-writer and more than eight hundred of the private letters he wrote, plus about ninety that were sent to him, have survived. In addition to his speeches and letters, Cicero published a number of works on rhetoric, politics, religion and philosophy, most of which we still have. And, finally, he was a keen poet, although we possess only a few, relatively brief extracts of his compositions.

Cicero's self-promotion, coupled with his unfaltering productivity as a writer, accounts for the majority of our knowledge about him. Yet this fact has not always played to his advantage. Seneca the Younger, a Roman writer living in the time of the Emperor Nero, wrote that Cicero praised his own achievements 'not without cause but without end'.[3] Indeed, he was obsessed with his own posthumous reputation: 'What will history think of me in a thousand years from now?' he once asked his friend Atticus.[4] Yet, more than two thousand years have passed and he is still being judged.

Very often the response has been unfair and unfavourable. His vain pursuit of glory has not won Cicero many friends among his modern readers; his desire for fame, praise and recognition for his achievements betrays a man who was obsessed with the idea of his own self-importance. But it mattered to a Roman that he was well thought of: his position among his peers depended, in large, upon his reputation. His lasting fame, or *gloria*, was as important to Cicero as it was to any man of high ambition. That he went too far in lauding his own achievements is beyond doubt, but that he did so at all was not unique.

The problem for Cicero is that, by the sheer variety and the nature of his published works, he is exposed, warts and all, as a human being with traits that we might not appreciate and flaws which we can easily criticize. One of the central paradoxes in studying him is that some of the scholars who have worked hardest to promote Cicero's life and works have simultaneously led the campaign in his character assassination. From his letters, in particular, Cicero emerges as erratic, fickle, insincere and shallow. If he is valued at all by such critics, it is for the light he sheds on the period of history known as the Late Republic (c.133–31 BC), a particularly bloody and stormy period in Rome's past. In these letters, as in his other works, Cicero provides a commentary to the events of his day, and he sketches fascinating portraits of his famous contemporaries: men like the dictator Sulla, the military conqueror Pompey, and the renowned Julius Caesar.

Cicero's works are of immeasurable value to anyone studying his life and times; yet they simultaneously make the task of the historian even harder. Personal likes and dislikes, which stem from values appropriate to modern political life, should be locked away before approaching an historical character. At the same time, it is necessary to be sensitive to what the evidence actually tells us about Cicero's character, and to divorce this from the pressing needs of his own times.

As an orator, Cicero delivered his many speeches in the law courts, in the senate house and at the *rostra* in the forum, from where he addressed the people of Rome on matters of foreign and domestic policy. He was both a politician and a lawyer, and we need to remember this before criticizing him too scathingly if he contradicts himself in words and actions. As a lawyer, we can be reassured that Cicero was not malicious, insofar as he considered it inhumane to prosecute innocent men – and, indeed, we know of only two prosecutions by Cicero during his whole career. Yet his actions in defending men who were either his friends or political allies are more complex, for he did not need to believe in their innocence, nor was he afraid to turn a blind eye to their guilt.

Cicero famously boasted that he 'shrouded the jury in darkness' after he secured the acquittal of a man called Cluentius, who was accused of poisoning his stepfather.[5] Whether or not this implies Cicero thought Cluentius was guilty of the entire charge is not clear; but we do know – from Cicero's own words – that he believed it was occasionally justifiable to defend a guilty man 'provided he was not a wicked and impious man'.[6] His frank approval of defending the guilty has raised eyebrows among Cicero's critics; however, it should be noted that his principles were not dissimilar to modern-day legal practice, where everyone has a right to be represented, and lawyers are often obliged to take on cases that fall within their field of expertise. Cicero was not bound by a legal code of conduct such as we have today, but he was bound by the traditional expectation that every citizen should have access to a patron. Furthermore, it mattered to Cicero that he protected patriotic men – men, he believed, who were useful either to himself personally or to the Republic. We may question his decisions, but they must be read within the context of a society whose lawyers were also its politicians.

Cicero's reputation as a politician has been harmed by the fact he was frequently on the losing side. Often his political beliefs have been seen as short-sighted. And he has been criticized for not developing any effective solutions to the pressing needs of his times. Yet he was not, and nor did he ever openly claim to be, the ideal statesman: this was a topic he reserved for his famous treatise *On the Republic*. But, in practice, he fought for his principles and his belief in the republican government (which is more than can be said for many of his contemporaries). Furthermore, even if we admit that his political foresight was limited, there were few, if any, men at Rome who demonstrated that they had the antidote to cure Rome's troubles. Even Caesar, who many might argue came closest to finding a way out, ultimately failed to unite a divided and dysfunctional system.

Furthermore, in his political dealings with other men of rank, Cicero at times appears fickle: one minute he fawns over Pompey, the next over Caesar. His private correspondence reveals a level of distrust of them both, and others like them, but Cicero needed the support of his peers in order to safeguard his own career and aspirations. He did not have to like the men with whom he co-operated; nor did he always have to co-operate with the same men: political alliances at Rome lasted only as long as each man needed the other. As we shall see in the following chapters, without the advantages of power, wealth and birth, which were necessary to succeed and win support from the aristocratic élite as well as the ordinary people of Rome, Cicero needed to play the political game adeptly. What too often goes unnoticed is the extent to which this level of flattery was reciprocated: in 50 BC when Rome was on the brink of the civil war between Pompey and Caesar, no other man was courted as much as Cicero was by the two combatants.

Finally, the criticism of Cicero results from our impressions of him as a man, in a way that none of his contemporaries has been, or can be, assessed. For after Cicero's death, Tiro – his friend, secretary and former slave – collected and published the remains of the correspondence we still possess today. It is clear that towards the end of his life, Cicero had envisaged that *some* of his letters should be made public. But what is important to remember is that they are essentially the private letters of a man who corresponded with his friends, family and acquaintances throughout both the triumphant and the turbulent periods of his life; during these times, in particular, he emerges either to blow his own trumpet or to wallow in the depths of his despair.

Cicero himself once remarked on the dangers that lay hidden in private letters: 'How many jokes are often found in letters which – if they were made public – would fall flat! How many serious thoughts there are which should never be divulged!'[7] Yet the snapshots that Cicero's letters provide – especially the frankest ones sent to his close friend Atticus – are all the more devastating for the fact they nearly all belong to the last twenty years of Cicero's life (63–43 BC). These were years in which his political ambition and former prestige were under constant challenge; that is to say, they belong to the years that scholars normally describe in terms of Cicero's failure and defeat. He does not always come across as we would like to have imagined him otherwise. And it is his letters, more than any of his other works, which have prompted adverse or, at best, mixed reactions. To take one example, Petrarch, an Italian scholar of the fourteenth century, read them, and he felt 'charmed and offended in equal measure'.[8] It is only fair to say that, when we read them today, we should remember the invasion we are making into his life, thoughts and moods. The letters sometimes reveal a side of Cicero which their author would have rather concealed.

How, then, should we judge Cicero? To start with, it should be noted that the evidence provided by Cicero himself does not present a complete picture. There is much in his life that the letters do not make known, and it is equally difficult to extrapolate fact from fiction in his other works. His political and legal speeches were deliberately published by Cicero after the occasion of their delivery – both to enhance his reputation and to put his side of events on the record. And his philosophical works were often largely written in dialogue form, with the result that Cicero's own opinion – if he had just one – is at times hard to determine.

The effect all this has on our assessment and reaction towards Cicero cannot be underestimated: his personality, as it emerges from his writings, speeches and especially his letters, has aroused and continues to arouse strong emotions. There is a huge mass of evidence from which to select, and the process of selection inevitably produces wildly different reactions, triggered by the biographer's own response to the subject. At various times and for various reasons, therefore, Cicero's popularity and prestige have either waxed or waned. In short, as one historian has pointed out: 'The verdicts will tell us more about the judges than about the judged.'[9]

Accordingly, it is not my intention to persuade the reader to like Cicero as a person, or to admire his political thoughts and actions, but rather to understand him, to appreciate his works and hopefully even to challenge the traditional obstacles, described above, facing anyone who studies Cicero in depth. Above all, I hope to demonstrate that Cicero – the man, politician and author – remains a valuable and exciting topic of study.

With this objective in mind, I have largely avoided engaging in the extensive debate that surrounds much of what I say; for those wanting to know more, notes and a bibliography are provided which will point the way to further study. Instead, the narrative which follows is given, as far as possible, as a unified presentation of my own views, which are driven by the conviction that Cicero was – as the Emperor Augustus described him – a master of words and a patriot. But it will also argue that a careful reading of Cicero's works can reveal something substantial about what motivated Cicero to behave the way he did, and how and why he achieved a predominant role in a political system that was, as we shall see, fiercely competitive.

The story of Cicero is, in many ways, also the story of the later Roman Republic. His life coincided almost exactly with the last six decades of this period in Roman history. To understand him, we must also consider how he viewed both the political climate at Rome and his role within it. And so, the first chapter will begin by tracing in broad outline the world into which Cicero was born, to explain how the Republic – his cherished ideal – functioned, and to understand the problems facing the society of his day. Chapter 2 will then continue the theme of Cicero's childhood and education, from his birth in Arpinum, which marked him as something of a political outsider, to the family's arrival at Rome. By examining the role of rhetoric and oratory at Rome, this chapter will also demonstrate why Cicero's skills in public speaking were to pave the way in his path to success – as well as how they helped him jump the hurdles facing him on the way there. The rest of this book will then continue in chronological order, departing only to provide essential background information to the events, places or people introduced. It will take us through the highs and lows of Cicero's career to explain how he became one of Rome's most wanted men on that fateful December day of 43 BC, for as far as possible looking at events through the narrow perspective of Cicero's eyes – but forever mindful of the fact that this picture is far from rounded.

1

The Senate and the People of Rome

THE BIRTH OF THE REPUBLIC

So, in those earlier times the senate administered the state in the following way: though the people were free, little public business was done by them; most of it was done on the authority of the senate, according to established precedent. The consuls held a level of power which was by nature and law equivalent to that of kings, but it was limited in length to one year. And what contributed most of all to the continuation of the aristocracy's power was this: the tradition was persistently observed that decisions reached in the people's assembly would not be endorsed if they had not met the approval of the senate.

(Cicero, *On the Republic* 2.56)

Throughout his life, Cicero remained a staunch supporter of the republican ideals he describes in the quotation above. Power over the city, its finances and campaigns was concentrated in the hands of the few: the aristocratic men that formed the backbone of the senate. To ensure that no one man ever held too much power in Rome, the magistrates who advised and directed the senate were elected annually. These men were the consuls of Rome, and there were two of them so that each could perform a check on the other.

The name given to this form of government was the 'Republic' from the Latin words *res publica*, which literally means 'the public business'. In many contexts the term Republic simply translates into 'government' or 'state', but the republican form of government was more than this: it was an ideal cherished by Romans up to, during, and for many years, after Cicero's lifetime. Its vast influence can still be seen scattered around the remains of the Roman Empire today; for the inscription SPQR is found on many street corners, buildings or milestones. It stands for *Senatus Populusque Romanus*: the 'senate and the people of Rome', and this is how Rome conceived of her power. Though neither element was independent from or equal to the other, the Roman Republic was a blend of aristocratic and democratic elements.

Before this, Rome had been governed by a monarchy. According to legend,

Senatus Populusque Romanus (Photograph © Hannah Swithinbank).

the first king of Rome was Romulus, who founded the city after competing against and murdering his brother Remus for the leading position. The period of kings (dated by the Romans to 753–510 BC) brought many benefits to Rome: it established the citizen classes and civil offices; religious rites, festivals and priesthoods were all introduced; and Rome began to expand over and absorb her neighbouring tribes. However, their reign was marked by cruelty and bloodshed, which led to a long-standing fear of the title *rex*: the Latin word for king. The final king, Tarquinius Superbus ('the Proud'), epitomized everything the Romans hated about monarchical power. He abolished some of the earlier constitutional reforms, and his tyrannical rule was characterized by violence and murder. The final straw came when his son, Sextius, raped a lady of noble birth and marriage called Lucretia. The Roman writer Livy records the event in his work *The History of Rome*. The result was that the Tarquin family were cast out of Rome, and her citizens vowed never again to suffer the rule of a king.

Thereafter the government was concentrated in the hands of the aristocratic families (the so-called 'patricians'), and the kings were replaced by two consuls, who received advice from the senate. The solution of the Republic did not erase Rome's political problems overnight. The period of the Early Republic (c.509–264 BC) was fraught with internal struggles, and its problems now were mainly due to the two-class system that had emerged. The patricians, who were the aristocrats, dominated the plebeian class, which was composed of peasants, farmers and craftsmen. But not all plebeians were poor, and those who had accumulated wealth through trade and farming led the fight for recognition and protection from the Roman élite.

As a result of what historians call the 'struggle of the orders', the plebeians gradually gained more of a say in the running of Rome's government. By the end of the Early Republic, they had their own plebeian assembly in which to convene, officers to represent them (called the 'tribunes of the plebs'), and the right to pass laws that were binding over the whole population (*plebiscita*). In reality, however, the concessions made to the plebeian class did not affect the everyday running of the Roman government. The men who had taken a stand against the aristocracy had been the wealthy members of the plebeian class, and they sought little more than recognition and a share in the élite's privileges. And so, essentially, the power was still in the hands of the wealthier members of society, but that now included a mixture of patricians and plebeians.

What was important about the Republic, according to Cicero, was that the tribunes who looked after the people remained respectful of the senate's authority. With the initial strife of the early period averted, the Republic functioned as a robust and tightly knit organization, and its leaders were regarded with great respect. The overwhelming prestige of the senate – termed *auctoritas* by the Romans – meant that its policies were implemented. This was the heyday of the Middle Republic (c.264–133 BC): the senate and the people of Rome united successfully to overcome armies and wars as great as those presented by the Carthaginians and Macedonians.

The Greek historian Polybius, who lived during these times, was amazed at the extent of Rome's military and political success; the two were always connected in ancient Rome. The Punic wars waged against Carthage and the Macedonian wars, fought against Alexander the Great's successors, had been pivotal in Rome's rapid expansion. But for Polybius the key to Rome's power seemed to rest in her constitution: 'Can any man be so indifferent or so idle,' he asked, 'that he would not want to know how and under what kind of government almost the whole inhabited world fell under the single rule of the Romans in less than fifty-three years?'[1]

The fifty-three years Polybius had in mind spanned from the beginning of the second Punic war to the end of the third Macedonian war (220–167 BC). By the end of this time, Rome had become so wealthy that her citizens no longer had to pay any personal taxes. And further changes had also taken place in the way power over the city was distributed, for other officials were gradually introduced in addition to the consuls: the quaestors, aediles and praetors. These men were the magistrates of Rome – responsible for her financial, social and legal welfare – and they all held power for just one year at a time. They were lower in rank to the consuls, but the 'ladder of offices' from the quaestorship to consulship, called the *cursus honorum* in Latin, offered a career path for Rome's most ambitious politicians, which still existed in Cicero's day.

It is important to remember that election onto the ladder of offices lay in the hands of the people – that is, the collective body of male citizens over the age of seventeen. This was one of the ways in which they contributed towards the political processes of the Republic. They also had the ability to enact laws and to act as a kind of law court, for every Roman citizen had the right of appeal before the people if he faced a capital sentence. Indeed, the people's power was such that Cicero once said that the '*res publica* was the *res populi*': in other words, the Republic was the property of the people.[2] This was something of an exaggeration, for their political independence was limited by the fact people could only take action on matters proposed to them by the senatorial magistrates. However, the people's role was not without influence, and politicians did not get far without their support.

Yet at the heart of the republican institutions there was the senate. In theory it was only an advisory body, but in practice its influence was vast, for all the men who had served as magistrates could go on to become members of the senate for life; it was Rome's only permanent political organ. Furthermore, provided that individual magistrates did not accrue too much personal power, the senate's role in the government of Rome was beyond challenge. On the whole, in the heyday of the Republic, the senators were supportive of each other both in their election for and in the conduct of office. While the senate itself was a permanent constituent, membership to this prestigious body was monitored by senior magistrates known as censors, who could expel men for moral lapses. In addition, the whole structure of the ladder of offices was designed to prevent any man from gaining an extended period of individual power.

Broadly, then, to return to Polybius, he saw that the government of the Republic was a mixed constitution comprised of the best elements of a monarchy, an aristocracy and a democracy – the system also favoured by Cicero. The annually elected consuls held the power equivalent to a monarchy, the senate formed the aristocracy, and the democratic element was the people, who were represented by the ten annually elected tribunes. In the sixth book of his *Histories*, Polybius explains the many ways in which each element served to check and be checked by the other. This led to a complex system that protected the rights and the power both of the people and their politicians. Yet, for as long as Rome remained a small and cohesive city-state, this system and its political institutions worked: the magistrates governed responsibly, Rome's leaders provided an able military force and the people did not protest.

As Rome expanded, however, her relationship with her Italian allies, coupled with the control she now had to exert over her subjects, raised issues with which Rome grappled throughout the late second and first centuries BC. To understand

Cicero's life and times, this rift in the political life of Rome requires explanation. Rome's growth, the great influx of wealth and the struggle between the classes – which was capitalized upon by power-hungry politicians – all contributed to the eventual fall of the Roman Republic and the emergence of the emperors. Before we consider the decline of the Republic and the world into which Cicero was born, it is first necessary to survey in brief the rise of Rome's wealth and power.

EXPANSION AND DECLINE

By 146 BC – forty years before Cicero was born – most of the Mediterranean world had come under Roman control. The shape of the Roman world had changed dramatically from its origins under Romulus and Remus, when men lived the 'life of shepherds' and 'depended on the labour of their hands', according to the picture painted by one ancient writer.[3] Rome's expansion had begun across the Italian peninsula spreading from the plains of Latium, in which she lay, to the neighbouring tribes of the other Italic people. By the middle of the second century BC, the map of Italy was a pastiche of communities who were under differing levels of Roman control: not all had full Latin rights but all were controlled by Rome, and they supplied men to fight in her campaigns.

Dispersed among the Italian communities were the colonies. These colonies were settlements of citizens, mostly veteran soldiers, who served as a security measure to protect against invading forces and help maintain Roman control. Some of the Italian communities were even absorbed into the Roman state, and their natives enjoyed the full privileges of citizenship, including the right to vote. Cicero later praised the Romans' policy and generosity in sharing their citizenship. In a speech delivered in 56 BC, he attributed this to the foresight of Romulus: 'Without any doubt, what above all founded our empire and increased the Roman people's name,' he claimed, 'was that our leader, the creator of this city, when he made a pact with the Sabines, taught us that we should increase this state by welcoming even those who had been our enemies; because of his authority and example, our ancestors never let the opportunity of granting and sharing their citizenship pass.'[4]

We should be careful not to attribute foresight to early Roman policy, for the case of the Sabines hardly illustrates Roman generosity and wisdom: instead, the Roman men, lacking wives, had initiated hostilities with their neighbours when they kidnapped their women and took them into their own homes. This particular quotation shows how Roman history could be glorified in the course of an oration. But Cicero's appreciation of the extension of Roman citizenship would have been genuine enough, for his own home town, Arpinum, had been granted full Roman citizenship in 188 BC. Indeed, in his treatise *On the Laws*, Cicero tells us that his grandfather even enjoyed a position of authority in Arpinum, which brought the family into close contact with Rome's leading politicians at an early stage.

As Rome continued her expansion across Italy, she gained control over southern Italy and this, in turn, brought her into contact with foreign foes. The two dominant superpowers of the times were the Carthaginians to her west and the Hellenistic kingdoms to her east, which had once been under the power of Alexander the Great. It was these campaigns, as we have seen, which lay behind the conflicts between Rome and her first major battles: the Punic and the Macedonian wars. These campaigns were long and protracted but, as a result of her successes, Rome began to acquire provinces abroad to add to her expanding power base.

In addition to the province of Africa that Rome created from the ruins around Carthage (roughly modern Tunisia), she acquired Sicily, Sardinia, Corsica and Spain (which she divided into two provinces: Nearer Spain and Further Spain). And from her campaigns over the Hellenistic kingdoms of the Greek East, Rome had gained control of Macedonia (including Greece) and Illyria (former Yugoslavia). Rome's conquest of both the eastern and western territories was further increased in 133 BC, when she acquired Pergamum in the rich province of Asia. Rome had achieved a political unity that mighty conquerors like Alexander the Great had dreamed about: in a short space of time she had become a world power.

Latin writers, including Cicero in his third book *On the Republic*, often idealize Rome's expansion. Indeed, Rome's initial conquests could to some extent be justified by the need to secure frontiers, protect allies and support trade. However, the appetite for wealth, power and glory in these years was hard to suppress. And what is important is the effect expansion had on the world into which Cicero was born, for the expansion in Rome's geographical empire was rapidly met by a decline in her internal political prosperity. The date 133 BC is traditionally seen as the beginning of the end for the Roman Republic, as it precipitated over a century of civil wars, violence and bloodshed. This is the period of the Late Republic, which arguably ended in 31 BC, when Octavian – the future Emperor Augustus – defeated the only man left challenging his domination: Mark Antony.

THE LATE REPUBLIC

It has often been noted that Cicero would have preferred to have been born a hundred years earlier, when the mixed constitution was at the peak of its success. Instead, writing a century after Polybius, he looked upon the Republic of his day as a 'magnificent picture now fading with age'.[5] Not only its original colours, Cicero complained, but even its basic form and outlines had changed beyond recognition. Furthermore, the cause of its decline was the men of his generation – men who had failed to preserve the customs of their elders (the *mos maiorum*) – for as the empire expanded, and the divide between the classes increased, the power of the senate fell under constant challenge in the period of the Late Republic (c.133–31 BC).

By 133 BC, the Romans dominated the Italian peninsula as well as the provinces mentioned above. This meant that Rome took on the burden of defending and fortifying her new territories, but she accumulated a lot of wealth in return. Tributes were exacted, great profits were accrued by the tax collectors, and the trade which accompanied Rome's territorial growth opened new opportunities for her businessmen. At the same time, plunder, slaves and confiscated lands all followed from her military conquests. These lands were made available for anyone wealthy enough to farm them, and Rome's senatorial class, the landed gentry, consequently took great advantage both of the vacant pastures and of the increased slave labour available to toil in them.

However, Rome's expansion did not bring a fair share of benefits to the rich and poor alike. In fact, the results were disastrous for the Roman and Italian peasants, who could not compete with the volume or variety of produce generated by these great estates. Many were displaced from their lands, and without their farms they were disqualified from serving in the army. This meant that the poorer men could no longer take a share in the spoils that Rome's wars bore, but the army too was suffering: the peasant class that had formed the bulk of her manpower was quickly decreasing. Instead, huge numbers of unemployed, impoverished and fiercely unhappy men flocked to the city in the hope of survival.

In 133 BC a tribune of the plebs, Tiberius Gracchus, saw these problems, and desperate times called for desperate measures. There was a need for some kind of reform, and Tiberius sought to introduce legislation redistributing the public land among the poor. However, his actions set a dangerous precedent for future generations. It all started when Tiberius broke with tradition. He realized that the tribunate offered a legal way around the traditional authority of the senate: the tribunes could take bills – to be passed as laws – directly to the people. Therefore, although he was a member of Rome's aristocracy himself, this is exactly what he did. We do not know what motivated him most – social reform, the quest for personal power, the unemployment, the army or other factors – but, intentionally or not, he had caused a revolution at Rome. From Tiberius' time on, the crowd played a crucial role as certain politicians courted popular opinion and support in their personal pursuits of power and reform.

Cicero later observed that the tribunate of Tiberius Gracchus, as well as his violent murder, 'divided a single body into two camps'.[6] The cherished ideal of the unity between the senate and the people of Rome was rapidly descending into a political nightmare of strife and discord: a tug-of-war between politicians, who claimed to act either in defence of the senate's authority or of the people's rights. The people's role, once limited, became lethal, provided that there was a man powerful and daring enough to speak against the senate's wishes. In the last years of the Republic, there were plenty such men and they championed causes which appealed to the common people: land redistributions, subsidies on the cost of grain, and special military commands for their favourite generals. It was a dangerous precedent to set, but perhaps Tiberius would not have needed to act in this way had the senators of his day not been quite so obstinate or corrupt.

Ancient writers offer a number of reasons explaining why Rome's expansion brought about the decline of both her society and the republican constitution. Some believed that it was Rome's contact with the East that exposed her people to luxuries which the Romans then copied and craved. Another idea suggests that the freedom from the threat of foreign invasions led to, or revived, internal power struggles. More recently, historians have argued that a significant reason for the fall of the Republic appears to be that Rome outgrew the form of government which had only ever been established for a small city-state. Rome had become the supreme power in the Mediterranean, yet the organization of power had not been changed to encompass her geographical development.[7]

Furthermore, the mixed constitution of the Roman Republic required the co-operation of all three of its constituents: the magistrates, the senate and the people of Rome could only function for as long as they each supported the other. But as Rome expanded, as we have seen, the divide between these groups deepened. And there were politicians ever ready to seize upon the opportunities this divide in society presented in order to promote their own prestige and power.

One area in which expansion certainly created a desire for power can be seen in Roman provincial administration. In her earlier conquests over the Italian tribes, Rome had granted citizenship or alliances to the territories she had acquired. However, this was not a suitable means of governing lands abroad, which were too far away to be under the controlling eye of the government at Rome. Instead, the management of the provinces fell to members of the senatorial class who had reached the praetorian and consular ranks on the ladder of offices. After their year in office at Rome, these men governed the provinces for a year as a proconsul or propraetor depending upon the post they had just held at Rome. Under a responsible governor, this system could work well. But it also opened the eyes of individuals to a power base beyond the confines of the senate. In their provinces, supported by junior colleagues and staff of their choice, governors held a larger amount of power and a greater degree of licence than they had ever enjoyed at Rome. This in turn had a negative effect on the political order at Rome, for individual senators and the political factions in which they grouped conceived of personal glory and a power above the collective authority of the senate.

Personal power was further obtained from military commands, with the result that the army became a major factor in Rome's political upheaval. For in the years of Cicero's infancy, at the end of the second century BC, the general and consul Gaius Marius reorganized the whole nature and composition of the army. Rather than the body of short-term conscripts which had existed before, the army was now composed of long-term professional fighters. What was of crucial importance was that these men pledged their allegiance to their general and not to the state. But they also depended on their leader to provide for them after their period of military service was over, for it was mainly the poorer citizens who signed up as soldiers, and they needed land and money upon their retirement.

These problems persisted throughout Cicero's time. Armies fought for their leaders, even if it meant engaging in civil wars. And their leaders fought to fulfil the promises of land and booty they had made to their soldiers. To this end, the competition for the best campaigns became ruthless and bitter. In his youth, as we shall see, Cicero was forced to witness Rome's first civil war between Marius and Sulla, in which the armies fought for their commander's personal power and dignity over the welfare of their country. Later too, Pompey and Caesar used their armies to settle political scores, while the civilian government buckled entirely in the face of the battle between Octavian and Antony.

The competition among the senatorial élite was the most destructive force in the unity of their order. However, the delicate political balance was further offset by the growing influence of a third rank of men: the equestrian order, which formed an increasingly powerful middle class in between the very rich and the very poor. Some equestrians – like Cicero – did progress into the senate. But others preferred to take advantage of the wealth they could accrue in business, for senators were forbidden by law to engage in trade and commerce. Landowning and farming were respectable occupations for the senators; however, it was considered beneath them to perform a service for others. The equestrians, on the other hand, had ample prospects for self-enrichment, and it was not long until they found that money also provided them with their own political leverage.

There were many industries opened up to the equestrians owing largely to the fact that Rome lacked a civil service or public body to manage her affairs. It was privatization on a massive scale, and men could become hugely rich by collecting taxes, lending money at high interest rates, as well as from general trades such as the slave trade or the import and export of luxury goods. When Gaius Gracchus – Tiberius' younger brother and tribune of the plebs in 123/122 BC – gave the equestrians the right to collect taxes in the new and lucrative province of Asia, he gave them a huge bounty. But it was not an act of pure generosity; he saw the political force that their support could offer against the dominant factions in the senate. By these acts and more, he knew that he had paved the way for further conflict: according to Cicero, 'Gaius Gracchus claimed he had thrown daggers into the forum to make the citizens fight like gladiators'.[8]

The conflicts and violence generated by the tribunates of the Gracchi brothers had not been quenched by the time Cicero was born. As we shall see in the following chapters, the revolution was to resume more fiercely in the years of his childhood, only to be fought more ferociously in his adulthood. Cicero was not only an eyewitness but also a key participant in these events, for oratory became an increasingly potent tool in the political processes of Rome, as the co-operation of the previous century turned instead towards counteraction and obstruction. The strife that arose between Rome and her allies, Rome and her provinces, the internal discord between her classes, and the competitions among her élite demonstrate clearly the power that a persuasive orator could accrue in the last years of the Republic. A politician could not expect to advance far without the power of persuasion.

Yet a politician could not expect to sit on the sidelines either, for the Romans' pride in their country, traditions and achievements was deep-rooted. The men calling for change challenged the traditional system, and criticized the monopoly of Rome's leading families. Their concerns were justified, yet their methods were often radical and destructive; some of the most dominant personalities in Cicero's lifetime – men like Pompey, Crassus and Caesar – were also the leaders of great armies, and their power launched an attack against the central tenet of republicanism, which prevented one man from having too much control at Rome.

For a conservative like Cicero, the changes brought about by these leaders represented a threat to the ideals of the old days: liberty and the freedom from monarchy. It was an ideal for which many, including Cicero, considered worth dying. As he stared into the demise of the Republic, less than a year before his own death, Cicero boldly declared that he had always acted – and would continue to act – as the champion of the Republic: 'I defended the Republic as a young man; I shall not desert her now I am old man . . . What is more, I would offer this body gladly, if in dying I might leave the Roman people free.'[9] When the chance came to live up to these words, Cicero did not back down.

2

The Making of the Man (106–82 BC)

WHAT'S IN A NAME?

The first of the family to be surnamed Cicero seems to have been worthy of report, which is why those who came after him did not reject the surname but embraced it, although it was derided by many. For the Latins call the chickpea *cicer,* and that man had, it appears, a slight nick in the end of his nose like the cleft of a chickpea, from which he obtained his surname. When, however, Cicero himself, about whom this book has been written, was first seeking office and tackling a political career, and his friends thought that he ought to shun the name and change it, he is said to have replied with youthful spirit that he would strive to make the name more famous than names like Scaurus and Catulus.

(Plutarch, *Cicero* 1.3–5)

Cicero does not tell us much about the early part of his life. Yet references scattered among the pages of Cicero's works, the personal letters he exchanged, and the biography of the Greek historian Plutarch, enable us to draw a fairly clear outline. The story of Cicero's upbringing and education has been pieced together many times, but it is essential for our understanding of Cicero's aspirations and success to examine how his early years laid the foundations for his political and oratorical career.

Marcus Tullius Cicero was born 3 January 106 BC. Like most Roman citizen-men he had three names. His first name (*praenomen*), Marcus, would only be used by his closest friends and family. His family name (*nomen*), Tullius, served to identify the wider family to which he belonged. This was also the name used in its feminine form (Tullia) to name his daughter. But it was his last name (*cognomen*), Cicero, by which he became famous. In Roman times the *cognomen* was like a nickname that passed down through the generations; in the examples cited by Plutarch above, Scaurus means 'swollen-ankled' while Catulus means 'puppy-dog'. Other men received their names in reference to qualities or achievements they either possessed or had earned. For example, the *cognomen* 'Magnus' ('Great') was given to the famous general Pompey for his accomplishments in battle. As Plutarch tells us, Cicero was advised to change his name but he was strangely proud of it, declaring that he would make the name as illustrious as any in Roman history – and he did. For by 63 BC, Cicero was at the top of his political game and he had reached the consulship.

Yet Cicero's dramatic rise through the Roman political system and his outstanding career as an orator was not without its struggles. To succeed in Rome a man needed the right family and a substantial fortune. By Cicero's time, the original distinction between the patricians and the plebeians was not as important as it once had been; but it *was* important that a man was descended from one of the noble families (the *nobiles*). These families – so-called from the Latin word *nobilis*, meaning well known or distinguished – were famous on account of their ancestry. They could point to at least one man, and often many more, in their direct family line who had been a consul before them.

The possession of nobility was a great advantage in politics, and the fortunate families jealously guarded the power which they regarded as their birthright. The main means of maintaining their authority included political alliances called 'friendships' (*amicitiae*), which were often very personal in nature. Marriage was often used to cement these alliances, and the production of legitimate children subsequently created another generation through whom the power was passed. If a man did not have any children of his own, he might adopt a male heir. It was not adoption as we think of it: the men had often reached adulthood by the time they entered another man's family.

Another central way to preserve a family's political importance was the patron–client system that lay at the heart of Roman society. Richer men (patrons) offered financial, legal or military protection to poorer men (their clients). In return the clients performed a number of services, including voting and canvassing for their patron or their patron's friends. Large troops of clients inevitably made a substantial contribution to a man's network of political supporters. And a man who did not have such a ready-made support base, either among the nobility or the voting populace, subsequently had to work harder to create one.

At the beginning of his career Cicero lacked these credentials. He was what was called a 'new man' (a *novus homo*). Although it was possible for new men to break into the ranks of the senate, they did not often progress much further up the ladder of offices than the first rank of the quaestorship. Furthermore, Cicero was not born in Rome but in a small town about 70 miles away, called Arpinum (now Arpino). Arpinum had been granted the full Roman franchise in 188 BC, which meant that its citizens were classed as citizens of Rome; indeed, by Cicero's time, Arpinum was thoroughly Romanized in its language and culture. However, these two factors – his ancestry and birthplace – bore heavily upon Cicero at various times in his career, especially when he confronted men from more distinguished families.[1]

That is not to say that Cicero's own ancestry was bad; in fact, he had a very priviliged upbringing. Attempts to trace Cicero's lineage back to Attius Tullus, a king of the Volscian territory surrounding Arpinum, are unlikely. At the same time, rumours that his father had been born and bred in a fullery can be dismissed as humorous slander. For the business of fulling was a disreputable career, washing clothes, as the Romans did, in urine and sulphur. Such jokes at a man's origins formed part of the stock-in-trade of Roman political abuse (called invective by modern scholars). There may have been a fullery on the family's estate, but it certainly did not provide their means of living.

Cicero's own self-presentation as a man from a respectable well-to-do family is the true picture. Little is known about his mother, Helvia, except that she was a thrifty housewife apparently of good birth and morals. Cicero's father was an educated man, who immersed himself in literature and learning rather than engaging in politics, but there is some indication that poor health was the reason for his political inactivity. Yet, despite his own avoidance of political life, the elder Cicero – 'a most excellent and intelligent father' – saw and nurtured the potential in his two sons: Marcus and his younger brother, Quintus.[2] He wanted them to succeed in achieving the rank from which his health had held him back, and the elder Cicero thought carefully about his sons' education.

BACKGROUND AND EARLY EDUCATION

Cicero's childhood and early years were spent in both Arpinum and Rome. Throughout his life he remained very fond of his birthplace: a small country house, which had initially belonged to his grandfather. However, by the time Cicero inherited it, the estate had been renovated and improved by his father. The journey from Rome to Arpinum typically took two or three days, but Cicero often retreated there when he needed an escape from the daily toils and strains of urban life. He loved Arpinum as much as he loved Rome, and he considered them equally as his homelands.

The house itself lay in a broad valley several miles outside the actual town so that it offered plenty of shade and tranquillity. When Cicero describes his home in one of his dialogues, On the Laws, he paints an idyllic picture: cool streams lapped the green and shady riverbanks. Poplar trees lined these banks, and there was an ancient oak tree which contributed to the natural beauty of the surroundings. In a letter to Atticus, written later in life, Cicero used a quotation from Homer's The Odyssey to describe how he felt about Arpinum: 'A rough land but it breeds good men; as for me, I can see no sight sweeter than my home.'[3]

Cicero's earliest years were spent in the family home, where his education would have been conducted under the supervision of his parents and nurses. While we know very little about this period of his life, we can imagine that it followed the stages of childhood development outlined in his work *On the Ends*. According to Cicero, after infancy, children learned to stand upright, use their hands and recognize their peers. They played games, became curious and delighted in listening to stories. A later Roman writer, Tacitus, dismissed some of the stories told to children by their nurses as 'rubbish tales'.[4] But this was probably an unfair criticism. For, in addition to moralizing fables, many of the Roman stories provided examples of good and bad behaviour through the deeds of men (and even some women), who had benefitted or betrayed their country. More important, listening to stories also helped train a boy's memory – a tool that later proved essential in Cicero's oratorical career.

Interestingly, Cicero believed that this was also the stage when children became competitive with their peers, and we know that this was certainly true of Cicero. In a letter to his brother Quintus, Cicero once wrote that his favourite motto from boyhood was a Homeric line: 'Far to excel, surpassing all the rest.'[5] Yet this kind of competitive spirit was not limited to Cicero himself; many Romans had the same desire to 'surpass the rest' – and it serves us well to remember that Cicero was not unique in this respect. In short, Cicero's description of the stages of childhood helps us some way towards an understanding of the formation of his own character from birth to the age of seven – as well as towards a more general appreciation of the qualities deemed necessary in anyone hoping to become a high-ranking Roman citizen.

After the age of seven, boys started on a curriculum which progressed through three levels of education, represented by the elementary teacher (*magister ludi*), the grammarian (*grammaticus*) and the rhetorician (*rhetor*), roughly following a pattern which had been developed by the Greeks several centuries earlier. In the elementary stages a Roman boy learned reading, writing and some basic mathematics before studying literature and language under the *grammaticus*. Typically, the secondary education took place between the ages of twelve and fifteen, but boys progressed through the three stages according to ability rather than age.

Again, Cicero tells us very little about these years. However, it was to equip his sons with this kind of traditional education that, sometime in the 90s BC, the elder Cicero moved his family to Rome. If we are to believe Plutarch, Cicero was a star pupil at school. He loved every form of literature and he was especially fond of poetry. This was a pastime that stayed with him as an adult, but even as a boy Cicero composed his own poems. Writing over a hundred years after Cicero's death, Plutarch claimed that a poem called *The Sea-God Glaucus* – written by Cicero when he was just fourteen years old – was still in circulation. And Plutarch believed that Cicero's ability was later enough for him to be regarded as one of Rome's best poets, even though there were many who mocked Cicero's compositions in his lifetime.

It was in his school years that Cicero also met his lifelong friend Titus

Pomponius, who was later called by the *cognomen* Atticus ('the Athenian'), which he earned from his love for Greece. Cornelius Nepos, who was both the friend and biographer of Atticus, provides some further clues about the boys' education. He states that Atticus was educated in all the arts, and these included the liberal arts – geometry, music and astronomy – which were taught alongside grammar and rhetoric. Furthermore, from the number of times that Cicero quotes Homer's epic poems, *The Iliad* and *The Odyssey*, in his letters to Atticus, it is clear that they must have studied these works intensively in their school years. Alongside the Homeric poems, works of early Roman poetry would have been studied and read aloud from memory. Pronunciation was particularly developed under the *grammaticus*, and Nepos tells us that Atticus could recite Latin poetry as well as he recited Greek. This was true of Cicero also. As anecdotes and events in his later life reveal, he could speak in Greek as fluently as any native speaker.[6]

By Cicero's time, almost the whole Roman education system was geared towards producing good speakers. Memory and delivery were two of the criteria that Cicero later identified for the successful orator, and it is important that these skills were nurtured at a young age. The Romans also added knowledge of law to their educational system, and Cicero tells us that he had to learn the Twelve Tables – Rome's earliest code of law – off by heart as a boy. Therefore, these years were critical in laying the foundations for Cicero's later life as a legal advocate and politician.

Later, in 62 BC, when Cicero defended the poet Archias, who possibly taught him Greek literature at this early age, he claimed to remember the start of his oratorical career taking shape:

> For when I look back into the past as far as my memory will let me, and recall the earliest memories of my childhood, whenever I cast my mind back that far, it is *he* whom I see before me, as the man who first inspired me to take up and to pursue the course of these studies [i.e. oratory and rhetoric].[7]

There may be some overstatement in the role that Archias himself played, but it is likely that a number of stimuli did indeed fuel Cicero's ambition in his early years. For in 107 BC – the year before Cicero's birth – another new man from Arpinum, Gaius Marius, had just been made the consul of Rome. He was no political genius, but his military success in saving Rome from two barbarian invasions cancelled out his ferocity and other shortfalls in the memory of successive generations. More important, the fact that he had risen through the ranks and achieved the position that he went on to hold a further (unprecedented) six times must have set Arpinum alight with pride and excitement. Local men of aristocratic families, like the Tullii Cicerones, who had powerful contacts in Rome, may now have had their eyes opened to the very real possibilities of a high-flying career at the hub of the Roman Empire.

For men, like Cicero, who had no desire to pursue a military career, the example of Marius was an unlikely role model. However, several years before Marius' time, Marcus Aemilius Scaurus had demonstrated that political ability could also be rewarded with distinction. While Scaurus was not a new man, his earlier family had been shamed and removed from the senate so that – in the words of an ancient commentator – 'he had to work as hard as any new man'.[8] And he did so effectively, for he reached the consulship in 115 BC. It was in this year that Scaurus met Cicero's grandfather, and his early personal contact with the Cicero family may go some way towards explaining why Cicero saw Scaurus as a model for his later political strategy. But in his early years – or so Cicero claimed – the example of Scaurus fired him with the hope that hard work, virtue and constancy might bring him the glory he so desired.

To this end, Cicero's father sought to provide his sons with the skills and the personal contacts they needed to be successful in life. This is the stage of his education which Cicero does feel worthy of record, and it begins shortly before the time when he assumed the toga of manhood (the *toga virilis*). This was an event of great significance, which normally took place on or around a boy's sixteenth birthday. He cut his youthful locks, shaved his facial hair and abandoned the lucky charm (the *bulla*) which he had worn from birth. More important, he exchanged the purple-banded toga, which he had worn as a boy, for the plain white toga worn by male citizens. It was at this ceremony that a boy became a man, and Cicero's time as a citizen of Rome could truly start to take shape.

RHETORIC AND ORATORY AT ROME

To be trained as a good orator, a young man had to study both rhetoric (the theory of speaking) and oratory (the performance of a speech). Neither of these were Roman inventions, for both aspects of public speaking – the theory and the practice – had enjoyed a fruitful life in the Athenian democracy of the late fifth and fourth centuries BC. As a result, Greek rhetorical handbooks and the published speeches of famed Attic orators formed a dominant backdrop to the Roman education system, and they exerted a heavy influence on Cicero throughout his life and career.

In his treatise on oratory, called *Brutus*, Cicero traces its origins back even further in time to Sicily, in the earlier part of the fifth century BC. The first practitioners were said to be Tisias and Corax, who saw the potential of arguing from probability. For example, if a small man attacked a large man and he had to defend himself in the courts, this argument was effective: 'Is it likely,' the small man could argue, 'that a man of my size would have attacked one of his size?'[9] The unlikelihood of a smaller man starting a fight with a larger one had the power to convince the jury, rightly or wrongly, that the defendant was probably not guilty of the charge against him. And it was not long before Tisias and Corax skilfully applied this simple means of persuasion to complex matters of litigation.

The art of oratory was subsequently believed to have been brought to main-land Greece, where it flourished under the Athenian democracy. Further means of persuasion were explored: how to appeal to the audience's emotions, how to use words and language creatively, and how to divide speeches powerfully. In short, speech became an instrument of persuasion, and so too of power. It is no wonder that rhetoric in the ancient world, as in the modern, was often regarded with suspicion.

The techniques and theory behind oratory continued to expand in different places across the Greek East long after the collapse of the Athenian democracy. Hellenistic schoolmasters systematized the theory of speaking, but the practical need for oratory did not die with the Athenian democracy. Rather, Hellenistic oratory flourished as the need for diplomatic embassies increased, and it was not long before Rome's expansion brought her into contact with Greek teachers and orators. The result, Cicero tells us, was that gradually Rome learned first to emulate and then rival the Greek art of oratory: 'When they had heard the Greek orators, got to know their literature, and had met their teachers, our men were fired by an incredible zeal for the art of speaking.'[10]

Here Cicero paints a rather rosy picture, for the Romans were initially distrust-ful of the sophisticated Greek culture. However, by Cicero's time, rhetoric and oratory were crucial for a rising politician. Many of Rome's most famous states-men made their name by speaking in the courts. These courts were held in the forum (the centre of all Roman activity) so that passers-by, as well as the senior members of the jury, formed a young man's audience. Furthermore, once a man had made his way onto the ladder of offices, his influence and rise through the ranks depended largely on his ability to give an effective oratorical performance: he needed to speak convincingly both in assembly meetings of the public and within the exclusive meetings of the senate. Accordingly, a young man's rhetorical education – the third and final stage in his curriculum – was of vital importance, and it consisted of a theoretical and a practical element.

Model speeches served to give guidance on what a good oration should look like, while the school exercises, called declamations, trained boys to argue on both sides of a given situation. For example, boys had to demonstrate that they could both praise a famous man and then blame him in another speech. Technical handbooks presented the theory of speaking, and they offered exhaustive instructions on how to invent, or rather find, the right argument for a given case (*inventio*), and how to arrange this material into a well-structured speech (*dispo-sitio*). However, the remaining tasks of the orator – eloquence (*elocutio*), memory (*memoria*) and delivery (*actio*) – had to be learned by practice and imitation.

Initially, Cicero the Elder's contacts at Rome made it possible for his sons to study at the house of Lucius Licinius Crassus, an ex-consul and highly influential member of society, who provided them with an exceptional start. An esteemed orator himself, Crassus oversaw Cicero's education and even questioned his teachers about the curriculum. In these years Cicero studied a range of subjects which he believed contributed to his success as an advocate. For, as he later observed in one of his treatises, the ideal orator 'must acquire the knowledge of a very great number of things'.[11] History, literature and philosophy all provided the material to 'educate, delight and sway' an audience, and these, in Cicero's words, were the three fundamental tasks of the orator.[12]

It was perhaps at this time that Cicero read Crassus' speeches. Indeed, he studied one of them so closely that he later described it as 'a sort of textbook' from his boyhood.[13] However, we can assume that Cicero's father often took the young Cicero into the forum to watch the great orators and statesmen in action – either in the open courts or in their addresses to the people. Crassus, by all accounts, was a rather static performer. But the other great orator of this period, Marcus Antonius, used the full range of gestures and actions to reinforce his orations. On one occasion Antonius even bared his client's scarred chest to the jury to remind them of the military services he had undertaken on Rome's behalf. Cicero watched Antonius in the courts, and he often questioned him on a number of subjects; between them, Crassus and Antonius had a profound impact on Cicero's rhetorical training.[14]

Cicero was not yet sixteen when Crassus died in 91 BC. However, through Crassus, Cicero's family were also acquainted with Quintus Mucius Scaevola Augur, an eminent legal expert. Now that he had retired from his distinguished political career, Scaevola was informally training a few promising students (despite his old age of eighty-four). And so Cicero joined them shortly after he had assumed the toga of manhood, so that he could build on his earlier studies in law.

His young 'pupils' used to assemble at Scaevola's house early in the morning to observe him giving legal advice to his clients. And Cicero, who had been instructed by his father never to leave the old man's side, also accompanied his mentor as he went about his daily business in the forum. He watched and listened as Scaevola discussed social and political issues with the great men of state; he was even privy to their natural conversations and exchanges. Cicero drew upon Scaevola's wisdom as much as possible and later, when Scaevola too died, he attached himself to his mentor's cousin, Quintus Mucius Scaevola Pontifex, to continue his studies.

In short, a general education in all the arts combined with rhetorical and legal training provided a sure and steady foundation upon which the student could build. His informal training with mentors broadened his horizons further by providing practical guidance in addition to the theoretical study he had undertaken.

For studying practical oratory, the young men watched famous and celebrated speakers presenting their cases in the forum to observe their delivery, gestures and overall performance. This was probably the most important part. Cicero says that when the famous Athenian orator Demosthenes was asked what the three key secrets of public speaking were, he replied: 'Delivery, Delivery, Delivery!'[15] Cicero frequented the forum on a daily basis to watch and listen to the leading orators of his day. But his own debut in the courts would have to wait another ten years, for Rome was in the grips of war and civil unrest.

A SOCIAL WAR AND A CIVIL WAR

As we saw in Chapter 1, the communities of Italy differed in their relationship to Rome, and by the time Cicero was fifteen, some of these allies had been clamouring unsuccessfully for a larger share in the benefits of Roman citizenship for many years. Frustrated by repeated attempts, they decided to revolt in what is known as the social war – from the Latin word *socii*, meaning allies. It started in 91 BC and, in the following year, Cicero was enlisted to fight against them. First, he fought under the consul Pompeius Strabo (father of the famous Pompey), then under Sulla. But this was the only military experience that Cicero gained in his early career; it was only forty years later that he again had to endure service, when he was forced to command troops as the governor of a province.

The social war was a rather pointless demonstration of obstinacy on the part of the Romans. They engaged in battle rather than grant the Italian communities the citizenship they requested. In the end, the Italians put up a greater fight than the Romans had anticipated and Rome backed down. As a result, the war was over by 88 BC and most of the Italian allies earned Roman citizenship. Cicero left the army to resume his education in Rome. However, he returned to a crisis, for the civil war between Marius and Sulla was going head-to-head in what proved to be a brutal and bloody episode in Roman history.

Tensions had been growing between the two men for many years; however, they came to a climax in 88 BC, when the newly appointed consul Sulla was about to lead a lucrative and prestigious campaign against Mithridates in the East. For one of the tribunes, Publius Sulpicius Rufus, stepped in and argued that the command should be transferred to Marius instead. This demonstrates one of the dangerous effects of the tribunes' power: the power to choose the commanders in war could be given to the people rather than the senate. And this abuse of the people's power was a problem that persisted throughout the struggles of Cicero's later career.

Cicero disapproved of Sulpicius' politics at the time, but he was greatly impressed by him as an orator. He lists Sulpicius among the orators whose public performances he followed in these years – even though he was later to reflect that many of the best men had been killed or were away from Rome. The result of Sulpicius' powerful orations, however, was disastrous. Sulla was stripped of the command against Mithridates, whereupon he became the first man in Roman history to march his army upon Rome, and he wrenched the power back from his startled opponents. Sulla rescinded the laws of Sulpicius, which had conferred the campaign against Mithridates upon Marius, and his opponents were branded as enemies: Sulpicius was executed, but Marius escaped and survived to fight another day.

Cicero – either for reasons of diplomacy or because of his dislike for military matters – is silent about his part in the civil war. But he certainly did not fight, and he stayed in Rome to continue his education as best he could. It was around this time in the 80s BC that Cicero composed his first rhetorical treatise: a work *On Invention* (the rhetorical art of 'finding' an argument). This work was not one of which Cicero was proud, for he later dismissed it as immature. Yet its survival today is hugely important for two main reasons. First, *On Invention* offers us a glimpse into the world of Cicero's early education and his rhetorical training. For in these books, Cicero systematically treats the parts of the speech, as well as presenting the complex rhetorical theory which guided an orator in his choice of argumentative strategy (*stasis* theory). Second, the work is important because, in his own words, Cicero shows the importance he attached to speaking well: 'From eloquence the state receives many benefits, so long as it is accompanied by wisdom – the guide of all human affairs; from eloquence, men can obtain glory, honour and dignity; from eloquence comes the surest and safest means of protecting your friends.'[16]

A political and legal career based on oratory was the goal which Cicero had set himself – to help the state and his friends respectively. However, in these years of civil war and unrest, the best Cicero could do was to engage in daily practice. If there was a positive outcome of the years in which Rome was at war in the East, it resided in the fact that there was an influx of Greek academics into the world of Rome, as they fled the troubles of their homelands. Leaders of the main contemporary philosophical disciplines – Stoicism and Epicureanism – together with Philo of Larissa, who had been the head of Plato's Academy in Athens, were among them. Cicero studied philosophy intensively and he often turned back to the subject later in life, both as a retreat and as an extension of his political activity. It also comforted him in moments of despair. Indeed, Cicero's use of philosophy as a distraction from the grim realities of life may have started in these years, for he later reflected that at that time 'the whole system of the courts seemed as if it had been abolished forever'.[17]

However, further bloodshed in Rome was not far away. In Sulla's absence, Marius returned to Rome with an army to seize his seventh consulship, taking

Lucius Cornelius Cinna as his partner. Fortunately, perhaps, Marius died less than three weeks into his term of office, but not before he had tracked down and killed many of his enemies, including the great orator Antonius. Several years later, Cinna too died – betrayed and killed by men from within his own ranks, whereupon Marius' son, Marius the Younger, took control of their faction, which was still dominating Roman political life.

When Sulla heard of Cinna's death, he returned from the East hot on the younger Marius' tracks. A fierce battle took place in 82 BC, from which Sulla emerged triumphant, but the younger Marius took his own life rather than face the brutality of his enemies. For, indeed, a devastating punishment awaited the Marians who had survived: Sulla outlawed them and put their names on 'proscription' lists. These lists derived their name from the Latin word *proscriptio* which simply meant 'putting up a notice', but Sulla's 'notices' were particularly shocking. They stated that any man who wanted could kill the 'proscribed' men with impunity; moreover, financial rewards offered an incentive to kill. It was legalized murder on a horrific scale. According to one source, at least sixteen hundred men were killed in this way, although the historian Orosius raised the death toll to nine thousand.

Sulla's actions were cruel in the extreme and Cicero was disgusted by the unjust ferocity of the proscriptions, but in the short term these methods were also effective. There was no longer anyone left to oppose Sulla in Rome, and he assumed the office of dictator for the purpose of restoring the republican constitution. This 'office' had not been used for many years, but it was essentially a safety valve for the Republic: in moments of crisis, one man could take supreme control for a specified period of time – up to a maximum of six months.

If we want to judge him by his motives rather than methods, it seems that ultimately Sulla sought to revive the failing Republic and to restore the senate to its place of authority. True, the years leading up to and including his dictatorship had witnessed bloodshed and devastation caused by men on both the Sullan and Marian sides. But the years of Sulla's rule did see some stability and order return to Rome after more than fifty years of political violence. He strengthened the senate and doubled its size from three hundred to six hundred men; at the same time, he also made the law courts greater in size and more efficient then they had ever been. As a result, in 82 BC, with the law courts beginning to function again, Cicero was ready and able to enter the world of oratory.

3

Climbing the Ladder of Offices (81–70 BC)

ENTERING THE FORUM

Laws and the law courts had been set in place. The Republic had been restored ... It was then, for the first time, that I began to plead both civil and criminal cases. For I had decided that I wanted to enter the forum not so much to learn my trade (as most men normally do), but, as far as possible, to enter the forum fully trained.

(Cicero, *Brutus* 311)

By 81 BC the face of Roman oratory had changed dramatically since the earliest days of Cicero's education. Many of the men whom he had admired in his youth had perished in the civil unrest. Crassus had died on the eve of the social war with the Italians. The other great orator, Antonius, had also perished under Marius' orders. But, despite the picture Cicero paints of an abandoned legal scene, he also adds that several lawsuits did take place during these years, and new orators rose to replace those who had been lost in the wars. Foremost among them was Quintus Hortensius Hortalus.

Hortensius represented a very new kind of oratory – a style of speaking that Cicero and his peers later labelled 'Asiatic' because of the Eastern influences which had been added to the traditional charm of classical Athenian (i.e. 'Attic') oratory. It was far more flamboyant and grandiose; as a result, it was only really considered suitable for a younger orator to speak in the Asianic way. At the same time, however, it was persuasive and forceful. On the back of this kind of oratory, and many other talents besides (not to mention a good deal of bribery), Hortensius had become Rome's leading orator. Cicero's description of him in *Brutus* is worth quoting at length, for it tells us much about what Cicero admired in an orator:

To begin with, he possessed a memory like I have never seen before: without the use of a script, he could deliver a speech in exactly the same words that he had prepared and jotted down in the privacy of his home. He was able to make such great use of this gift that he could remember off the top of his head not only what he had said (whether it had been written down only in note form or fully prepared), but even what his opponents had said. He was fired by such ambition that his devotion to his studies burned brighter than anything I have ever seen. He could not let one day pass without either speaking in the forum or practising outside it. More often than not he would do both on the same day. He brought a style of speaking to the forum that was quite unordinary; indeed, he was unique in two respects: first, he would divide up what he was going to say under headings and, second, he provided summaries of what had been said by his opponents. His choice of words was brilliant, he combined them skilfully and he expressed them abundantly: a result of his great talent coupled with the most rigorous training. He always knew his case off by heart and divided it sharply into parts; he almost never passed over anything in the case that could either strengthen his argument or refute that of his opponent.[1]

There is an agenda behind Cicero's praise written in 46 BC: by expanding upon Hortensius' abilities, Cicero, who supplanted him as Rome's best orator in 70 BC, was simultaneously magnifying his own talent. Yet there is doubtless still a large element of truth in the sketch of Hortensius it provides. It was against Hortensius that Cicero finally appeared (and probably lost) in a complicated suit in 81 BC. Hortensius was famous, experienced and thirty-three years old. The case was not Cicero's first, but it was his first major appearance.

Cicero clearly regarded his performance in this trial as worth recording; for he published a version of the speech he had delivered, *For Quinctius*. The trial revolved around a complicated business partnership between the defendant and his opponent, and Cicero's mastery of the legal technicalities in this speech clearly stands testament to his ambition, quoted at the beginning of this chapter, to enter the courts fully trained. At the same time, his decision to disseminate a written record of the speech shows the use Cicero made of this medium to advertise his name and build a reputation. And, although the speech itself has not won much favour among Cicero's modern critics, his strategy evidently worked: just a year later, he was asked to take on the case which launched the beginning of his career – the defence of Sextus Roscius of Ameria.

MAKING A SPLASH: THE DEFENCE OF ROSCIUS OF AMERIA

To lose a first case was not unusual, and many young men who entered the courts had to wait for their moment of triumph. Just as some today would say that all publicity is good publicity, it was the fact that a man had entered the forum, rather than his success, that was important for the would-be politician. It was for this reason that a lot of men, such as Julius Caesar, started their careers with a high-profile prosecution. However, it was not gentlemanly to pursue a career of prosecuting. The key to achieving glory, Cicero believed, lay in the act of defence.

And for Cicero, coming from an unknown family from a town outside Rome, it was more important to make friends by defending men than to risk his reputation by prosecuting them.

Roman society operated very much on a principle of reciprocity: the giving and taking of favours. Yet Cicero was legally forbidden from charging a fee for his work as an advocate. And so, when Cicero offered to defend men, they owed him something – other than money – in return: that is, his payment was in kind, and it should be clear that it was in his interests to defend wealthy, influential politicians. A powerful man could offer to support Cicero in his electoral campaigns, thus providing Cicero with the network of supporters which he lacked as a new man.

The fact that advocates could not charge a fee may seem strange, but it fits in entirely with the Roman view of how the educated élite should behave. For all men of senatorial rank were forbidden from engaging in trade and business: they were only allowed to profit from their farms, and were not to be seen offering other services for payment. There were ways around this ban, such as the hefty 'loan' Cicero received in 62 BC from one (rather disreputable) client. However, for the most part, Cicero drew political support and prestige from the men he chose to defend, with the result that his actions nearly always had a political agenda.

Cicero's first major triumph came in 80 BC, when he was asked to defend Sextus Roscius, a young man who was charged with the hideous crime of patricide: the murder of his own father. It was Cicero's first appearance in a criminal, as opposed to a civil, trial. Moreover, it was a very high-profile case. The courts had received a facelift under Sulla, who established seven permanent courts to deal with the major crimes that were rife in the Rome of his day. One of the courts that had received particular attention was the court established to deal with crimes of poisoning and murder. And the trial of Roscius was the first to be conducted within it.[2]

One of the hurdles that Cicero automatically faced was that, after years of bloodshed and the recent proscriptions, the people were anxious for a conviction to demonstrate some return to law and order. The courts were situated in the open space of the forum, and the orator, Cicero tells us, had to be prepared to speak come rain or shine. People of all walks of life – students, passers-by and anyone with an interest in the case – used to assemble to watch the orator in action. On the day of Roscius' trial, Cicero refers to the excitement it had generated:

> Look at the great crowd of people which has gathered to watch this trial. You can see what they are all hoping and longing for: strict and severe verdicts. This is the first murder trial for a long time, yet the most awful and despicable murders have been committed in the meantime.[3]

Looking back on this speech later in life, Cicero believed that it was the first to
launch his oratorical career. But we may question what made the case so successful besides the interest it generated. For, while we only have Cicero's version of
events by which to judge, the case against Roscius seems positively weak.

The defendant had lived with his father, Sextus Roscius the Elder, who was
a wealthy man from Ameria (about fifty miles north of Rome). Yet Roscius the
Elder had lots of friends in Rome whom he often visited, leaving his son to
manage his thirteen well-positioned and prosperous estates. But one night in
81 BC, Roscius the Elder was returning from a dinner party he had attended in
the city, when he was brutally attacked and murdered in the streets by a group of
unknown thugs. The only witnesses were the slaves who accompanied him; the
defendant, Roscius the Younger, was in Ameria that night, and there was nothing
to connect him to the crime which had happened in Rome.

However, two of the defendant's relatives, Titus Roscius Magnus and Titus
Roscius Capito, apparently sought and succeeded in depriving Roscius the
Younger of his vast inheritance. They did this in collaboration with a man called
Chrysogonus, who was a favourite freedman of the dictator Sulla. Together, the
three men – Magnus, Capito and Chrysogonus – had the name of Roscius the
Elder posthumously inserted into the proscription lists, with which Sulla had
outlawed and murdered his opponents the year before. Once a man had been
proscribed, he could be killed with impunity, his family would lose their inheritance and any property would be auctioned at a cheap price. And the addition
of Roscius the Elder's name onto the proscription list provided the means for
the trio to obtain his property, even though he had never been an enemy of
Sulla. Under this feigned proscription, the younger Roscius was evicted and
Chrysogonus bought the farms cheaply at auction. Three of the farms were given
to Capito, while Magnus looked after the remaining land on Chrysogonus' behalf.

Chrysogonus, Magnus and Capito clearly expected to get away with this:
they were intimidating and powerful in comparison with the young Roscius.
However, with the support of the local people of Ameria, Roscius attempted to
clear his father's name and regain his property. Chrysogonus and his accomplices
now realized they had wildly underestimated the young man and sought to find
another way of silencing him. It was at this stage that the trio decided to hire a
prosecutor called Gaius Erucius, and it was only now that they trumped up the
charge that Roscius had murdered his father. Their desperation and the subsequent contradiction in their actions stands as the greatest argument in favour
of Roscius' innocence: if Roscius' father *had* been officially proscribed, his murder
would not have carried a punishment under Sulla's law.

Fortunately for Roscius, his father had cultivated powerful connections at
Rome. One family, the Metelli, were particularly influential and, although Cicero
dwells on their failure to speak in Roscius' defence at the trial, they had provided

some support – including accommodation and a little legal assistance – to their friend's son. It was the Metelli who probably turned the case over to Cicero, and they presumably told him to tread with caution. In particular, they told him not to criticize or incriminate Chrysogonus, for this would also be viewed as an attack on Sulla. But Cicero ignored their warnings. In a daring move, which he records in the published version, Cicero recalls the charged atmosphere of the court when he, speaking as a relatively young orator, mentioned the forbidden name:

> It hadn't occurred to Erucius that I would be acting in Roscius' defence since I had never spoken in a criminal case before. But as soon as he found out that no one more able and experienced was going to speak, he became so relaxed that he would sit down whenever it took his fancy to sit down or, the next minute, he would start wandering around. At several points, he even called a young boy over to him – to order dinner, I suppose. To cut a long story short, he was treating this jury and court of law like it was one big, empty space. Finally he brought his speech to an end. He sat down. I stood up. He seemed to breathe a sigh of relief because no one more powerful was speaking. I began to speak. I even spotted him joking, gentlemen, and doing other things besides. That was before I mentioned Chrysogonus. The second I said his name, our man got up at once, he looked shell-shocked. I knew what had struck him. So I named Chrysogonus a second time and a third time. From that point on, men ran this way and that – non-stop – I guess to report this to Chrysogonus: there was a man in Rome who dared to speak out against *his* will; the trial was not going according to *his* plan; that the purchase of Roscius' property had been exposed as a sham, the 'partnership' with Magnus and Capito was under heavy attack; that his influence and power were being brushed aside; the jury were paying close attention and the people were judging the whole affair a scandal.[4]

The atmosphere must have been electric even if we allow for some exaggeration on Cicero's part. But, in ancient Rome, it was not enough to expose one side as a farce. Cicero had to put forward a plausible alternative to encourage the jury to acquit the defendant, for a horrific penalty potentially faced Roscius. Rome only used the one prison she had for detaining men on a temporary basis, and so most legal sentences resulted in a fine or the exile of the condemned man. However, the laws for patricide had preserved a curious tradition: if Roscius was found guilty, he could have been tied up into a sack together with a cock, a dog, a monkey and a snake, and then thrown into the sea to meet a most gruesome death.[5]

Throughout his speech, Cicero draws great rhetorical mileage from the hideous nature of both the crime and the punishment to highlight the weakness of the prosecution's case: 'Do you really think you can prove such a crime has been committed, to jurors such as these, when you have not even produced a motive?' Cicero asked his opponent.[6] For Erucius, supported by Titus Roscius Magnus, had based his case on the allegation that the younger Roscius did not get on well with his father, and that he had arranged his father's murder because he was afraid of being disinherited by him. Cicero obviously denied all this, but he also argued that Roscius was too naïve and too devoted to his father to be able to commit, or to have considered committing, the crime. Furthermore, he was not in Rome at the time and thus had neither the *character, motive* nor *opportunity* to kill his father.

For all we know, Cicero's version of events may be little more than a powerful figment of his imagination. Some of his argument certainly dissolves under inspection; for example, Roscius the Younger could have arranged for someone to kill his father, and he did not have to be in Rome himself to accomplish the deed. Cicero dismisses this possibility on the grounds that Roscius was a loner, a country bumpkin, who did not have the friends or the acquaintances to contract a killer. Yet he is saying this about a man who raised enough resistance in Ameria to challenge the unlawful purchase of his lands, and who took his protest to Rome, where he received support from one of her wealthiest families, the Metelli. However, Cicero ingeniously argued that Magnus and Capito were more likely to have murdered the victim based on these three considerations: they were savage and greedy *characters*; they wanted the deceased man's property and thus had a *motive*; Magnus was in Rome at the time of the murder and had the *opportunity*, either to kill the victim or to hire a killer. This type of counterargument was a standard rhetorical trick in defence cases, and it appears in many of Cicero's speeches.

The accusations against Magnus and Capito did not need to be true, but they needed to appear true. And so, to lend weight to his speculations, Cicero deployed the argument of *cui bono* ('who stood to gain?'). Here, by arguing a cause from effect, Cicero established a motive from the benefit Magnus and Capito had derived from Roscius the Elder's death: the possession of his farms. Their scheming and devious characters, when coupled with the support offered by the greedy and powerful Chrysogonus, meant that they were more likely to commit the murder than Roscius the Younger.

All of Cicero's arguments were based on probability; he did not prove that Magnus and Capito *actually* killed Roscius the Elder (or even arrange for him to be killed), but he did provide the jury with a possible, and plausible, alternative. It has often been debated whether or not the Romans believed in the verdicts that they passed in court. But the lengths to which Cicero goes to establish an alternative scenario would suggest that, at the least, the more scrupulous jurors did have to believe in something other than the defendant's alleged guilt.[7]

Furthermore, Cicero's case does derive some support from two other curious details about the events surrounding the murder. Why, at the moment of the murder, did a messenger rush all the way to Ameria (making the fifty-six mile journey in less than ten hours), to announce the death of Roscius the Elder *not* to his son but to Capito? (Capito had fallen out with Roscius and his son many years before.) And, why did Magnus and Capito now refuse to hand over the slaves, who were with the victim at the time of his death? In Roman law, their testimony (only acceptable after they had been tortured first to check that they were telling the truth) could have provided valuable evidence.

The case against the younger Roscius (as far as we can tell) seems weak, but this does not undermine Cicero's achievement in securing the result he did: Roscius seems to have been acquitted of the crime (we do not know whether he recovered his property), Chrysogonus falls out of the history pages, and Cicero was increasingly called upon to undertake new cases. As for Sulla, by a master-stroke of persuasion, Cicero absolved him of any knowledge of the crime – like the god Jupiter, Sulla could not be aware of everything that happened on Earth. Even with this level of tact, we should not overlook Cicero's courage in delivering and publishing the speech. It was clearly a political oration in the sense that it touched upon and criticized Rome's leading politician, whose henchmen were immoral, unscrupulous and out of control. At the end of the speech Cicero makes an appeal for an end to the evil cruelty that has taken hold of Rome. When we remember the deaths of all the men whom Cicero had admired in these years, we can imagine he meant it.

Plutarch states that Cicero had to leave Rome for fear of Sulla's wrathful vengeance following the attacks he had made on Chrysogonus, but most scholars now dismiss this suggestion. Cicero did leave Rome shortly afterwards but, by then, Sulla had resigned his position as dictator. Moreover, in an amazing piece of autobiography, Cicero explicitly tells us that his reason for going was to prepare himself physically for the demanding nature of the oratorical career he desired:

> At the time my body was slender and weak; my neck was long and thin. This kind of physique is often regarded as almost perilous if you work too hard and lay too much stress upon the lungs. All the people who cared for me were all the more worried by the fact that I used to speak without pause or variation using the full power of my voice and the strength of my whole body. Although my friends and doctors urged me to put an end to my activity in the law courts, I decided that I would rather undergo any danger than abandon my ambition to achieve lasting fame as an orator. But, when I weighed it up, I realized that I could both avoid this danger to my health and acquire a more controlled manner of speaking if I relaxed and moderated my voice and changed my whole habit of speaking. In order to change my way of speaking, then, I decided to leave for Asia. And so, after two years of pleading in legal trials, when my name was already famous in the forum, I left Rome.[8]

MORE STUDY, A MARRIAGE AND A MAGISTRACY

'Study abroad' was a relatively new phenomenon at Rome. It later became conventional for young men to extend their academic studies, and a trip to Greece was more like leaving home for university than the modern gap year. But in 79–77 BC, probably at their father's expense, Cicero and Quintus left Rome for the Greek East and Asia Minor (the west coast of modern Turkey). Their cousin Lucius, with whom Cicero was very close, went with them together with some other friends, including Atticus.

It is possible, though by no means certain, that Cicero's young wife also made some of the journey with him, for he had married Terentia shortly after the Roscius trial – in either 80 or 79 BC.[9] In ancient Rome, men could marry any time from the age of sixteen, and their bride could be as young as twelve. Some men, like Julius Caesar, did marry in their teens, but many waited until their mid to late twenties. In Cicero's case, a later marriage made sense; for he needed to show his senatorial potential if he wanted to attract a good marriage prospect. Selection criteria were more geared towards political rather than romantic considerations, and a man looked for a wife who could bring a good dowry as well as new family connections. Therefore, at the age of about twenty-six or twenty-seven, Cicero married Terentia, who was eighteen (give or take a couple of years).

Little is known about Terentia's immediate family but she was clearly wealthy, for her dowry was rumoured to have been over four hundred thousand sesterces. By Roman standards this was a very ample amount, for it was the same sum of money that made a man eligible for entry to the wealthy equestrian class. But she also owned a lot of property in her own name, which may mean she was an heiress. As regards her family, some of her relatives even belonged to the Roman nobility. Terentia's half-sister, Fabia, was a vestal virgin – one of the highly honoured priestesses within the Roman religious system, open only to the most aristocratic women. Cicero had married into a good family, and his success as an orator and the potential he showed for the future must have played some part.

To return to Cicero's travels abroad, he first arrived at Athens, where he studied with the philosophers and rhetoricians. By sitting at the feet of famous philosophers and travelling to the spot where the famous Plato had lived, breathed and taught, Cicero and his companions witnessed the past coming to life before their very eyes. His love of philosophy remained with him throughout his life, and Cicero was later instrumental in making Greek philosophy accessible to a Roman audience. Afterwards, he travelled through Asia Minor, before moving to Rhodes where he attached himself to Apollonius Molo. It was here that Cicero noticed a great change in his oratory taking place, and it was the transformation he needed to succeed in his career:

Molo was distinguished as an actual speaker and as a speech-writer for others; but, as a teacher, he was also excellent at criticizing and correcting errors. He made it his aim to check, if possible, the overflowing abundance of my style which was flooded with youthful excess and decadence, as if he were preventing a river from bursting its banks. Thus I returned, after two years, not just better trained but almost transformed. The strain in my voice had subsided and it was as if my language had been stopped from boiling over. My lungs had gained strength and my whole body was more robust.[10]

In the middle of 77 BC, Cicero returned to Rome a better speaker: he could control his voice more effectively, there was more strength in his lungs, and he had put on some much-needed weight. Plutarch states that Cicero did not engage in advocacy immediately because he had received a warning from the Delphic oracle. He also suggests that Cicero was not popular with the people, who called him a 'Greekling' and a 'swat'.[11] But it is doubtful that Cicero avoided oratory given his new-found confidence. Indeed, Cicero himself tells us that in the first year after his return from Asia he pleaded some famous cases, and we have evidence of a number of forensic trials in which he participated. He needed to continue his advocacy: this was part of the so-called 'new man's industry', for he still had to expand his network of personal supporters.[12]

Cicero now had a firm eye on his political career, and he was in the ideal position to begin his campaign to be elected as a quaestor – the first rung on the ladder of offices. His marriage to Terentia had increased the size of his family and support base. She personally also seems to have supported, encouraged and shared his political ambitions. And Cicero himself had become significantly richer after being left a huge sum of money in a legacy, which was almost equal to the dowry that Terentia had brought with her to the marriage.

In 76 BC, as the people of Rome and Italy assembled to cast their votes, Cicero secured his election to the quaestorship. The election day itself was probably a mixture of the excitement and frustration that busy, hot events incite among those who attend. For the elections took place in the heat of June and the voting-pen (a wooden, roofless frame) offered little shade to the thronging crowds who gathered on the plain known as the 'field of Mars' (the *campus martius*). Voters were lured to Rome by the games and festivals that were staged at this time, and probably also by the chance to make a profit off the back of the extensive bribery and corruption that was customary in Roman politics. Cicero does not appear to have resorted to such desperate lengths in his own career, and later in life he even passed a law against electoral bribery. But others employed bribe-distributors extensively, and they would only have added to the whole hullabaloo of the day.

Roman citizens, all men of free birth over the age of eighteen from across Italy, were divided into thirty-five tribes for the purpose of voting. However, a remarkable feature of the voting system was that a simple majority was never taken. Instead, the voters entered their vote into the communal pool of their tribe. A majority of individual votes sealed the decision for each tribe and, in turn, a majority of the tribes settled the vote for the whole assembly. As soon as a candidate received eighteen votes from the thirty-five tribes, he was considered elected, even though he might not have polled the largest number of votes if every vote had been counted.

We do not know how Cicero felt as he waited to find out the results of his election, but we can gauge some of the nerves and excitement from the scene he would have witnessed. The day was long and drawn-out, starting early in the morning when the citizens assembled for a public meeting. Afterwards, to add to the grandeur of the occasion, the consul presided over the elections taking his seat on the special chair made of ivory (the curule chair). The consul's lictors stood around him: these men were the twelve attendants who each carried the symbol of his authority, the *fasces* – a bundle of rods, tied together with strips of red leather, surrounding a single-headed axe. It was the consul's job to preside over the public meeting, introduce the candidates, and also to order for the omens to be taken.

Rome was deeply concerned with the taking and interpretation of a range of omens and prophecies, such as the flight and the cries of the birds, any unusual activity in the weather or by the inspection of the entrails of sacrificial animals. Positive omens and prophecies granted divine support to their actions, negative ones could result in the abandonment of the proceedings or the disqualification of newly appointed magistrates. The omens must have been good on the day of Cicero's election, as the proceedings went ahead as usual.

First, the voters were marshalled into the correct division of the voting-pen: the huge structure was roped off into thirty-five sections so that each tribe had its own area. Here, they were provided with a wooden tablet, coated in wax so that the voters could inscribe the name, or perhaps just the initials, of the candidate they wanted to win. Next, they proceeded in single file across raised gangways to drop their tablet into the voting urn. It apparently took some time for the votes to be counted, but the opportunity to canvass for next year's elections did not escape prospective candidates. They eagerly circled the field scouting for support, while the herald announced the results as they went along.

As soon as a candidate received the majority votes needed, he swore an oath to obey and observe the laws. The votes continued to be counted until all twenty posts had been filled. But, fortunately for Cicero, he did not have to wait long: he was voted 'in first place'.[13] Furthermore, he was just thirty years old, and he had achieved this distinction at the earliest age permitted to him by law (what the Romans called election *in his year*). Cicero was now a magistrate of the Roman Republic – and he had earned his place in the senate for life. Instead of one of the urban praetorships, he was allotted the post of quaestor in western Sicily, and on 1 January 75 BC Cicero entered office for the first time.

LESSONS FROM SICILY

Sicily was Rome's oldest province. Roman occupation of the province had started in 241 BC, and since that time the Sicilian farmer had been taxed with the duty of providing a share of his harvest to the Roman authorities. The result was that Sicily had acquired an important reputation as 'the nation's storehouse'; the province was once described as 'the nurse at whose breast the whole Roman population is fed'.[14]

The year Cicero entered office, and for many others afterwards, there were shortages in the grain supply at Rome. This shortage in grain led to increasing demands being made upon the farmers to raise the supply they made to Rome, but this was never a popular request. For, without anything like a civil service to collect this tax, the job was hired out to private companies of tax farmers, who were often extortionate and bullying in their bid to make a lucrative profit. Roman magistrates could either overlook or actively participate in these schemes depending on whether they were unscrupulous or diligent governors of their provinces. Yet Cicero's evident care for the provincials and his eye for justice made him the most popular quaestor among the Sicilians. He did raise the amount the farmers needed to send to Rome, but his sense of fairness and leniency won Cicero many friends.

Other than a few anecdotes – such as one recording Cicero's joy at discovering the tomb of the famous Sicilian scientist, Archimedes – we know little about Cicero's activity as a quaestor.[15] In itself, the job, which involved matters of financial administration, was more important for the support it offered senior politicians. Years later, in 64 BC, one of Cicero's junior contemporaries, Cato the Younger, caused astonishment for the diligence with which he approached the role. And it was the fact that, in Cicero's day, this office brought automatic membership to the senate, which made the quaestorship particularly significant. However, Cicero's year in this post was crucial for three main reasons that should not be detached from a study of his political and oratorical career.

First, as we have seen, Cicero was ever aware of the need to create a personal support group to compensate for his lack of ancestral ties. Important Sicilians, who were protected by the patronage of noble Roman families or military dynasts, offered direct access to the inner core of the Roman élite and the powerful men of Cicero's day. The distinguished house of the Marcelli had been the traditional patrons of Sicily since 212 BC. And a number of prominent figures – including Pompey and Hortensius – had close connections with the Sicilian provincials. Cicero may have had a view to furthering his political ambitions at Rome through the ties that he forged in Sicily. He certainly made efforts also to support the Roman businessmen who had settled in the area. These businessmen formed a large part of the equestrian class, and they were always useful support-ers to have in politics.

A second and related advantage of Cicero's quaestorship was the opportunity it opened in his oratorical career. In the speech that Cicero delivered at his fare-well ceremony, he promised to serve as a patron of the Sicilian people himself, if they ever needed his services as an advocate. By 70 BC, after three years of suf-fering at the hands of a corrupt governor, Gaius Verres, they were calling in the favour, and Cicero obliged. As we shall see, the subsequent prosecution of Verres was arguably one of the greatest trials of Cicero's career. At the same time, look-ing back on his career, Cicero also felt that the end of his Sicilian quaestorship marked a watershed in his oratory. He had undertaken a number of cases there, and practised his oratory often. Whatever talent he had possessed before Sicily, he later claimed, was fully rounded and completed by the time he returned.

Finally, Cicero's time in Sicily taught him one of the most valuable points in his career: there was a great value to be placed on seeing, and being seen at, Rome every day. In an anecdote that he humorously directed against himself over twenty years later, Cicero recalled his astonishment when he returned from Sicily. The shocking event is best expressed by Cicero:

> At the time I thought that the whole of Rome was talking about my quaestorship. For I had sent a huge amount of grain to Rome when it was more expensive than ever; yet I had been civil to the businessmen, fair to the traders, generous to the tax farmers and temperate towards our allies. Everyone thought that I had been most conscientious in every aspect of my duties; some unprecedented honours were devised for me by the Sicilians. When I left my province, then, I was wishfully thinking that the Roman people would rush forward to bestow all kinds of honours on me. But, a few days later, I hap-pened to arrive at Puteoli on my way back from Sicily, just at the time when all the most fashionable and wealthy people generally flock there. I nearly fainted, gentlemen, when someone asked me when I had left Rome and whether there was any news to report from the city. And, when I replied that I was on my way home from my province, he said: 'Gosh, of course, you're on your way back from Africa aren't you?' I swallowed my anger, and said: 'Sicily, actually.' At which some know-all said: 'you mean you don't know that Cicero has been the quaestor of Syracuse [i.e. eastern Sicily]?' What else can I say? I gave up being angry and just became the same as all the other seaside tourists. But that whole incident, gentlemen, definitely did me more good than it would have done had everyone congratulated me. From that day on, I realized that the Roman people had deaf ears, but sharp and observant eyes. I stopped worrying what men would hear about me; I made sure that from that day, every day, on they would see me in person. I have lived in their sight; I have never left the forum; neither a closed door nor shut eyes have prevented me from seeing anyone.[16]

The joke may be exaggerated, but this is exactly what Cicero did: for the rest of his life he only left Rome under compulsion, first by a brief spell in exile in 58 BC and, later, by an obligatory provincial command in 51 BC. In the meantime, it was necessary for Cicero to make his influence felt back at Rome: he was thirty-two years old by the time he returned from this adventure. His quaestorship had made Cicero a senator but he had far more to do if he wanted to progress further up the ladder: Cicero's name and reputation at Rome were established, but they were not yet distinguished.

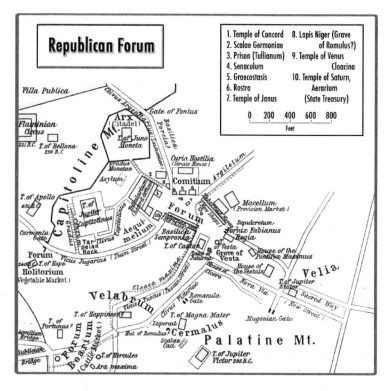

'I have never left the forum': a plan of the Roman forum
and the surrounding area at the time of the Republic (drawn by PB Productions
based on an original in W. R. Shepherd's *Historical Atlas*, published in 1923).

4

Cicero on the Attack (70 BC)

PROVINCIAL MISMANAGEMENT

When I returned from Sicily a year later, it seemed that whatever talent I had possessed beforehand was fully rounded and to have reached a certain maturity . . . And so after five years of activity, in which I pleaded many cases against some of the leading advocates, I finally came head-to-head in a trial of great magnitude against Hortensius – I was an elected aedile facing an elected consul.

(Cicero, *Brutus* 318)

In the year 70 BC, Cicero began his campaign for the aedileship hopeful that he would be elected 'in his year' for 69 BC. At the same time, a remarkable opportunity came his way. In one stroke, if he was successful, Cicero could become Rome's leading orator, establish a political 'line' and win the popularity he needed to secure his election to the aedileship. If he failed, he would make powerful enemies and jeopardize his whole career. Cicero – never afraid to burn what he called the 'midnight oil'[1] – put in every hour of the day and night to secure this triple triumph. It all started when Gaius Verres, a notoriously corrupt politician (as Cicero would have us believe), was appointed the governor of Sicily in 73 BC.

Cicero's political career had proved very promising so far, but it was not exceptional. He was not the first new man to break through into the ranks of the senate, although very few ever progressed much further up the ladder of offices than the quaestorship afterwards. Indeed, it had been a long time since the last new man had made it all the way up to the top rung of the consulship. Cicero's oratorical career had certainly started off brilliantly. But it is interesting to note that, despite his successes, his clients to date had primarily been men, and some women, of the same ilk as himself: that is, well-to-do Italian families rather than the men of senatorial rank. While the support of the former was valuable, the backing of the élite was crucial. If Cicero wanted to play at their level, he needed to raise his game. He was not just looking forward to his election as aedile: he was looking beyond this to the more remote prizes of the praetorship and consulship.

It was his talent as an orator, again, that enabled Cicero to push through the barriers ahead of him. Speakers gained the greatest publicity from criminal trials. And so, if you really wanted to draw attention to yourself, it did not get much better than the prosecution of a senior politician and senator. Cicero was thirty-six when he decided to make his debut prosecution, and it was this case that launched his career once and for all.

As Cicero later reflected in his work *On Duties*, many young men obtained distinction in the law courts, and many of those men had established their reputation by prosecuting another. These men were sometimes as young as eighteen or nineteen, and Cicero was thus relatively old to be making his first attack. But there was still much to be earned. While defence was always the most honourable action, there were reasons for which even a prosecution could be well regarded: a man could justifiably prosecute another if he had the interests of the state in mind, if he wanted to avenge wrongs or if he felt compelled to protect Rome's provincials. Indeed, Cicero claimed to be acting from the last of these motives in his prosecution of Verres: 'Although it looks like a prosecution,' he maintained, 'it should be reckoned more as an act of defence than one of prosecution. For I am defending many men, many communities; in fact, I am defending the whole province of Sicily.'[2]

Gaius Verres was the ideal object of Cicero's attack. He was emblematic of the corruption for which the senate had been criticized since the time of Sulla. He was a senator of Rome who was supported by men from some of the noblest families. But, crucially, he was not an integral member of the inner clique that controlled Rome's senatorial élite. Rather, Verres' family was fairly new to this rank. His father had been a senator, but not a very influential one. If we are to believe Cicero, Verres was more of an upstart of the Sullan regime. He had started off on Marius' side in the civil war, but he later betrayed him and bought his way into Sulla's favour with bribes of stolen treasure. Verres was later rewarded with property and power by Sulla, and he had since wangled his way up the ladder of offices, as far as the praetorship. He had betrayed those who trusted him, and won influence by the distribution of his ill-gotten gains. The truth is probably not that far off, but this would only make Verres as bad as many of the other men of his day.

As we saw earlier, advocates were not allowed to charge for their services. In the same way, politicians were not paid either, despite the fact that politics was an expensive business. Senators had to support their clients, provide shows for the people and finance an election campaign (often, illegally, resorting to extensive bribery). Many got into debt, for they had to borrow vast sums of money at the beginning of their careers: Julius Caesar is reported to have said that he needed to make twenty-five million sesterces, just to break even. We may ask why they bothered. Cicero's answer was that a political life brought: 'rank, prestige, splendour at home, a reputation and esteem abroad, a purple-bordered toga, an ivory curule seat, marks of distinction, the *fasces*, an army, commands and provinces'.[3] These were the goals which fuelled many men's ambitions.

The two highest magistracies, the praetorship and the consulship, brought the extra opportunities that Cicero cites last: the right to command an army abroad (*imperium*) and a provincial governorship (a propraetorship or a proconsulship). And these two benefits of political life – military and provincial commands – did not just carry great prestige: they were the only real way that a senator could (legally) make any money at Rome on top of what he earned from his estates.

Commanding an army brought the biggest rewards: if successful, a general could sweep up a huge amount of plunder and booty. This was shared among his troops, but the general doubtless took the lion's share for himself. Alternatively, if he was appointed to the governorship, a senator could recoup the expenses of his election campaign the year later in his provincial role. This was not because men were expected to extort money from their provinces, but because the lump sum granted to them for their expenses was far more than they needed. Cicero personally managed to earn over two million sesterces in this way, and it was all 'within the limits of the law'.[4]

However, since military commands and magistracies were few and far between, some went to town during their year of office. In the provinces, the opportunities for corruption were endless: crooked deals with the tax-farming companies, the acceptance of bribes in legal suits, and other ingenious means could be devised to extract huge amounts of money from defenceless natives, whether they were provincial inhabitants or Roman businessmen operating in the area. It is hard to believe that Cicero was exaggerating that much when a few years later he recalled the unpopularity of the Romans abroad:

> It is difficult to put into words, citizens, just how hated we Romans are among foreign peoples, because of the greed and the damage our governors, men sent by us, have done in recent years. For in all those lands, do you think there is any shrine that our magistrates have regarded as sacred, any state they have regarded as inviolable, any private house they have regarded as locked and bolted?[5]

The case of Verres demonstrates the nature and extent of provincial mismanagement in Cicero's time. For in the three years he had been the governor of Sicily (from 73 to 71 BC inclusive), the rumours of Verres' widespread extortion had been overwhelming. The first year had been bad by any standards, but matters spiralled out of control when Verres' governorship was extended. Reports were flying around Rome; however, the senate could not call him back as there was no one available to replace him: the slave war with Spartacus was raging in southern Italy, Sicily was vulnerable, and a former Marian soldier called Sertorius was wreaking havoc in Spain. It was a time of extreme chaos, and Verres capitalized on the welcome extension to his command.

One man, in particular, did his best to expose Verres' crimes during these years: Sthenius of Thermae, who had escaped from Sicily to seek help and refuge from Cicero and his other patrons. Verres and Sthenius had initially been on amicable terms, for it was customary for a governor to be lodged, fed and entertained by a town's wealthiest citizens whenever he made a tour of the province. And so, when he was visiting Thermae, Verres had stayed with the eminently wealthy Sthenius. However, if we can trust Cicero, Verres first stripped Sthenius' house of all its worldly possessions before turning his attention to some precious statues belonging to the city. Sthenius allegedly bore the loss of his personal possessions in silence, but he prevented Verres from acquiring the public treasures.

In revenge, Verres conspired with some of Sthenius' enemies and he guaranteed them success in any legal action they could think to bring against his former host. When they charged Sthenius on the grounds that he had forged an official document, the latter fled to Rome in fear. For all we know the charge against Sthenius may have been true, but Verres pursued his vendetta further. He even supported a capital charge which was trumped up against Sthenius, and – even though he was not in Sicily to defend himself – Verres pronounced him guilty of that too.

This version of events, or something similar, had become known at Rome as early as 72 BC, when the senate met to discuss the legality of putting Sthenius on trial in his absence. Shortly later, too, Cicero delivered a speech in Sthenius' defence against a new piece of legislation, which banished from Rome anyone who had ever been convicted of a capital charge. Under this bill, Sthenius needed to leave the city. However, Cicero successfully pleaded the injustice of Sthenius' conviction, and he was allowed to stay. It was only natural that, when more and more men wanted some remuneration for the losses they had suffered under Verres, the Sicilians turned to Cicero, who was only too happy to oblige.

LAUNCHING THE PROSECUTION

Despite the fact that crime was rife at Rome in Cicero's day, the Roman Republic lacked both a police force and a public prosecution service. For civil cases, where one party had been wronged by another in a business transaction, inheritance suit, land dispute or similar, the recourse to law and arbitration was a natural means of settling private affairs. But for the larger criminal offences – crimes against the state – the onus to prosecute a man fell upon the volunteer prosecutor: that is, any man who wished could file a suit requesting the right to prosecute another.

Furthermore, there were a series of rewards and incentives available for the successful advocate. The details of these rewards are vague, but it has been argued that a prosecutor who won his case even earned the right to take the defeated man's standing in the senate. Conversely, severe penalties awaited those who undertook malicious or sham cases. These men were labelled *kalumniatores* ('pettifoggers' or 'phonies'). If a man was found guilty of being a *kalumniator*, the letter 'k' was scorched onto his forehead as a permanent tattoo of his crime. For an orator undertaking a prosecution, therefore, it was imperative to show that his motives were sound and honourable.[6]

Given the publicity that a high-profile prosecution brought, coupled with the rewards that were on offer, it is little wonder that another man, Quintus Caecilius Niger, also came forward and requested permission to prosecute Verres. This led to a preliminary trial, called a *divinatio*, during which a panel of jurors first had to decide between the rival prosecutors. The trial to decide between the two would-be prosecutors took place at the end of January 70 BC; the speech Cicero delivered, *Against Quintus Caecilius*, survives as the first in the *Verrines* collection.

The nature of the trial, however, caused Cicero some anxiety: he had to prove that he was the best man to act as prosecutor while simultaneously avoiding the impression that he was a malicious prosecutor, eager to further his own career off the back of Verres' misfortunes. Furthermore, self-praise was not a task to be undertaken lightly. As Cicero himself claimed in the *divinatio*, 'vanity of every kind is insufferable; but that concerning talent and eloquence is by far the most hateful'.[7]

Instead, Cicero focused his attention on proving that Caecilius was the worst choice: he was a 'straw man', Cicero alleged, hired by the defence to put on a shambolic prosecution.[8] For Verres' supporters, including Hortensius, wanted to spare Verres the full force of Cicero's attack. Whether Caecilius was, or was not, a collusive prosecutor is impossible to know; indeed, he may have had good grounds for wanting to prosecute Verres. Therefore, Cicero also needed to convince the jury that his opponent was unsuitable for the task. Caecilius, he argued, was too dependent on the rules of rhetoric and the model speeches that everyone knew from their boyhood. Cicero, on the other hand, was more of a match for the defence advocate, Hortensius. In the speech that he delivered in the *divinatio*, Cicero argued this point in actions: he did not just claim to be the better speaker, he demonstrated it.

As he stood in court, arguing against the choice of Caecilius as prosecutor, Cicero imagined all the rhetorical tricks that Hortensius would deploy in his defence of Verres in the main trial: 'How many times he will put the power in *your* hands to choose between two alternatives – something either happened or it did not, something is either true or false – but whichever one you choose, you're done for.'[9] This was called a dilemma, and a good orator was a whizz at trapping his opponent in a catch-22 situation. Only moments later, Cicero used precisely this trick against Caecilus to discredit his motives for prosecuting Verres. Caecilius had frequently joined Verres for dinner when they worked together in Sicily, he argued: 'You must choose whether you want to be considered a treacherous friend or a treacherous advocate. Either way, you must be one of them.'[10]

Cicero also evoked Hortensius' amazing ability to recall an opponent's speech from memory: 'What about when he begins to break up and smash your speech for the prosecution: he will tick off each part of your case on his fingers as he goes along?' Even Caecilius would start to believe that he was prosecuting an innocent man, argued Cicero: 'Take care, I beg you. I cannot help worrying that he will not only strike you with the power of his words, but that he will dazzle your mind and senses with his gestures, making you forget all that you planned to say and do.'[11] Finally, in a devastating display of sardonic wit, Cicero lay down the ultimate gauntlet before his opponent:

> I think a decision on this matter can be settled straight away. For if you can actually reply to *me* today, and you can reply to what *I* am saying, and if, just once, you can tear yourself away from your textbook – you know, the one full of other people's speeches that some schoolteacher once gave you – then I shall admit that you might not be a failure in the main trial as well: maybe you *can* do justice to the case and your duty. But if you come to nothing when you are only exchanging blows with me, what kind of opponent can we expect you to be in the actual battle against a most bitter foe?[12]

A good prosecutor, Cicero demonstrated, needed a whole range of skills. For instance, he had to structure his speech effectively – according to rhetorical theory, an orator's weakest argument had to be buried somewhere in the middle of his speech. He had to be able to tell a good story; his audience should not just be listening: they should be on the edge of their seats. And, of course, he had to prove his guilt using the evidence of witnesses and documents. To these, he should add all the weapons from his rhetorical armoury: emotion, humour, character assassination and cultural references. As a man, the prosecutor needed to have worked hard, trained thoroughly and be able to combine education with ability. Cicero had the full package, and Caecilius did not stand a chance. He was 'a nobody who can do nothing', Cicero argued – and the jury agreed. When Cicero won the right to prosecute Verres, Caecilius was not even accepted as his *subscriptor* (the advocate's assistant).[13]

A GOD-GIVEN OPPORTUNITY

Several reasons account for Cicero's zeal to prosecute Verres. First, as we saw in the quotation cited at the top of this chapter, it brought him 'into a trial of magnitude' against Rome's foremost orator, Hortensius, who was speaking in Verres' defence. Second, Cicero was doubtless looking ahead to his aedileship should he be successful at the polls. In a year where he would have to keep the cost of grain low in order to please Rome's populace, the support of Sicily – the 'nation's storehouse' – would be a great help. Third, however, the prosecution of Verres provided Cicero with the platform from which he could advertise himself both as a supporter of senatorial standards and as a critic of the corroding influence which some of its members were exerting. As Cicero claimed at the very beginning of his prosecution speech:

> The very thing that was most surely longed for, gentleman, and the one thing that will help more than anything else, in reducing both the hatred felt towards your order and the disgrace of your judicial verdicts, has come at a moment of great political crisis: it has not come about by human planning, but it is, as it were, a gift bestowed on you by the gods. For a belief, destructive to the state and dangerous to you, has become deep-seated not only at Rome; it even spreads like wildfire among foreign nations. They say that these courts, as they stand at the moment, will never convict a man, however guilty he may be, so long as he has money. Now, at this moment of crisis for your order and your courts, a defendant has been brought before you: his name is Gaius Verres – a man already condemned in everyone's minds by his life and deeds; already acquitted, according to his own hopeful predictions, by his immense wealth.[14]

If the trial of Verres demonstrates one thing in particular it is that corruption was widespread in ancient Rome, and it went to the top levels of society. The year 70 BC was a year of crisis for the senatorial order. As the quotation above shows, Cicero claimed the senate needed a gift from the gods to recover its name and dignity. This gift was the trial of Verres. For, in the face of mounting hostilities and suspicion, it was a chance for the senatorial order to quench the widespread rumours of their fraud by convicting one of their peers. To understand how things had got this bad, we need to go back in time to the years of Sulla's dictatorship and the reforms he made regarding the staffing of the law courts. First, however, we need to see why Sulla himself felt the reforms were necessary.

Since the double tribunate of Gaius Gracchus (123 and 122 BC), the rising wealth and influence of Rome's 'middle class' had caused some tension between, what were now, the two upper levels of society: the senators and the equestrians. While they engaged together socially, politically they were at loggerheads. The equestrians had become remarkably rich off the back of commercial opportunities that were closed to the senatorial order. Some equestrians, like Cicero, did become senators; but many, like Cicero's friend Atticus, did not take a share in Rome's government. Instead, they were Rome's businessmen, and their mounting wealth was, in turn, increasing their amount of social and political clout.

Rivalries between the two orders reached a climax when Gracchus deprived the senatorial rank of its monopoly over the law courts, transferring it instead to the equestrians. His reasoning was that the senatorial juries had proved inadequate in convicting their peers tried before them on charges of extortion. At the same time, however, the equestrians were themselves engaging more and more in provincial matters, for Gracchus had also provided them with lucrative business opportunities collecting the taxes in the new province of Asia. What he failed to recognize was that the equestrian order, too, were unlikely to deal with extortion as effectively as they should. For a governor who took a backhander, or who turned a blind eye to high levels of taxation, only served their business interests. They were as bad as the senators, and the law courts became what one scholar has described as a 'political football' being passed between the two sides, while each fought for possession.[15]

When Sulla assumed the dictatorship in 82 BC, the courts had been in the hands of the equestrians for twenty years. This was one of the ways in which he felt the power of the senate had been weakened. In addition, the senate was short on numbers, for many men had been killed in the civil wars and proscriptions, and the tribunes of the plebs had learned to exercise their powers to an alarming, even dangerous, degree. If we can talk in terms of a political programme, Sulla essentially made it his aim to restore strength to the now dwindling senate. New members were added to the senate from the equestrian rank, the powers of the tribunes of the plebs were dramatically curtailed, and full control over the increased number of courts was handed back to the senators. However, this last move had disastrous results upon justice and morality in the years that followed.

By the time of Verres' trial, over ten years later, morality was demanding to be restored. For in previous years, one way of monitoring the behaviour of the élite had been through the appointment of censors: every five years, two former consuls held this office for a maximum of eighteen months. Their main duty was to scrutinize every man's membership to the senate and to eject those they deemed unworthy of the honour. But this office had fallen into disuse in recent times, with the result that it was not an effective deterrent. Without any censors to monitor the standards of behaviour in the senate, the senators could and did behave as they wished. The criticism of morality in Cicero's early speeches was not empty rhetoric; when the office was finally reinstated in 70 BC, a staggering sixty-four senators were expelled in one go.

As for the standards of justice in the law courts, Cicero preserves some horrific stories of their maladministration in the ten years between Sulla's reforms and the trial of Verres: 'What words can I find to deplore that shameful and ruinous tarnish upon our whole rank?' Cicero asked referring to a notorious incident in 74 BC: 'The fact that in this very land, when the senators were the jurors of our courts, the voting-tablets of sworn jurors were marked with coloured wax?'[16] Not only were the jury dishonest enough to accept bribes in the first place, they were so dishonest that even the bribery agents did not trust them. For this reason they had marked the tablets to check that the jurors, who had accepted bribes, were keeping to their side of the deal.

In short, two measures of social control – the censorship and the threat of prosecution – had effectively been removed by the Sullan reforms. The threat of prosecution had traditionally been efficient in the sense that criminal trials, in particular, had the power to end a man's political career once and for all. Crimes such as murder, extortion, bribery and treason were capital offences: if a conviction looked inevitable, the guilty parties saved their lives by escaping into exile, but there was still no return to political activity for them thereafter. Yet, Cicero claims in the speeches *Against Verres*, rumour has it that no one will be found guilty, if he has enough money. Indeed, Verres allegedly boasted that he had extorted enough money 'to use the first year's profits to enrich his own fortune; the second year's to pay his advocates and defence team; and that those of the third year – the richest and most profitable of them all – would be reserved for his judges'.[17] It is no wonder that there was a new need for a reform of the juries, and this was the political crisis lurking in the background of Verres' trial.

Moves were being made towards a solution by the time Verres came to court, and one proposal had been made by a praetor called Lucius Aurelius Cotta. Cotta's bill planned to split the control between the senators, equestrians and a third class of wealthy men called the treasurers, who were only slightly beneath the equestrians in status. But the uncertainty surrounding the future staffing of the courts enabled Cicero to direct the jurors' attention towards the political implications of the trial: 'Who will there be to prevent the transfer of the courts,' he imagined the nobility asking among themselves, 'if Verres is acquitted?'[18]

Indeed, Cicero made great mileage out of the political context of the trial for rhetorical effect; for the claim that the case of Verres was a god-given opportunity for the senators to prove their integrity runs throughout the published speeches. But, even if the senate's monopoly of the courts was under threat, this did not prevent some of Rome's greatest names from rallying around to support Verres – including Hortensius, whose efforts to sabotage the trial form a key part in Cicero's self-presentation as a new man fighting against the dominant factions of the nobility.

THE TRIAL OF VERRES

On 5 August 70 BC, the trial of Verres finally commenced, but in the meantime Verres and Hortensius had used many tactics of obstructionism and intimidation against Cicero – their junior in age, rank and wealth. Originally, the trial had been due to come to court around the beginning of May. But the timing for Verres was disastrous: the jury and the praetor, who presided over the court, seemed to be more honest and upright than most of their day. There was only one day in his entire life, Cicero claimed, that Verres felt afraid, for 'he had stumbled upon the courts at a time when it was almost impossible to corrupt them'.[19]

However, the members of the defence team were well aware that, if they could somehow delay the trial until the next year, it would potentially be a lot easier to secure Verres' acquittal. Hortensius was hoping to be the consul for that year, and Verres' other friends, including several of the distinguished Metelli family, were also canvassing for positions of high power. This provides an interesting glimpse into how the powerful members of society could pool their efforts to protect each other. For a plan to save Verres was hatched. Although it seemed ages away until the end of the year, there was a way that the trial could be stalled until the beginning of 69 BC.

The Roman calendar was full of holidays, and these were particularly clustered towards the end of the year. And so, in reality, if they could delay Verres' trial so that it started in August, rather than May, there was every chance that the large number of games and festivals would prevent it from coming to a vote before the following January – by which time all of Verres' friends would be in high office. Hortensius and Verres saw an opportunity: all they needed to do was to get another trial for extortion placed on the waiting list of trials to be heard before Verres'.

The plans of Verres and Hortensius were possible because the role of the prosecutor went beyond just presenting the case. The prosecutor in Cicero's day also had to do the investigatory work of the detective and the police: it was his job to gather the evidence and witnesses needed to secure a conviction against his opponent. In cases of provincial mismanagement, this entailed some time abroad if the job was to be done thoroughly. To this end, Cicero was granted one hundred and ten days to collect his evidence from Sicily – including the time needed to travel there and back. Yet Hortensius and Verres instigated another extortion trial, against the former governor of Achaea; moreover, the prosecutor, whom they allegedly hired, only asked for one hundred and eight days to collect his evidence. This prosecution would come to court before Verres' trial, and it threatened to cause a troublesome delay to Cicero's plans.

Cicero was forced to work in a hurry. When he set off for Sicily, together with his cousin Lucius, he was determined to gather the evidence as quickly and as thoroughly as possible. And he did it in record time. After just fifty days in the province he returned, armed with a phenomenal amount of evidence against the former governor. In the end, witnesses, documents and deputations from all over Sicily were gathered in an impressive monument to Cicero's hard work. But the defence team did not relax in their efforts to sabotage the trial. For when Cicero returned to Rome with his evidence, they even told his witnesses that they should just give up. Cicero, the rumour spread, had accepted a large bribe to make a complete sham of the case. It was all a lie; fortunately for Cicero, however, the Sicilians did not believe the vicious reports.

The month before the trial started, the elections for the following year's offices took place. And, again as Verres and Hortensius had hoped, the results were favourable. Whether by luck or by bribery, Hortensius and Quintus Metellus were to receive the consulships in January 69 BC, while another of their clique, Marcus Metellus, was appointed the president of the extortion court. Buoyed on by this news, it was now vital to delay the conclusion of Verres' trial until the following year. With his friends in high office, Verres would never be found guilty. According to Cicero, when the results of the elections were announced, men were congratulating Verres rather than the successful candidates: 'I hereby declare,' said one man to Verres, imitating the style of the official announcements, 'that according to the election held today you are officially acquitted.'[20]

Cicero had to take drastic action: the lengthy Roman court procedure would have to be abandoned. Typically, a trial was heard over the course of two hearings, each taking the same format. The prosecutor opened with a long speech, and the defence answered at equal length. The witnesses for either side were then cross-examined, and there may have been a chance also for the opposing advocates to enter into a debate with each other. An adjournment followed, and after a day's interval it all happened over again: further speeches were given and additional evidence could be called. It was only after all of this that the verdict was passed and, if necessary, the assessment of damages taken. To save time, Cicero had to weigh up the cost of glory against securing a quick conviction:

> If I was to use the full time allotted to me by law for making my speech, I would certainly reap the fruits for my painstaking and meticulous work; for my conduct of this prosecution would show that no one in the memory of mankind has ever come to court more prepared, more vigilant, more ready than I do today. But there is the very real danger that, in going for glory, I might let the defendant slip through my fingers. So what can I do? I guess it is clear and plain to see: I must save the fruits of glory that could be reaped from a long speech for another day. For now, I intend to prosecute this man by means of account books, witnesses, and public and private documents and decrees.[21]

We can only imagine the defence team's reaction at the sight of all the document boxes, as well as at the crowds of witnesses and envoys from nearly every city in Sicily. Furthermore, although there was nothing illegal in Cicero's decision to cut short his speech, his strategy was unusual. Within the first hour of the trial, Cicero later tells us, he had cut short any hopes the defence still had. By the second day, they had given up, and on the third day Verres pretended to be ill. For the rest of the hearing, which lasted nine days in full, the evidence produced from Rome and Sicily continued to overwhelm the deflated and despondent Verres. At some point in the middle of the trial, perhaps before the second hearing started, Verres took a Roman's prerogative: he escaped into exile for the rest of his life, taking what he could with him.

Although Verres had managed to take some of his treasures with him into exile, trials for extortion were followed by an assessment of damages, and some restitution was made to the victims of provincial mismanagement. Plutarch states that Cicero assessed the penalty at three million sesterces; this amount was dramatically lower than the forty million he earlier claimed Verres had extorted. Cicero – or so the story later went – was subsequently accused of scheming to reduce the assessment, but we need not take this claim too seriously. Rather, it may reflect the extent of Cicero's exaggeration of Verres' misconduct in the speeches he delivered against his opponent, or Plutarch has got his facts wrong (and doubtless they derived from a hostile tradition against Cicero anyway). Either way, the Sicilians were evidently pleased with the compensation they received, for they remained loyal supporters of Cicero, whose patronage of Sicily now brought him a valuable base of political supporters for the future.

Cicero's success had depended a lot on his speed in preparing the case, as well as his flexibility in jumping over the hurdles that the defence team threw in his way. But Plutarch's statement that Cicero won 'not by speaking but by actually not speaking'[22] dramatically devalues the superb range of oratorical weapons that Cicero brought to bear on his opponents.

The speech for the first hearing was as entertaining as it was shocking, emotional and tragic. Apparently, Hortensius was moved to complain when a young boy, a victim of one of Verres' inheritance scandals, was paraded in shabby attire before the court to elicit the jury's sympathy. Everyone laughed when Hortensius complained that he did not understand Cicero's riddles. Cicero responded, 'you ought to, you have a sphinx at home', alluding both to the famous riddle of the sphinx and a marvellous ivory statue that Verres had given Hortensius as a gift.[23] The audience was allegedly outraged, as Cicero told the story about some pirate captains whom Verres had failed to have beheaded: he had turned a blind eye to their guilt and the safety of Rome for the sake of a tidy backhander. Even Verres had jumped up to defend himself against the witnesses Cicero produced. In short, Cicero had promised a spectacle, and this is what he delivered – even if he did not get to deliver all of it.

All the speeches from this trial survive under the title of the *Verrine Orations*, and they include the speech that Cicero had planned to say in the long second hearing, if Verres had not gone into exile. There were no standards of relevance in a Roman court: a man was expected to expose all the scandals of a man's life, and this is precisely what Cicero did. Verres was a man marked by his lust, cruelty, violence, arrogance and more. He was a pirate, a tyrant and a national enemy. In Cicero's words:

I have brought before your court not only a thief, but a wholesale robber; not only an adulterer, but a ravisher of chastity; not only a sacrilegious man, but an open enemy of everything sacred and religious; not only an assassin, but a most barbarous murderer of both citizens and allies. And so, I think he is the only criminal in the memory of man who is so atrocious that it would even be for his own good to be condemned.[24]

This is the published speech for the second action, which allowed Cicero to cover the charges against Verres in full: he detailed his early career, his abuse of the judicial system in Sicily, his extortions from the Sicilian tax system, his plunder of precious works of art, and his inefficiency as a military commander and Roman governor.

At the same time, Cicero's publication of the speeches enabled him to lay claim to the glory that his hard work had earned. This was a conscious act of self-promotion, not only as an orator, but as a politician. For publication in ancient Rome was not a commercial enterprise; nor was it handled by professional companies. Instead, a publication was produced when a writer – nearly always a man – decided to copy out and circulate his works. As an orator, Cicero wanted his work to be studied as a model prosecution case. Yet, in writing his speeches up for publication afterwards, Cicero also put his political views on paper for all to see and read. He had established a political 'line' so to speak, and he thus showed his readers what he stood for. He was deferential to the institution of the senate, but his disgust at the state of the courts and the nepotism of the élite inner circle marked him out as a politician for the people, fighting against the nobility's corruption:

> Your 'friendship', Hortensius, and the 'friendship' of all the other great men of noble birth, is more freely available to a man like him, brazen and impudent as he is, than it is to any of us honest and principled men. You hate the new men's industry, you despise their honesty, you scorn their sense of decency, you want to see their abilities and virtues crushed down and destroyed: Verres, on the other hand, you love! Oh, I get it: he may not be virtuous, hard-working, blameless, shameless *or* pure; but you do enjoy his conversation, culture and good taste do you? You cannot: he has no such quality. Everything he does is tarnished not only by extreme indecency and disgrace but by exceptional stupidity and vulgarity.[25]

Cicero had defeated Hortensius and he was now regarded as Rome's leading orator. It meant that he could now lay aside the suspicious task of prosecuting; for it was not an activity in which senior politicians were meant to engage. But the prosecution of Verres had served its purpose: afterwards, Cicero's services were in demand from men of senatorial rank, and the following years witnessed a huge surge both in the number and the importance of the clients he was commissioned to defend.

Hortensius continued to speak in the law courts until his dying day, but at the same time he retired increasingly into a life of leisured luxury. Cicero always remained slightly distrustful of him, but often he and Hortensius spoke on the same side. Indeed, looking back on their years in advocacy together, Cicero said: 'For twelve years after my consulship, Hortensius and I engaged in some of the greatest trials side by side. I always regarded him as my superior, he held me as his.'[26]

As for Verres, he stayed in exile for the rest of his life. By an ironic twist of fate he met his death in the same proscriptions as Cicero in 43 BC: the precious items which he had so painstakingly acquired in Sicily had caught Mark Antony's eye. When Verres refused to part with them, he signed his own death warrant. But not without the satisfaction that Cicero had died first.

5

The New Man at Rome (69–67 BC)

CICERO'S AEDILESHIP

> Meanwhile my election began to take place: Verres thought he was master of that too, along with all the other elections that were taking place this year. Running from tribe to tribe, with his charming and popular young son at his side, the all-powerful Verres made his rounds: he was canvassing and summoning all his family friends – that is, rather, all his bribery-agents. But, as soon as the Roman people noticed this and realized what he was doing, they wholeheartedly made sure that I was not cast out of my office by the money of a man whose wealth had failed to distract me from my duty.
>
> (Cicero, *Against Verres* 1.25)

As we saw in the last chapter, the elections for office in 69 BC had taken place the month before the trial of Verres opened. And just as Verres' money had doubtless helped his friends obtain the highest offices, so he tried to sabotage Cicero's chances of election to the aedileship. Yet Cicero's name was the first to be called out: he was at the top of the polls and the most popular candidate for that year. We might ask what accounted for his popularity and ensured his success if, by Cicero's own admission, his quaestorship (the only office he had held to date) had failed to make the headlines. His name had been made, as we have seen, in his earlier defence cases, but that was ten years ago now. The prosecution of Verres must have been the final push his career needed.

For the decade before the trial of Verres, Cicero had worked hard to establish the network of political friendships which came naturally to men of nobility, but from which his ancestry and birth deprived him. Yet he had taken advantage of the powerful support he could gain from the equestrians (his own original class), and added clients from the provincial towns he defended. The prosecution of Verres, however, had also demonstrated that he was the kind of politician that the people could admire, yet whom the senate did not need to fear. This delicate balance of people-pleasing was vital if he was to be sure of continued success at the polls. And Cicero's decisions in the years leading up to his consulship demonstrate a sound calculation of the need to cultivate an elaborate nexus of supporters, drawn from all the sectors of society.

This can be seen most clearly in his decision not to stand for office as a tribune of the plebs. Every year, the assembly of the people elected ten men to stand as their representatives vis-à-vis the rest of the senate. The task of these representatives, the tribunes, had originally been to protect the plebeians against overbearing or aggressive magistrates. But over time, and particularly after the tribunate of Tiberius Gracchus in 133 BC, their powers made them potential political opponents of the senate's traditional authority. While it was possible to use the office in the senate's favour (as Cato the Younger later did in 62 BC), Cicero may have fallen under suspicion if he, a new man, had chosen this route.

Instead then, Cicero had waited for the aedileship, which was a safer means of winning favour among the general populace. For the aedile of Rome was responsible for putting on the games, maintaining the grain supply and for the supervision of public buildings and places – all the things that mattered to the average man on the street. Unlike the other posts on the ladder of offices, the aedileship was optional. It could be a costly venture because the aedile was expected to subsidize the public budget out of his own pocket, but – for a man who wanted to progress further up the ladder – it had its advantages. Much as politicians today attempt to sway voters with promises of lower taxes and social reform, the politician in ancient Rome could make his name memorable by lowering the cost of living and increasing social happiness.

This year was one that passed well for Cicero. His aedileship ran smoothly, for he provided games and kept the cost of living low. In this last task Cicero was particularly helped by the grateful Sicilians, who sent him all kinds of foodstuffs to pass on in his official capacity. Yet he never lost sight of the need to broaden his support base. After his time as an aedile, Cicero had to wait another two years until he was legally old enough to serve as a praetor. In the meantime, he returned to the tool with which he had carved his success so far: oratory. But Cicero also returned to the act of defending. Now was the time to make friends, and he did so by defending senators, equestrians and men from the lower classes too – both at Rome and across Italy.

It was during the year of his aedileship in 69 BC that Cicero undertook his first defence on behalf of a senatorial client, Marcus Fonteius, who had until recently been the governor of Transalpine Gaul. However, this case also highlights one of the problems in judging Cicero as a man; for Fonteius was being tried on the charge of extortion. Thus, within a year of haranguing Verres and denouncing the behaviour of Rome's magistrates in the provinces, Cicero was defending a man who was, in all likelihood, guilty of the same crime (albeit on a much smaller scale). By this act, Cicero can all too easily be condemned for being hypocritical, immoral and inconsistent. Yet his own conscience was clear; as he once reflected later in life: 'In lawsuits, the jury should always search for the truth, but an advocate may occasionally defend what looks like the truth, even if it is not strictly accurate.'[1]

Furthermore, as we have seen, the Roman rhetorical education was geared towards producing speakers who could argue on both sides of the same case. Indeed, although the speech *For Fonteius* only survives in fragmentary form, several passages do well to highlight Cicero's forensic skill in countering the same hurdles that Hortensius had faced when he defended Verres. For the prosecutors of Fonteius had witnesses who could testify against Cicero's client – and it was imperative for Cicero that these men should not be believed.

One way of dealing with the prosecution's witnesses was simply not to cross-examine them. Hortensius had largely remained silent while Cicero produced the streams of witnesses against Verres, and Cicero used a similar tactic in the trial of Fonteius for two main reasons. First, as Cicero candidly admitted, it was not wise to give 'an angry man a platform to speak'. Second, because an advocate who protested too much actually 'attributed some authority to a greedy man'.[2]

However, the prosecuting advocate *would* have cross-examined his own witnesses; and it was the task of the defence to dismiss any testimony they gave. Here, Cicero drew an immense advantage from the fact that Fonteius had at least taken steps to protect the interests of the Roman businessmen operating in the area. These men rallied to Fonteius' side, and they defended him in front of a court which now consisted largely of equestrian jurors. On the other hand, all of the prosecution's witnesses were Gauls – one of Rome's traditional enemies in days past – and racial attacks seem to have proved an effective means of discrediting foreign witnesses.

In the *Verrine Orations*, Cicero had guarded the reputation of his Sicilian witnesses by stressing both their individual uprightness and the loyalty of the province as a whole. And so, if Fonteius was lucky that his province was notorious for the historic unruliness of its inhabitants, he was certainly fortunate to have an advocate who successfully exploited every Roman prejudice to diminish the credibility of the Gauls' accusations: 'What do we need a wise jury for? What need is there for a fair president of the court, or a clever advocate?' Cicero ironically asked in a series of rhetorical questions: 'The Gauls say Fonteius is guilty – so it must be true!'[3]

To add to the portrait of the slanderous Gauls that he had thus created, Cicero linked their character and famed disorderliness to the traditional warning of the consequences a wrongful verdict might bring. The prosecutors had argued that Fonteius' *acquittal* would result in 'some new Gallic war' – a claim Cicero traced back to the Gauls themselves who 'stroll happily, with their heads held high, from one end of the forum to the other, uttering threats, terrifying men with their barbarous and savage language'.[4] But in fact, Cicero argued, the real danger lay in what would happen if the Roman jury gave in to the Gauls' threats and wrongfully *condemned* Fonteius; for there would be no limit to their impudence thereafter.

We are again reminded of how important the argument from character was in the Roman courts. However, in a defence case, it was also vital to appeal to the jury's sympathetic side. Cicero excelled at such emotional appeals and the case of Fonteius shows him in one of his best performances. It was typical for the Roman defence advocate to parade the distressed family of the accused, but Cicero could go one step beyond the normal in this trial. Fonteius' sister was one of the esteemed and prestigious vestal virgins who guarded the sacred fire of Rome: 'Beware,' Cicero warned the jury, 'in case the eternal flame, saved for so long by Fonteia, who watches and waits over it every night, is extinguished by the tears of your priestess.'[5] It was one of Cicero's boldest pleas and Fonteius, it seems, was acquitted.

The case of Fonteius not only presents us with an illustrative example of how Cicero exercised his oratory in the different roles of prosecution and defence; the trial served Cicero several useful purposes in his political career. Fonteius was a senator who had protected the interests of the equestrians well during his term of office, and in one go Cicero had extended his services to men of both orders. However, Fonteius also brought Cicero into the favour of his family's original homeland, Tusculum (near modern Frascati). Like all the Italian towns which possessed full Roman citizenship, Tusculum had the right to vote. Their political support was part of the elaborate matrix of networks that a Roman politician needed, and Cicero's work in the courts continued to help him establish further ties across Italy.

In addition to the case of Fonteius, Cicero acted in the interests of another wealthy Italian, called Aulus Caecina, in a hugely complicated inheritance suit. But he did not ignore the lower sectors of society in his quest for friends and political allies; for Cicero himself tells us how he defended Matrinius – a 'humble aedile's clerk' – who had been wrongly dismissed from his office.[6] In sum, while delighting in his new senatorial clients, Cicero had not forgotten to curry favour with the larger body of voters. At the same time, he demonstrated that he had not become imprudent in the face of his initial successes.

A PRIVATE MAN WITH A POLITICAL AGENDA

Away from the public glare of the forum and the law courts, a man's personal life also contributed heavily towards his political career. Marriage in particular was a powerful resource in the accumulation of friends and connections, and by the time of his aedileship in 69 BC, Cicero's marriage to Terentia was in its eleventh year. They had seen the birth of their first child early on in their marriage, around 78 BC. This was their young daughter, Tullia, the apple of her father's eye. Later, in 65 BC, Cicero and Terentia also had a son to follow in his father's footsteps, and his name too was Marcus Tullius Cicero.

Children, Cicero believed, were a gift from the gods, and love for them was a natural instinct. It is no surprise that fatherhood came easily to him, and it is warming to see Cicero's very genuine capacity to give and receive affection. Several years later, when his close friend Atticus had a daughter, Cicero took a great share in his delight:

> I am delighted that your little daughter is bringing you such joy, and that you agree with that Greek doctrine that 'it is natural to feel affection for children'. For if this is not the case then there can be no natural tie between one human being and another; if that is taken away, the whole essence of society is removed.[7]

At the same time, having a family brought several political advantages. Cicero could rank himself among the responsible citizens, whose domestic affairs did not escape the notice of the public eye. Reports of his stable family life would spread, and they provided a benchmark from which his political reliability and reputation could be assessed. For these reasons and more, Cicero was equally keen to ensure a good match for his younger brother, Quintus.

It was probably in the year of his aedileship that Cicero and his friend Atticus arranged for Quintus to marry Pomponia, Atticus' sister. For by 68 BC, in the earliest of the surviving letters from Cicero to Atticus, it emerges that the couple were already experiencing marital problems: 'I have been greatly concerned that my brother Quintus should feel towards her as a husband ought', Cicero complained. 'Thinking that he was rather out of sorts, I sent him a letter in which I calmed him down as a brother, advised him as my junior, and scolded him as a man in the wrong.'[8]

At the time of their marriage, Quintus was about thirty-four and Pomponia may have been slightly older than her new husband (it is commonly thought that it may have been her second marriage). He was short-tempered, while she was a jealous and moody woman. Yet a marriage was as much a union between men as it was between a husband and wife, which is why we see Cicero and Atticus anxious to make the match between Quintus and Pomponia work. Their stormy relationship forms a recurrent feature in Cicero's correspondence with Atticus, for amazingly the marriage lasted until 45 BC. The couple also had one son named, as was usual, after his father – Quintus Tullius Cicero.

Just as the elder Quintus' marriage to Pomponia was a sign of the friendship between Cicero and Atticus, having a daughter also enabled Cicero to strengthen his political alliances. Tullia's engagement too was arranged the year later, in 67 BC, when she was just eleven years old. Her fiancé was an excellent young man called Gaius Calpurnius Piso Frugi, whose ancestors had been praetors, and his great-grandfather had even been a respected consul and censor. And, although the marriage itself did not take place until Tullia was about fifteen, the relationship between Cicero and Piso's family was cemented at the time of the betrothal. It was only natural that Cicero was thinking ahead to ensure his daughter's happiness, but he was also thinking of his bid for the praetorship.

To gauge from a letter of advice that Cicero later sent Atticus, however, it seems that more than political considerations were in play in his selection of a son-in-law. Certainly a young man's personality, family and financial position were all important criteria. But he also added the necessity of knowing the man personally, and of liking his father too. Piso was about ten years older than Tullia, and so it is possible that he had been one of Cicero's students at some point. Cicero had certainly observed and admired his talent and potential; when Piso was young 'he made so much progress that he seemed to fly not run', he later wrote.[9]

However, it should be observed that the match between Tullia and the young Piso was quite a coup for Cicero, who had still not even reached the praetorship himself. The marriage alliance probably owed its success, first and foremost, to Cicero's skill as an orator. Cicero may only have been a new man, but he had demonstrated that he and his family would become worthy of a noble union. The shared values, evident in Cicero's admiration of Piso's hard work and enthusiasm, certainly also played a part. Yet there was another factor that may also have contributed towards Cicero's ability to arrange such a good marriage for Tullia: his father had just died, leaving Cicero significantly better off in terms of his wealth and position.

The evidence for this is a brief mention in a letter, dated to the end of 68 BC, which states simply: 'We lost our father on 23 November.'[10] The brevity of this announcement has led many to suppose that Cicero and his father were not close. This is mere speculation. However, the passing away of one's father in ancient Rome was always a practical, if not an emotional, milestone in a man's life. For Roman society was patriarchal, and at the top of every family was the 'father of the household' (the *paterfamilias*). In theory, the *paterfamilias* had the power of life and death over his family, including his children and slaves. He held the financial purse-strings. When Cicero married Terentia, for example, her dowry may have gone to Cicero's father rather than to her new husband. For as long as Cicero's father was alive Cicero remained dependent on him, but all this now changed. The death of Cicero's father made him a far more independent and rich man.

Immediately, Cicero began to invest in property; a lifelong occupation in which he took great pleasure. His favourite property for years to come was a villa he bought this year at Tusculum, just south-east of Rome. This was a country home where Cicero often went to take comfort in his books. He even built and decorated a *gymnasium* there – a lecture hall with a series of colonnades and walking grounds – in the fashion of Plato's Academy, which he had visited in his study-tour of Greece a decade earlier. Later he built a second library, called the Lyceum after the school of Aristotle. For now, Atticus helped him furnish the Academy – choosing and acquiring choice works of art from Greece: statues and the portrait heads of deities like Hercules and Minerva, the goddess of wisdom.

In time, Cicero added several more villas, about half a dozen in total, which he called the 'jewels of Italy'; on top of these he owned several small lodges.[11] This was typical of Cicero's day. Without anything like the modern hotel (there were only disreputable taverns and inns), a man needed to own a few villas and apartments, where he could stop overnight on his travels, lodge his friends or take his holiday. Yet Cicero's investment in property was also a political venture. A big house in the city of Rome was essential for a politician, who needed the large open space of the hallway (*atrium*) to receive his clients and associates. On the other hand, the properties around Italy enabled Cicero to make vital friends in these communities, which in turn added to his network of supporters. These municipal contacts were as useful as any of the ties that could be claimed through political alliances, the patron–client system or the obligations of hospitality. And they helped Cicero gain a foothold in a number of the voting districts, in addition to the strong support he received from his native Arpinum and other local areas.

By the beginning of 67 BC – the year his election was to be held – Cicero was in the ideal position, personally and financially, to bid for the praetorship. His political career had flourished in his performance as an aedile, his first official role to be conducted before the eyes of Rome. His oratorical career now also benefitted men of all classes with the result that his network of personal supporters was increasing in both size and prestige. At the same time, preparations in his private life and his own increased fortune all meant that Cicero was confident in the run-up to the elections. However, the race was only just beginning and the competition was going to be tougher than most for a new man: Cicero needed to manage his campaign carefully, and this included making decisions on whose friendship to accrue and what alliances to make.

CICERO, POMPEY AND THE CAMPAIGN TO BE PRAETOR

As the year 67 BC opened and Cicero's campaign for the praetorship geared towards its climax, a major proposal was presented to the people by one of the tribunes for the year, Aulus Gabinius. This bill, the Gabinian law, proposed an extraordinary command to deal with the very real problem of piracy in the Mediterranean, but it was clear to everyone at the time that it had been framed with one man in mind: the general Gnaeus Pompeius (known to the modern world as Pompey). The bill proposed to place a huge amount of power in the hands of just one man, and there were many men at Rome who were determined not to let this happen.

To say something about Pompey, he was born in the same year as Cicero, and the two men had almost certainly met while serving for Pompey's father in the social war, when they were just seventeen years old. In all likelihood, they may have come into contact with each other long before this, as both their fathers owned properties in the Carinae district of Rome, on the Esquiline hill. However, they do not seem to have formed any sort of early friendship, for their paths took Pompey and Cicero in different directions in the 80s and 70s BC. During the years in which Cicero was studying at Rome, Pompey had become something of a national hero.

Pompey the Great.

Pompey was ruthless and ambitious from the start. In his early years, he was nicknamed the 'killer boy' when, at the age of just twenty-three, he raised a private army of his own to help Sulla in the civil war.[12] It was from these campaigns that he earned the *cognomen* Magnus ('the Great'); and after this initial taste of public glory, Pompey continued to fight in a number of high-profile campaigns. First, he quelled a potential civil uprising in 77 BC. From 76 to 71 BC he then fought in Spain against the illustrious general Sertorius, who was taking a stand against the Roman government. Finally, Pompey returned to Italy in time to help crush the remnants of Spartacus' troops in the south – the seventy thousand slaves and gladiators, who had surprised Rome with the level and determination of the battle they fought between 73 and 71 BC.

For Pompey, military prowess proved to be a far quicker route to the top than oratory and sticking to the rules had proved for Cicero. And when he made it to the top, he stayed there for a long time. The name of Pompey dominated the political scene at Rome over the 70s, 60s and 50s BC – as, indeed, it did over the corresponding years of Cicero's life. The years of Cicero's political rise are also the years of Pompey's ascendancy; and so it is important to get to know Pompey better, as well as to be aware of the resistance he faced from many in the senate, if we are to understand the decisions Cicero made both at this stage and in the rest of his career.

Pompey's battles had brought him a huge amount of personal fame and influence. However, they had also come at a huge cost to the senate, who had short-sightedly granted Pompey these extraordinary commands. Through fear, no doubt, of Pompey's personal army, a highly irregular and illegal enterprise, the senate had given Pompey everything he had ever asked for. He had never held a single magistracy on the ladder of offices, yet the senate had granted him the power of *imperium*, and the standing equivalent to a consul. They had panicked when warfare struck and the senate used Pompey when they needed him; however, they had given him a disproportionate amount of strength in return. When he finally returned to Rome in late 71 BC, Pompey refused to start at the bottom of the ladder, as his contemporary Cicero had done. He demanded the consulship, and a weakened senate had little choice but to grant the thirty-five-year-old's wishes.

By all the laws that Sulla had established to prevent precisely this kind of anomaly, Pompey should not have been given the consulship. He needed to be forty-two, and he needed to have held the quaestorship and praetorship first. Pompey's success in the race for office, coupled with his immense popularity with the people, earned him the distrust of the nobility for years to come. That is why in 67 BC the senate's leaders did not want Pompey to gain yet more influence; on the other hand, the equestrians and the general populace gave their unreserved support for the bill, which nominated him as the commander of the Roman troops against the pirates.

The senatorial resistance to Pompey's appointment ultimately proved futile. In the end, amid violent remonstrations during the voting procedure, Pompey did receive his command. Furthermore, he astonished even his critics by clearing the seas of piracy in just three months. Reflecting on this achievement a year later, Cicero told the Roman people that 'one law, one man, one year not only freed you from the dire and humiliating situation you were in, but even brought about one in which you truly seemed to be the ruler of all people and nations on land

and sea'.[13] But, crucially, however much Cicero praised Pompey in hindsight, he avoided engaging in the debate at the time – and what Cicero did *not* say or do with regard to the Gabinian proposal paradoxically tells us much about Cicero's political strategy.

Scholars disagree on when exactly Pompey and Cicero first took notice of each other as political colleagues; yet a hint from Cicero suggests that it was not until some time *after* his election to the praetorship. Even in the run-up to his consular campaign, over two years later, Cicero was still very much unsure of whether or not he could count on Pompey's support: 'Tell *him* I shall not be angry if he does not come to my election', Cicero instructed Atticus; for he was afraid that Pompey might have his own candidate to promote.[14]

The temptation for Cicero to support Gabinius' bill must have been hard to resist, for there was much to commend a political alliance between him and Pompey. Indeed, although they were fundamentally different in their military aspirations and experience, Cicero and Pompey were perhaps destined to be closely linked in life – as later events showed them to be. Not only were they born in the same year, but their family backgrounds, status and connections had much in common.

To begin with, both men were born outside of Rome. Cicero, as we have seen, was born in Arpinum while Pompey's family came from Picenum, just on the other side of the Apennines, to the north-east of Rome. Unlike Cicero, Pompey's family *had* been ennobled by the election of family members to the consulship. But, even so, his connections with the noble families in the senate were loose, and Pompey was more closely aligned with the equestrian order. These factors may explain why Cicero later felt more drawn to Pompey than to other men of rank. Yet now was not the time to risk alienating Pompey's opponents in the senate, and so Cicero – aware as ever of the need to win senatorial support – chose not to speak in favour of the bill, and he delayed an outward show of support for Pompey.

In 67 BC, therefore, we see Cicero cautiously engineering his campaign to avoid displeasing the nobility. This was especially important because the elections to the higher offices (the praetorship and consulship) were held in the centuriate assembly, which was heavily biased towards the votes of the wealthier citizens. He was so confident in his strategy, in fact, that Cicero could tell the influential Atticus not to return to Rome on his account alone: 'There are more important things for you to be doing at this time than being present at my election.'[15] And he was right. When it came to the time of the elections, Cicero's name once more came at the top of the polls. And not just once but three times, for the elections were twice interrupted that year.

The so-called 'new man's industry' had paid off, and Cicero's efforts to cultivate a political support base had rewarded him handsomely. On 1 January 66 BC, he entered into office as one of the eight praetors for the year. His success can be attributed to his energy, political instinct and oratory. And in his year of office, these skills and more were called upon as Cicero edged ever closer towards his political dream of the consulship.

6

The Climb to the Consulship (66–64 BC)

THE PRAETORSHIP AND POLITICAL ORATORY

Until today I have never dared to speak from this place of authority on account of my age, and I was determined that I should not deliver anything other than a speech rounded-off by a matured ability, and polished by experience: before now, I thought that I should spend all my time assisting my friends in their times of need. And so, while this place has never lacked men ready to defend your interests, my hard work, which has been honestly and openly dedicated to defending private citizens, has received the highest possible reward by the vote you have taken.

(Cicero, *On the Command of Pompey* 1)

Cicero's year as a praetor of Rome was a crucial stage in his career. Not only had he reached one of the two highest magistracies in republican Rome but also he now had the chance to demonstrate what he stood for and to show the senate and people of Rome what kind of consul he would make. It was in this year that, for the first time in his life, Cicero stood before the people of Rome and addressed them from the *rostra*. This elevated platform was a highly honoured spot. It was from here that senior politicians of Rome addressed the citizen body in *contiones* ('public meetings'). Very often *contiones* were held to discuss new or proposed legislation, and this was the context of Cicero's first appearance – for there was a new bill on the proverbial table, and it sought to give Pompey another all-powerful command against Rome's oldest and most formidable enemy: Mithridates.

For several years the campaign had been led by one of Rome's leading citizens: Lucius Licinius Lucullus. He was an able general but Lucullus had stretched his troops too far. The men operating against Mithridates were in disarray, and there was need for a new improved Roman presence in the East. It was for this reason that the tribune, Gaius Manilius, now proposed that the command against Mithridates should be transferred to Pompey. Pompey was already in the area following his campaigns against the pirates, and his military successes made him the obvious man to take the lead. It was also now that Cicero decided to deliver his first ever political oration: the people, he urged, should support Manilius and Pompey.

Cicero's speech *On the Command of Pompey* is the first of its kind to survive in Latin literature; namely, it is an example of deliberative oratory, which recommended a course of action for the assembly's consideration and vote. Deliberative orations still had to persuade their audience, but on matters of policy rather than crime, and so they required a slightly different kind of oratorical approach to the forensic speeches Cicero had so far delivered in the law courts. That said, the majority of the Greek and Roman rhetorical handbooks were geared towards providing advice for legal trials. Cicero himself, as we have seen, composed one such manual in the 80s BC – his work *On Invention* – and it is clear in the current speech that Cicero did not deviate far from the system he knew.

The speech is a model of clarity, structured around the typical elements that Cicero believed were necessary in a good oration: the *exordium* (introduction), in which a speaker aimed to win the audience's goodwill; a *narratio*, or a short narrative, detailing key information and background events; and a *partitio*, in which the speaker listed how he intended to treat his subject matter. These were followed by the two elements that strengthened a speaker's case: the *confirmatio*, setting forward his own argument, and the *reprehensio* or *refutatio*, which aimed to destroy that of his opponent. This was all rounded off with a *conclusio* (a peroration), which typically, as we have already seen, paid particular attention to arousing the emotions of the audience.

Winning the assembled people's goodwill, Cicero claimed, was an easy task in the speech *On Pompey's Command*. After all the topic was in praise of their hero: 'It will be more difficult to finish speaking than to begin.'[1] Yet, as we saw in the quotation above, Cicero felt like he had to defend his decision to enter the political arena – he had not 'dared' to speak on a political matter before. Strange as it may seem, that a politician would have to justify his decision on when and why he spoke to his countrymen, Cicero may have had some cause for uneasiness.

Although Cicero was now much higher on the ladder of offices than most, it was by no means expected that a praetor should embark on political oratory. Instead, Cicero had made a deliberate and calculated decision to make his debut in political oratory at this time, for this was not just a political speech, it was a political move: Cicero was using the occasion to proclaim his alliance with Pompey's faction – and to win the backing of Pompey's supporters. At the same time, he had to be careful not to offend Pompey's opponents.

Speaking against the bill was a small handful of highly influential senators. These were men from within the innermost clique of the senate, often referred to by Cicero as the *optimates* (the 'best men'), who grouped around Lucullus, Hortensius the orator and their highly esteemed ally, Quintus Lutatius Catulus.

The decision to speak against this inner faction on a bill that sought to wrench the prestigious command away from the nobility was risky, but Cicero had chosen his time to speak wisely. Enough of the senate were in favour of the proposal, and so this was the ideal opportunity for Cicero to show his political hand.

To begin with, Cicero would not alienate the senate by speaking up for Pompey in this instance; he just needed to tread carefully on the sensitive toes of Lucullus' circle. But, on the positive side, he was promoting a line of action that was very popular with the people as well as the equestrians, whose revenues were suffering as a result of the war. Indeed, one of Cicero's themes in this speech was the need to make Asia Minor a safe and prosperous province, both for Roman finance generally and her businessmen specifically. The latter's revenues, he said, were the 'sinews' of the Republic: 'Believe me,' Cicero warned, 'and believe what you can see for yourselves: this entire system of credit and finance, which operates at Rome, in this forum, is tied up and dependent on the money they have invested in Asia.'[2]

A further factor which may have influenced Cicero to speak was the opportunity that this speech offered for making an oratorical extravaganza. For Cicero always had an eye on his posthumous reputation, and a written record of a political speech, which could be read for years to come, would be a great addition to his list of publications. As both an orator and a politician, Cicero was a rival for any of the great Athenian men of the past – men like Demosthenes, whose speeches Cicero greatly admired and emulated. A published version of a deliberative oration to complement his forensic speeches would make Cicero the Demosthenes of his generation. Furthermore, the topic of Mithridates was a gift to any orator with a flair for imagination.

It was now the third and last war that the Romans had fought against Mithridates – the greatest threat to Rome since the days of Hannibal. In the past he had shown himself to be a cruel and savage aggressor. On the outbreak of the first war with Rome (88–85 BC), Mithridates had brutally executed a Roman general by pouring molten gold down his throat. In the same year, he ordered the deaths of thousands of Roman citizens – men, women and children – all on one day. It was a tragic moment in Rome's history and Cicero made sure he exploited it:

> More than any other nation, you have always sought after glory and have been eager for renown. You must therefore wipe out the stain of that disgrace incurred in the earlier Mithridatic war, a stain which has seeped in too deep, and sullied the reputation of the Roman people for too long. I am talking about a man who on one day, across the whole of Asia, in so many cities, with one letter, and with one command could order for Roman citizens to be killed and butchered. Not only has he never paid a penalty to fit his crime, but that was twenty-three years ago – and he is still ruling. And he rules in such a way that he refuses to lie hidden in the dark shadows of Pontus or Cappadocia. Indeed, he

wants to break out of his own country and kingdom, and encroach upon the lands that pay you taxes: that is, into the bright light of Asia.[3]

At the same time, Cicero's speech was a masterpiece of tact. True, he argued that Pompey should replace Lucullus as the commander of the forces against Mithridates. But he was generous in his praise of Lucullus – even more so than the men defending Lucullus' position, Cicero claimed. In this way, he won favour with the crowd, he fought for the businessmen's interests, but he also remained cautious not to offend the powerful men fighting in Lucullus' corner.

We may wonder how genuine Cicero was being in this speech. Yet, however high-flown his language may have been in praise of the famous general, Cicero always remained one of Pompey's most loyal admirers. Even though he was personally disappointed and let down by Pompey at several key moments in his later career, Cicero stuck by him to the end. And perhaps, already in 66 BC, Cicero saw in Pompey a glimmer of the hope he would long hold for him. At the same time, Cicero's eyes were firmly fixed on the consulship. And his public declaration of support for the people's darling at this stage of his career had been an opportunity that he could not let slip.

LOOKING BEYOND THE PRAETORSHIP

Obtaining the praetorship had been a reward in itself, but we must remember that it was still only a rung on the ladder. For the men who had made it this far, the ultimate goal was the consulship. Cicero's whole political life had been gearing towards this moment, and his best chances of winning the consulship lay in the practice at which he had excelled so far: the law courts. For this was also considered a public service like any other task devoted to community improvement – be it the funding of major building works, service in the army or the provision of legal advice. Cicero did not need to make any more political orations for now; nor could he afford to risk offending senior political figures, upon whose support he would soon heavily rely. Instead, Cicero knew that he could continue to create a political profile by defending clients, as well as by conducting his praetorship carefully. And for the rest of 66 BC this is precisely what he did.

One of Cicero's most famous speeches belongs to this year: his defence of Aulus Cluentius Habitus, who was accused of poisoning his stepfather Oppianicus. This case, which Cicero presented in a way that was as scandalous as it was complex, formed part of a long-running series of family disputes. For, eight years previously, it had been the other way around: the stepfather, Oppianicus the Elder, had been prosecuted for attempting to murder his stepson, Cluentius.

In the earlier trial, Oppianicus the Elder had been successfully convicted by just one vote, but everyone knew that the jury had been bribed. The result was that popular opinion was generally against Cluentius; even his natural mother, Sassia – a depraved woman, if we are to trust Cicero – had turned against her own child. Consequently, when her husband died just two years later, Sassia allegedly conspired with Cluentius' stepbrother (Oppianicus the Younger), to bring a charge against her son: this charge was that Cluentius had poisoned Oppianicus the Elder by injecting a cocktail of drugs into his bread.

The evidence for the poisoning, without the medical advances we have available today, rested largely on the testimony of slaves, coupled with the suspicious circumstances surrounding Oppianicus' sudden and unexpected death. But even if he did die suddenly – as many people do – Cicero argued, there was no proof of poisoning. The true cause of Oppianicus' death, Cicero claimed, was that he fell off his horse. Here, again, we see that Cicero's ability to come up with an alternative version of events was tantamount to his success in the case. Yet he also needed to disprove the slaves' statements – extracted, as was customary, under torture. And, indeed, Cicero rose to the challenge by providing a brilliantly vivid account of the conspiracy against his client, which he made believable by the characters he created for the main protagonists in the trial.

Sassia was a cruel woman, Cicero argued, who had plotted her own son's downfall and railroaded the younger Oppianicus into prosecuting him; furthermore, this was the second time she had tried to ruin Cluentius. On an earlier occasion, Sassia had brutally tortured her slaves to give evidence against her son; yet the slaves claimed to know nothing about a plot to poison the deceased man, and her plan failed. However, three years later, when the opportunity arose to resume the trial, Sassia jumped at the chance to renew her attack. Two of the slaves, who had been tortured in the first inquiry, were examined again; however, this time they appear to have said whatever Sassia wanted them to say, and the minutes from this second inquiry had been submitted and read aloud to the present court.

Cicero's narrative – which forms only a part of his long speech – is a highly charged account of deception, brutality and betrayal revolving around Sassia. The minutes from the inquiry were a fabrication, he claimed: 'If she got the chance, the hand that forged the charge would be the hand that slaughtered her son.'[4] Her evil deeds continued in the gruesome conclusion to this episode: one of the slaves got off scot-free, but the other, whom Sassia distrusted, had his tongue ripped out and was crucified. Cicero's vilification of Sassia may have been a small piece of the darkness that – according to his own boast – he cast over the jury in this trial. But, by attacking Sassia, Cicero could simultaneously lessen the attack on the men involved. Oppianicus the Younger was an affluent equestrian from an Italian family, and now was not the time for Cicero to be losing support from the wealthy municipal regions.

Yet, at the same time that it provided a shockingly entertaining narrative, the speech *For Cluentius* also contained a very clear political message. It was a political ideal for which Cicero later became famous: the *concordia ordinum* ('the harmony of the orders') – that is, the need for co-operation and concord between the highest-ranking citizens of the state. 'All those senators who live an honest and honourable life,' Cicero claimed, 'want the equestrians to be bound to them in the most harmonious relations and to be second only in position to the senatorial order.'[5]

As we have already seen with regard to the staffing of the juries, contentious issues could arise between the senatorial and equestrian ranks, and so it would only take business and politics to clash for another dispute to arise. Cicero's stance was probably not an entirely original one, but it does demonstrate that he was very alert to the dangers of the system. If the Republic was to survive then this unity, he believed, needed to be achieved.

A further reason why Cicero had to tread carefully in this speech was that, now, his jury included men from the three wealthiest classes – the senators, equestrians and treasurers – all of whose support he would need in years ahead. However, Cicero's own plans to keep every sector of society happy did not always run smoothly, and two incidents in particular caused Cicero some embarrassment during his year of office: the trials of Gaius Licinius Macer and Gaius Manilius.

In his role as the president of the extortion court, a job allotted to him in his capacity as praetor, Cicero had to supervise the trials of these two men. Yet both Macer and Manilius were popular with the masses, and this meant that Cicero had to balance his judicial integrity with the need to retain their favour. At the same time, he could not afford to alienate the senatorial élite. In the first of these cases, he succeeded. Macer was condemned, but the people – to Cicero's great surprise and relief – approved: 'I managed the trial of Gaius Macer to the quite incredible and unique approval of the people', he later wrote in a letter to Atticus.[6]

However, the trial of Manilius – the very same man whose proposal Cicero had backed in the speech *On Pompey's Command* earlier that year – was more problematic. By this time it was December, and Manilius applied for several days' postponement, hoping to delay proceedings until the next year. Yet Cicero granted him just one day's adjournment, and his refusal to delay the case further annoyed Manilius' plebeian supporters. They thought Cicero was acting unfairly towards a man he had once supported, and the tribunes immediately summoned a meeting at which they questioned his decision. But Cicero, thinking on his feet, appeased them: he had wanted, he claimed, to try the case of Manilius himself – so that he could provide a sympathetic hearing while he still held his authority as praetor.

The people had called Cicero a 'turncoat' for failing to support Manilius, but now the crowds cheered; they even begged Cicero to defend Manilius when the

trial came to court. The defence of a populist politician had the potential to alienate Cicero from the ruling classes, but there was little he could do except agree.
As it turned out, however, the case of Manilius never came to trial, and Cicero
came away from the whole incident with his reputation intact. But the result was
that Cicero ended his praetorship on a high note, with the crowds applauding
him. He had turned the tide of opinion in his favour, and he could now hope it
would carry him to the top.[7]

PLAYING THE POLITICAL GAME

It was another two years until Cicero could legally become a consul when he
retired from his praetorship in December 66 BC. At the beginning of 65 BC he was
still forty years old; yet he needed to be forty-two if he was to be successful, as he
most surely wanted to be, 'in his year'. But as he looked ahead to the consulship,
Cicero put into practice one of the lessons he had learned from his time in Sicily
many years before: it was better to stay in Rome, where he could live his life in
the eyes of the people. And so, while most ex-praetors left directly to govern one
of Rome's provinces, Cicero turned down the opportunity to go abroad as a propraetor. At the same time, Cicero may also have demonstrated a very profound
point by staying in Rome. Unlike other politicians, who used their year abroad
to recoup the financial losses they had made in their electoral campaigns, Cicero
could afford not to go. In short, he had not bribed his way to the top.

However, despite Cicero's impressive rise through the ladder of offices, aiming
for the consulship was another matter entirely. To begin with, the competition
was tougher: only two consuls were appointed, compared with the eight praetors
and twenty quaestors. But the rank of consulship was also jealously guarded by
the noble families. In fact, it was over thirty years since the last new man had been
elected to the consulship. Nor did the other new man from Arpinum, Marius,
who had held the consulship six times between 107 and 100 BC (before seizing it
for a seventh time in 86 BC), do anything to allay the nobility's fears. A new man
was a 'pollution' to the consulship – or so the Roman writer Sallust once wrote.[8]

It was Cicero's status as a new man that was to hamper him most in the years
ahead. But Cicero was not just any new man – he had a unique talent as a public
speaker, and he had used this gift to remarkable effect. He was unrivalled in the
law courts, he had elevated his standing in the eyes of Rome's political élite, and
he had mustered a huge network of personal supporters. Yet the ability to speak
well came with a price: one had to defend the right people, and support 'honourable' policies – for the risk of offending the wrong people was an ever-present
danger. In short, one had to play the political game carefully, as a unique pamphlet on electioneering, often thought to be written by Quintus Cicero, points out:

> You must cultivate [the aristocrats] diligently. You must call upon them, persuade them that politically we have always been in sympathy with the *optimates* and have never in the least been supporters of the *populares.*[9]

To put this advice into context and to understand the obstacles that faced Cicero, it is time to be aware of how politics worked at Rome. For not all senators were equal in the eyes of its members, and those wishing to advance in their political careers worked in very different ways.

The *optimates*, as we saw earlier, were the 'best men' – the wealthy ruling class who sought to uphold the traditional authority of the senate and the power of the aristocracy. Up until the end of the 60s BC, this clique was dominated by Hortensius, Catulus and Lucullus, until, as we shall see, they began to champion Cato as their dominant member. However, challenging the influence of this inner élite, there was also a group of politicians who advanced their aims and careers on the support they received from the people. A politician that pandered to the mob in this way was labelled a *popularis* (a 'people pleaser') by his opponents: that is, he was a populist politician in contrast to the *optimates*, the conservatives, who sought to uphold the senate's influence.

But the networks in which politicians operated were not political 'parties' in the modern sense of the word, with the result that it is nearly always impossible to identify or classify politicians in Rome within strictly demarcated groupings. In addition, just as our concept of political 'parties' fails to describe the alliances formed at Rome, we should also avoid mapping the terms conservative and populist onto modern ideas of right-wing or left-wing programmes. They did not share a 'party' programme, a common agenda or a uniting philosophy. Politics was, and so it remained in Cicero's day, a shifting network of personal allegiances which were as easily broken as they were formed.

Cicero himself used the terms *optimates* and *populares* flexibly, and so – despite the tendency of twentieth-century scholars to use these labels – it has more recently been argued that they do little to enhance the modern reader's understanding of the political climate in the first century BC.[10] However, what is clear is this: the populists had developed in response to, and often as a challenge against, the control exerted by Rome's most aristocratic families. Some populist politicians doubtless had the interests of Rome and social reform in mind. But there were many who manipulated and utilized the mob to further their own careers, either by becoming tribunes themselves, or by operating behind the schemes of tribunes. That is why Cicero had to tread carefully in how he presented his political stance, for he needed to earn the support – not the distrust – of the nobility.

During his praetorship, Cicero had admittedly lent his support to populist causes. For, as we saw, the *On the Command of Pompey* speech he delivered was in support of a tribunician bill that had not met the full approval of the ruling élite. Yet Cicero knew how to play the game of diplomacy, as can be seen in a controversial case which came his way in 65 BC. This trial was the defence of a former populist tribune called Gaius Cornelius, yet Cicero's handling of the case – as far as we can tell from the fragments that remain of the speech – was the product of a master tactician.

The period of Cornelius' tribunate in 67 BC had met with staunch resistance from the most powerful members of the senate generally, but the specific charge facing him was treason. Opposing Cornelius was a formidable array of faces, including Hortensius, Catulus and Lucullus, who claimed that he had committed a crime against the majesty of the Roman people. For, when a bill that Cornelius proposed had been vetoed by a fellow tribune, Cornelius continued to read the bill out loud. This was an affront upon the sacrosanct power of his fellow officer. But did Cornelius' disregard of a veto really make him a radical tribune, Cicero asked, sidestepping the issue of his actual guilt. For this was the question which Cicero opened up for Catulus to decide:

> Suppose, as one friend to another, I wished to ask Quintus Catulus, a most learned and humane man, the following question: 'Out of the two, which tribune was less tolerable: Gaius Cornelius or – (and I shall not name Publius Sulpicius, Lucius Saturninus, nor even Gaius Gracchus or Tiberius, who are generally regarded as seditious tribunes) – but, tell me, Quintus Catulus, who was less tolerable: Gaius Cornelius or your own uncle, a most distinguished and patriotic man?' – What do you think his reply would be?[11]

In this way Cicero made a valuable point, for Catulus' uncle had proposed legislation that was against the interests of the aristocracy during his tribunate too; but that did not make him a radical tribune. In one of his favourite rhetorical tricks – called *praeteritio* – Cicero promised not to recall all the tribunes (Sulpicius, Saturninus, the Gracchi, etc.), who had been extremely antagonistic towards the senatorial order. But in making the point that he would pass over their names, Cicero did mention them. And these men's tribunates had witnessed riots and death, thus enabling Cicero to put Cornelius' 'crime' into perspective. By the same stroke, he excused his decision to defend a tribune for his anti-senatorial actions.

Cicero had pulled off an incredibly tricky case. In other fragments, we see that he managed to both flatter Pompey (who was associated with Cornelius) and soothe Pompey's critics (notably Hortensius and his circle). And, at the same time, he criticized the office of the tribunate, while defending a tribune. According to the rhetorician Quintilian, he gave an extraordinary performance. Cicero's speech met with thunderous applause from his listeners: 'He blew their minds; forgetting where they were, they burst with delight.'[12]

However, although he may have managed to avert the suspicion of having negative populist leanings in the trial of Cornelius, Cicero still had a bigger point to prove before embarking on his campaign properly: he needed to show that he could also speak in the interests of the nobility and that he could serve their ends, if he was to succeed in winning their support. The chance came later that same year when an ever-ambitious and hugely rich man, Marcus Licinius Crassus, started to interfere with the affairs of Egypt. There were many in the senate who were not impressed with Crassus or his populist tendencies, and Cicero used the occasion to deliver his first speech in the senate.

To say a word about Crassus first, he seems to have been an unlikeable fellow for whom Cicero had little time. He was the son of the great orator, whose speeches Cicero admired greatly. But his ancestry may have been his only redeeming factor, for boundless anecdotes recall Crassus' scurrilous greed and desire for power. They tell of how he inserted the names of innocent men onto Sulla's proscriptions lists, just to get his hands on their property. Or they record how he recruited his own fire brigade to salvage burning houses after buying them, as well as any others in the surrounding area, at knock-down prices. Rome was full of wooden houses and fire was a constant hazard; the owners would have been happy to take anything in the face of abject poverty. And, indeed, Crassus was rumoured to have bought most of the property in the city in this way. These were all tales of a ruthless, self-serving villain. Yet, whether we choose to believe them or not, they do preserve a hint of how Crassus was perceived by those who knew him.

From the fragments of the *On the Egyptian Kingdom* speech that Cicero delivered, it appears that these two factors – Crassus' ambition for money and power – figured heavily in Cicero's argument. For Crassus was either proposing or supporting a motion to add the rich kingdom of Egypt to the Roman Empire. Furthermore, the proposal may have envisaged that a young Gaius Julius Caesar (the future dictator) should be the commander. There were many advantages in it for Crassus. Egypt was not only a wealthy land but also it played a key part in Rome's grain supply and other commercial enterprises. If he was successful, the equestrian class would be eternally grateful to Crassus. And Crassus, in turn, would have great influence in, and the rich pickings of, a highly desirable province.

Yet Crassus was rich and powerful enough and, for some time, he had used his enormous wealth to buy political supporters. He lent money at large to aid bribery in the courts, and even funded the careers of younger men in whom he saw the potential for a powerful alliance based on popular support. It was for these reasons and more that Cicero joined the nobility in arguing against, and successfully blocking, Crassus' plans. Cicero had by no means entered the inner clique of the senatorial élite; however, he had demonstrated that he could and would support them.

Cicero's speech *On the Egyptian Kingdom* was one step towards earning the backing of the traditionalists within the senate, or at least towards settling any anxieties they may have had regarding his own political intentions. But it was no guarantee that they would actively promote his bid for the consulship – especially since Cicero's competition included men from far more prestigious backgrounds. For, in the year ahead, Cicero had to campaign long and hard against men who, in the eyes of some, had more of a 'right' to be consul than the new man from Arpinum did.

COMPETITION TO BE CONSUL

In July 65 BC Cicero was already looking ahead to the management of his consular campaign. He was planning to start canvassing in the middle of that month, a whole year before the elections, but this did not stop Cicero speculating on who his competition would be for Rome's two premier positions: 'The rivals who seem to be certain,' he famously wrote to Atticus, 'are Galba, Antonius, and Quintus Cornificius. When you read this last I think you will either laugh or cry. So you will smack your forehead now: some think Caesonius may stand too! . . . As for Catilina, if the jury decide that the sun doesn't shine at midday, he will certainly be a candidate.'[13]

From the jocular tone of his letter, it seems that Cicero's competition was not as tough as it could have been. However, two names did stick out in particular: Gaius Antonius Hybrida and Lucius Sergius Catilina (referred to as Catiline by modern writers). Both Antonius and Catiline were members of the nobility; indeed, Catiline was even a patrician. This meant that he could trace his ancestry back to the legendary beginnings of Roman history, and to the one hundred *patri* (or 'fathers') – the original senators chosen to advise Rome's first king, Romulus. Since that day, the descendants of these *patri* had maintained their powerful influence over politics at Rome, and they regarded it as their birthright. The result was that, although no one in his family had held the consulship for several years, Catiline's name was as noble as it could be.

Yet, from the extract of the letter quoted above, it seems that Cicero had all but discounted Catiline from the race for the consulship. For Catiline was pending trial for crimes committed as a governor in Africa the previous year, and any man facing criminal proceedings in Rome was forbidden from standing as a candidate in electoral campaigns. Furthermore, it seems his guilt was obvious to all – as obvious as the fact that the sun shines at midday, according to Cicero's private note to Atticus. But Catiline was desperate to reach the consulship. He was two years ahead of Cicero on the ladder of offices, yet he had missed out on the position once before already – again on legal grounds. He planned to stop at nothing, and within a month something obviously changed to make Catiline's acquittal look like a foregone conclusion. Indeed, all of a sudden, Cicero even started to consider defending him.

Cicero evidently hoped that he could win Catiline's support by acting in his defence – they could even pool their efforts and campaign together as a duo. But this was not to be. For reasons that we do not know, Cicero did not defend Catiline. Maybe Cicero got a pang of conscience and changed his mind again; or perhaps Catiline was confident that he could bribe his way out of trouble, as Verres once had been. Catiline evidently did not think he needed to rely on the services of Rome's leading orator, and he was right. For Catiline was acquitted: his prosecutor had been induced to put on a bogus trial – or so the rumour had it.

Whatever reasons there were to explain the detachment between Cicero and Catiline, it is clear from subsequent events that there was never going to be a union between the two men. In fact, Catiline and Antonius formed an alliance and campaigned together for the two consular positions – against Cicero. Not only did Cicero have to counter their joint nobility, but he even had their lavish deployment of bribery to face. Indeed, their bribes grew so extensive that there is every chance that Crassus was funding their campaign. On the other hand, Cicero's only resources lay in the hard work and industry he had used to date in building up his network of supporters.

Cicero's campaign was tireless and his preparations were thorough. He dispensed with the services of a *nomenclator* – the slave whose job it was to announce men's names to his master when they came to greet him. For Cicero believed that a good politician should know his fellow citizens personally, and apparently he did; if we can trust Plutarch, Cicero could even point out the houses of everyone he knew across Rome and Italy.[14] Furthermore, he travelled all over the country, even visiting the military troops in Gaul when the courts were quiet. And, finally, he enlisted the help of his friend Atticus who, although only an equestrian by rank, had a circle of friends larger than any man's in Rome. Over time it included everyone from the most aristocratic of senators to staunchly populist politicians like Caesar and Mark Antony. As well as being a dear friend to Cicero, Atticus was one of his most useful supporters.

The pamphlet on electioneering had stressed the need for a candidate to collect support from all levels of society – and this is exactly what Cicero did. He had opened the year of his praetorship by championing Pompey; he had continued to look after the interests of equestrians and senators alike; and he had demonstrated to the traditionalists, the so-called *optimates*, that he could be trusted to preserve the senate's influence. Catiline would have done well to do the same, but, instead, our sources tell us that he openly courted the masses by paying out huge amounts of money as a bribe. The result was that Catiline raised such suspicion by his open display of populist policies that, even though he was a 'noble' man, the nobility distrusted him.

The doubts raised by Catiline's actions only added to the rumours that were rife about him: accusations of murder, incest and an affair with one of Rome's prestigious vestal virgins – Cicero's own sister-in-law, Fabia, if later reports can be believed. And as the competition and bribery grew more fierce and intense in the days leading up to the election, Cicero had to resort to the most power-ful weapons he knew: his words. He delivered a speech known as *In the White Toga*, referring to the particular brightness (*candidatus*) of the clothing worn by candidates, from which we derive the modern word.

In this speech, he lampooned the characters and shameful pasts of both Antonius and Catiline, but against the latter Cicero made vicious accusations: 'Catiline has sullied his body with every form of sexual perversion and vice', he doubtless boomed at the top of his voice. 'He has stained himself with the blood of his evil slaughters, plundered our allies, and violated our laws and law courts.'[15] He even hinted that Catiline had been involved in a plot to kill the consuls of the previous year as well (a plot that is often referred to by historians as the 'first Catilinarian conspiracy', for reasons that will become clear).

There were no limitations on political invective: it was an art form in ancient Rome – the polar opposite of extreme praise. Cicero could rake up every piece of scandal, and more, that had ever existed against Catiline in the hope that some of it would stick. There was probably little truth in some of these accusations, but the speech worked. For their part, Catiline and Antonius tried to strike back, but the only blow they could strike was Cicero's 'low birth (his *novitas*)'.[16] Catiline did not stand a chance; when the votes were counted, he came third in a race that only offered two positions: Cicero was voted in first place, and Antonius – despite a shameful past of his own – came second.

Cicero's campaign had been successful, but we should not attribute it solely to the fact that his rivals were weak or corrupt; nor should we compare Cicero's attack on his rivals to the modern smear-campaign. For the speech Cicero deliv-ered was born from desperation, and it was also in line with ancient conventions of political abuse. Instead, Cicero's election was the result of a number of reasons. True, luck played its part, but so did the hard work, determination and patriot-ism which Cicero had displayed in his rise through the ladder of offices. No one could prepare him for the events he witnessed during the dramatic year of his consulship – yet all these factors were called upon as Cicero faced one of the most challenging periods of his career.

7

A Consulship and a Conspiracy (63 BC)

A CONSUL FOR THE PEOPLE

> I am the first new man that you have elected as consul in a very long time, almost within our living memory. With me as a leader, you have broken open that position which the *nobiles* used to hold under lock and key and which was fortified in every way. You have shown that in the future you wish its gates to be open to those who deserve entry.
>
> (Cicero, *On the Agrarian Law* 2.3)

Cicero was notoriously happy to expound upon his own successes; even to an ancient audience, who were more accustomed to and acceptable of such braggadocio, Cicero seemed capable of excessive immodesty. To some extent it was natural, even expected, for a man to blow his own trumpet; for *dignitas* ('dignity' or 'worth') at Rome – which included a man's status, position and authority – depended upon both his own achievements and those of his ancestors. But if, like Cicero, a man did not have noble ancestors then he had to sound his own achievements louder. At the beginning of his consulship, however, Cicero had more reasons than most to feel proud: he had won his election to every single appointment at the first opportunity and, even more impressively, he had done so without recourse either to a ready-made support base or bribery.

Yet the Rome Cicero inherited from the grasps of the nobility was on the brink of chaos. Far from the days of decadence that we may imagine whenever we think of ancient Rome, with its lavish banquets, luxurious villas and convivial citizens, the city in Cicero's day was crowded, dangerous, dirty and unhappy. The poor lived in high-storeyed building blocks that were likely to collapse and burn under the perpetual threat of fire; the levels of sanitation were appalling in these crowded flats, where men, women and children had no access to bathing facilities, toilets, cooking appliances or even drinking water. Many fell into huge debt, and the only provision made for them by the state was a subsidy on corn. Even this they still had to pay for, however, and the prices forever fluctuated in the unstable market.

In such circumstances, a man who could represent himself as a politician for the people stood to gain much; this goes part of the way towards explaining why Cicero wanted to divorce himself from the *nobiles* and emphasize that he was not just another self-serving aristocrat. Indeed, he often used populist language when he addressed the assembled mob, but in 63 BC, at the beginning of his consulship, there was a further reason why he needed to pitch his oratory to the tune of the people. For there was another man ambitious for political advancement this year: Gaius Julius Caesar – and he had recently launched his career with a spectacular commitment to the popular cause.

In the years prior to Cicero's consulship, Caesar had made himself a very difficult man to ignore. His family was certainly well known, for the Julian clan boasted descent from Julus, the son of Aeneas (one of Rome's legendary founders after Romulus), who was himself believed to be the son of the goddess Venus. However, despite these impressive links to Rome's heroic and mythical past, none of Caesar's immediate family had reached political prominence in recent years. He was not yet the rich and famous leader that he came to be; this meant that Caesar needed to be creative in the political identity he chose to construct in order to gain the glory he craved.

Our picture of Caesar, even more so than most of his contemporaries, has been heavily distorted by writers who either romanticized his life or vilified his career after his death. Yet the personal ambition and self-confidence reflected in the biographical tradition certainly seem to stand behind the remarkable skill with which Caesar entered and manipulated the political game. For, despite the political obscurity of his own immediate family, Caesar's aunt Julia *had* been married to Marius, the notorious opponent of Sulla – and this provided Caesar with a firm foundation upon which he could build his reputation as the new champion of the Roman people. When his aunt died in 69 BC, Caesar paraded images of Marius in her funeral procession, which made its way through the streets of the city and right into the centre of Rome. Four years later, during his aedileship, Caesar even decorated the forum with statues and memorabilia commemorating the victorious general's campaigns.

Caesar represented the kind of populist politician that had long been feared. His patrician birth fuelled him with the desire to make his family's name great again; his early taste of military success – even winning the prestigious reward of the civic cross at the age of just twenty – increased his appetite for personal glory; and his oratory, admired by Cicero, gave him the power of persuasion. In short, he had everything he needed to succeed in political life, and in the forthcoming decades he utilized these advantages to a remarkable degree. For the time being, however, he was still in the shadows of men like Pompey and Crassus; yet it was now, in 63 BC, that Caesar showed he did not intend to stay there. Rather, he intended to fly on the wings of their success, and Caesar's decision and subsequent alliance with the multimillionaire Crassus spelled trouble for the year of Cicero's consulship.

CICERO, CAESAR AND THE QUESTION OF LAND REFORM

First on the agenda for 63 BC, the tribune Publius Servilius Rullus raised an issue that had been buried for many years and which was always associated with popular reformers. This was the topic of land reform, and Cicero was most probably right to suspect that Caesar and Crassus were operating behind the scenes. For in the past, agrarian bills – which proposed to redistribute land and provide farming pastures for Rome's poorer or retired citizens – had always been a crowd-pleaser. The current bill certainly offered an attractive and much-needed solution to Rome's poverty, yet there was something suspicious about Rullus' proposal.

The law envisaged that ten men were to be appointed as commissioners for a period of five years; their authority would be immeasurable, and such power was potentially devastating in the wrong hands. Plutarch lists among the commissioners' rights the authority to sell property belonging to the state, to try any man they thought fit, expel exiles, found new colonies, take money from the public treasury as needed, and maintain and levy army forces as and when they required them.[1]

Cicero's fellow consul-elect, Antonius, was expected to support the bill – and even perhaps be one of the ten commissioners, and this was the problem facing Cicero as he assumed the position of consul on the *kalends* (the first) of January. But fortunately for Cicero, the tribunes had assumed their duties almost three weeks earlier, as was usual, on 10 December. More important, they had declared their intentions for social reform and legislation immediately; this time gap gave Cicero a valuable head start in preparing the best line of attack.

Cicero needed to win Antonius' support promptly, and it was now that he either made or hinted at a deal with his colleague. Cicero's bargaining chip was the rich province of Macedonia, which he was due to govern after his consulship expired. The allocation of provinces was always made a year before the term of office started, so that Cicero was well aware of the advantage he had in his hand – and he played this advantage by offering to exchange Macedonia for Antonius' co-operation. It was a great coup for Antonius in the light of the huge debts he had accumulated during his consular campaign, for he could recover his financial losses through the routine practice of extortion. But it also suited Cicero down to the ground: he did not have to leave Rome after his consulship, and nor did he have to face any opposition from his co-consul during their joint term of office.

With Antonius' help assured, Cicero spoke vehemently against Rullus' proposal to the senate on the very day he entered office. Yet he faced a trickier audience when he attacked the bill in a meeting of the people, for Cicero had to persuade them against voting through a measure which was essentially to the people's advantage: 'I said in my very first speech to the senate on 1 January, in the very place where such an expression would not go down well, that I would be a consul for the people', Cicero reassured the crowds that flocked to hear his first address to them as consul. But, in the wake of the new populist policy proposed by Rullus, a redefinition of what it meant to be a people's politician was required: 'When I use the phrase *for the people* I need your wisdom to give it the correct meaning and interpretation', Cicero urged. 'For a critical blunder is perpetrated by those men who cover up their treacherous plans: they pretend they are acting in the people's interests when they make their speeches, but really they are acting against the interests, and even the safety, of the people.'[2]

Cicero's ingenuity in convincing the people that a bill proposed to benefit them was actually a fraud is remarkable. The ten men appointed to redistribute the land would have the power of kings, Cicero had warned an audience ever hateful of words associated with monarchy, kingship and tyranny. Moreover, the elections would be a sham because only seventeen of the thirty-five tribes were going to be called on to vote. In all actuality, the seventeen tribes would have been selected by lot, so there was probably nothing sinister in this particular clause of the bill, but Cicero could present it as a contrived effort to mismanage the voting procedure. Finally, there was a clause that he could play on to great effect. The bill stipulated that any candidates, who wanted to act as one of the ten commissioners, had to register in person. What was the point of this proviso, Cicero asked, if not to prevent Pompey, who was still campaigning in the East, from entering as a candidate?[3]

Cicero had trumped every card his opponents had in their favour: a populist agenda, the favour of Pompey and public benefit were all played down. Cicero surely exaggerated the dangers in the plan, but he was evidently worried about the intentions of those framing it – as well as the dubious financial implications of the scheme, which sought to privatize important public assets, as well as to purchase additional land from the state's treasury. The people were similarly afraid and the bill was swiftly dropped. It was an important victory for the new consul, but it was not the last challenge to the senate's authority that he needed to counter in the year ahead.

CICERO, CAESAR AND THE TRIAL OF RABIRIUS

Several other measures proposed by tribunes kept Cicero busy in the first part of the year: he seems to have quelled a proposal that aimed to cancel all debts, as well as another one which offered restitution to the sons of men proscribed under Sulla's brutal regime, and he even restored order after a riot broke out at the theatre. Yet before the first six months of Cicero's consulship had passed, an even more serious attack was launched against the senate when an elderly senator was prosecuted for a crime allegedly committed some thirty-seven years earlier.

The aged defendant was a man called Gaius Rabirius, but the object was not justice or retribution: the prosecution, instigated by the tribune Titus Labienus – and certainly inspired by Caesar – sought to undermine the authority of the senate. In particular, Labienus/Caesar wanted to question the senate's powers in issuing and implementing its 'ultimate decree' (the *senatus consultum ultimum*). This decree was an emergency measure that effectively invoked a kind of martial law; when passed, it stipulated that the consuls of Rome had to take extraordinary action 'to see to it that the state came to no harm'. It did not specify what actions the consuls could take, and it did not provide legality to their actions. But it did provide a worrying cloak of security under which violent actions could be condoned if they were deemed necessary.[4]

In short, the ultimate decree gave magistrates the power to use force against any citizen who was threatening the Republic; it was the passage of this decree that had led to the murder of a tribune, Lucius Appuleius Saturninus, in 100 BC. For when Saturninus and his henchmen were imprisoned in the senate house, they were brutally slaughtered as the mob (thinking that they too had some protection under the ultimate decree) tore the tiles off the roof and pelted them. Labienus now alleged that it was the tile thrown by Rabirius that had killed Saturninus all those years ago.

To make matters worse, Saturninus' status as a tribune of the plebs had meant that he was legally sacrosanct; his body was protected by the majesty of the Roman people and he was thus inviolable. So, it was not any old murder charge with which Labienus/Caesar now charged him: it was high treason. The penalty facing Rabirius was scourging and crucifixion, and he was to be judged by just two men: one was Caesar, the other was Caesar's cousin. The trial was to take place before the people, in an assembly meeting on the field of Mars, where hostile judges, an executioner and a cross all awaited Rabirius.

Modern historians disagree on what happened next. Many believe that Rabirius was found guilty and faced an appeal before the people, while it has also been argued that the harsher sentence was quashed and replaced with a more lenient procedure. Either way, the case was dropped before a verdict could be passed. Moreover, it was abandoned in a manner that was as bizarre as the rest of the trial, for the quick-thinking praetor, Quintus Caecilius Metellus Celer, recalled an ancient method of halting proceedings in the city.

In the early history of Rome, a red flag was waved on one of Rome's seven hills, the Janiculum hill, whenever the assembly was in session. If the flag was lowered it meant enemy invaders were about to attack, and any public business was brought to an immediate close. At the crucial moment of Rabirius' trial, when the speeches had been heard for the prosecution and the defence, Metellus Celer made the decisive announcement: the red flag on the Janiculum hill had been lowered, and the trial was stopped. Interestingly, the charge was never resumed – but Caesar and Labienus had made their point in a most emphatic manner.

Why, then, had Rabirius been put on trial in the first place? 'So that in future,' Cicero answered, 'the senate will have no authority; the consul will have no power; and the verdict of all good men will have no strength against the pernicious pests of society.'[5] This prosecution had been political not personal: the populists had been staging a dramatic protest against the executive power of the ultimate decree. But the protest was also extremely well timed, for murmurs of plots, conspiracies and dissent were in the air. And by the end of the year, Cicero too was faced with the agonizing decision of how and when to implement the ultimate decree.

THE CONSPIRACY OF CATILINE

Despite the prominence of Caesar and the opposition of the populists in the early part of his consulship, Cicero's year in office is most famous for the events surrounding the last half of 63 BC: the conspiracy of Catiline. For, as can only be expected, Catiline had not taken his rejection at the polls the previous year lightly. He was a patrician and it was his 'right' to be a consul of Rome. His ambition to attain the top position, coupled with the knowledge that this was his last chance to achieve it, led him to undertake a no-holds-barred election campaign.

Because Catiline had lost the support of many among the nobility in his previous campaign, he had to look elsewhere to get the backing he needed. And so he turned increasingly towards the people, and especially those plagued by debts and other difficulties – a ready and ample crowd both at Rome and across her empire. Aware of this, Cicero had kept a watchful eye over Catiline for some time, but rumours of an unofficial 'election speech' were enough to make him take action. 'That wicked gladiator allegedly made a speech in a meeting held at his house', Cicero later recalled. 'He said that it was impossible for a man to be a loyal defender of the poor unless he was poor himself; that people who were broke and in trouble should not trust the promises of men who were successful and fortunate.'[6]

The next day, Cicero called for the elections to be postponed and he questioned Catiline in the senate. But far from denying the rumours, Catiline gave a chilling response: 'He said that the state had two bodies: one weak with an infirm head, the other firm but with no head at all – to the latter, provided that it showed itself deserving of him, he would provide the head so long as he was alive.'[7] The first body was the senate, the second the masses – and Catiline was declaring his intentions to champion the mob. It was an alarming claim but the senate, perhaps proving Catiline's point, did nothing but groan. He, on the other hand, left the meeting triumphantly.

However, if Cicero failed to convince the senate to take action against Catiline with his words, he *did* succeed in persuading the voting populace of the imminent threat posed by Catiline. For on the day of the elections, Cicero made a show of wearing body armour beneath his toga: his breastplate was visible to all, as was the armed band of supporters that stood by to protect him. His plan, in Cicero's own words, was 'for all the loyal citizens to take notice and to rush to offer their help and defence, both out of fear and from the sight of their consul in danger.'[8] And it worked. Once more a desperate Catiline was beaten at the polls, and – if we can trust the sources that describe the dramatic events that follow – his thoughts turned more and more towards revolution.

Indeed, if he had not considered it earlier, Catiline certainly now began to hatch the conspiracy for which he has become notorious. His goal was to seize power at Rome by means of violence, and Cicero first heard about his plans through a woman called Fulvia (not, it should be noted, the same Fulvia who later married Mark Antony). Instead, this Fulvia was the upper-class mistress of Quintus Curius, who was one of the typical men who followed Catiline – 'a man of no mean birth, but immersed in vices and crimes', in the words of the Roman historian Sallust.[9] And for the rest of 63 BC Fulvia remained Cicero's informer.

Later too, Curius was swayed to supply Cicero with the information he needed, but for a long time Cicero had only the word of a shady mistress to go on. To judge from anecdotes Cicero later told against himself, he was often mocked when he announced to the senate: 'I know for certain that . . .'[10] But one night in late October, the proof that Cicero had been waiting for came to light, for some anonymous letters had been left at Crassus' door. One letter was addressed to Crassus, which he duly opened and showed to Cicero. It said that Crassus should leave the city at once, and warned that Catiline was planning to attack and slaughter many of the leading senators, including Cicero.

The next day, Cicero convened the senate and distributed the rest of the letters Crassus had received, still unopened, to their intended recipients. Cicero asked for them to be read aloud and they all contained the same message of impending doom. The question was: who had written them?

To this day it remains a mystery. Some scholars have suggested that maybe Cicero wrote the letters as a ruse to test Crassus: Crassus had, after all, openly supported Catiline in the past, and it would not be wildly unthinkable to connect him with Catiline now. Others have suggested that maybe Crassus stage-managed the whole business to place himself above suspicion. But it is more likely, considering how clumsily Curio had leaked the plans to his mistress in the first place, that some of Catiline's conspirators were simply just careless enough to warn their friends.[11] Yet, as subsequent events revealed, there was no smoke without a fire in the case of Catiline. And it perhaps does not matter too much *how* the conspiracy was exposed; what was more important was that the senate was finally ready to believe its consul.

Cicero had other news to report: Manlius, who had been a centurion in Sulla's army, was raising troops at the mouth of Etruria in a place called Faesulae (about five miles north-east of modern Florence). Cicero was even able to predict with some confidence, or so he later boasted, that Manlius' troops would rise on 27 October 63 BC and begin their march upon Rome. The unsettling news was enough to compel an anxious senate into action, and on 21 October they passed the controversial ultimate decree: Cicero now had 'to see to it that the state came to no harm'.

A number of immediate measures were taken. The large companies of gladiators were removed from the city, and Cicero armed a strong force of volunteers, who garrisoned strategic points across Italy and Rome. On 1 November 63 BC, these forces were even able to thwart an attempt to seize a stronghold, Praeneste, which was only twenty miles from Rome. However, there was still nothing to connect Catiline firmly with the reports of a conspiracy. The letters were, after all, written anonymously. And nor was there any evidence linking Catiline with Manlius' troops. It was true that Manlius had supported Catiline politically in the past, but rumours and suspicions were not enough for Cicero or the senate to take direct action under the ultimate decree.

For now, the best anyone could do was to charge Catiline formally under the laws against public violence. One man seized on the opportunity to prosecute him; however, under Roman procedure, Catiline was still a free man until he came to trial. He could attend the senate, take part in their debates, and nobody could stop him. In a bold protestation of his innocence, Catiline offered to place himself under the house arrest of any senator who would watch him. But no one, including Cicero, wanted to have him. So he stayed with a friend, an unlikely 'guard', and Catiline continued as normal.

This friend did not prevent Catiline from attending an all-important meeting on 6 November. In the darkness of the night, Catiline made his way through the narrow streets of Rome and came to the scythe-makers' district – to the house of Marcus Porcius Laeca. This meeting was a secret gathering of Catiline's conspirators and their aim was to complete the plan they had hatched. At this meeting Catiline divided up the regions of Italy, telling each man where he would be posted. Others were to stay in the city. As for Catiline, he proposed that he should leave Rome to join Manlius' troops immediately, but he would only leave when he knew for certain that Cicero was dead.

Our main source for these events is Cicero's impassioned account in the speech known as his *First Catilinarian*. But his claims should not be dismissed as empty hysteria, for on the morning of 7 November, two of the conspirators did indeed attempt to kill Cicero. Their plan, we are told, had been to get close to Cicero during the early morning call traditionally held in the consul's house. 'I knew all of this,' Cicero boasted to Catiline, 'scarcely a minute after that meeting of yours dispatched!'[12] Fulvia's warnings had enabled Cicero to foil the attempted assassination, but he no longer felt safe with Catiline still in Rome. He called an emergency meeting of the senate the very next day, and Cicero used all the power of his oratory to drive his enemy from the city.

'O TEMPORA, O MORES'

'O the times, O the customs', Cicero lamented in one of his most famous speeches (the *First Catilinarian*). Catiline's guilt was obvious, everyone knew it, yet there he was – in a meeting of the senate. Perhaps no one expected Catiline to attend that day. Indeed, Cicero's words certainly seem to convey his surprise as he rounded on Catiline: 'How far, I ask you, Catiline, will you test our patience? For how long will that madness of yours continue to frustrate us? At what point will your rampant audacity stop flaunting itself about?'[13]

If we can trust Cicero's portrayal of the event, no one dared to sit near Catiline and the benches emptied around him. The meeting was not in the senate house that day; instead, the senators had been instructed to assemble in the temple of Jupiter near the Palatine hill. The temple was far easier to guard, and a large number of equestrians and other loyal citizens all trooped to support Cicero. The location served a rhetorical point too. At a moment in which Cicero wanted to exaggerate the dangers facing the senate and Rome, the sight of the armed men surrounding a place of sanctity could be used to great effect.

At several points in the speech, Cicero draws attention to the surroundings. The senators were gathered inside the temple, and a large statue of Jupiter dominated the interior. Twice Cicero addressed Jupiter Stator directly. 'Stator' means stayer or stabilizer – and Jupiter was the god who protected Rome and her empire. It was a very sacred spot but it also had a long history – especially in times of military crisis. The site of the temple and its erection evoked memories of the foundation of Rome, as well as the earliest battles fought by Romulus and his men. This was the essence of Roman history and it would not have escaped the notice of the senators called to assemble there. The denunciation of Catiline was brilliantly stage-managed, and the choice of venue dramatically added to the force of Cicero's words.[14]

We can only imagine the scene from the speech that Cicero later published, as well as from the accounts of Sallust and other historians; however, emotions were evidently charged. Cicero led a sustained attack on Catiline but he criticized the senate too, as well as his own hesitation:

> This is now the twentieth day on which we have let the sharp edge of the senate's author-
> ity become blunt. We have the senatorial decree, but it is filed away in some study like a
> sword buried in its sheath. You should have been killed by this decree, Catiline. Yet you
> live, and you live not to lay aside but to strengthen your audacity.[15]

Cicero was not calling for the immediate execution of Catiline, but he was urging Catiline to leave Rome. And that evening he did. Taking a different route out of the city than expected, Catiline said he was going into exile in Massilia (now Marseilles), but that was a trick. He shortly joined Manlius, as Cicero knew he would, in Etruria. Dressed in the consular robe of which he felt he had been deprived, Catiline raised the military standard that had belonged to Marius – a magnificent silver eagle. According to one source, he had managed to raise twenty thousand men in his ranks.

Now that Catiline and Manlius were in open revolt against Rome, they were declared 'public enemies' and the senate hesitated no further. Cicero's colleague, Antonius, was sent to lead the forces against them in the field; however, Catiline's departure from Rome did not spell the end of the conspiracy. A large number of Catiline's supporters – the 'dregs' as Cicero called them – were still in Rome: 'How lucky Rome would be,' he reminded the people in his *Second Catilinarian*, 'if it could flush all of this scum from the city!'[16] For Cicero could not forget the plans that he had heard from Fulvia – plans of fire, slaughter and the demolition of the city; moreover, he was terrified at the thought of enemies within the very walls of Rome.

Not everyone, however, shared Cicero's anxiety. In fact, the usual quarrels between the aristocratic élite resumed as quickly as Catiline had departed, and chief among their disputes was the outrageous amount of bribery employed in the recent consular elections. Cicero had even passed a law increasing the penalty for electoral bribery to ten years' exile in an attempt to curb the corruption; yet this had not been enough to prevent its occurrence. And as soon as the city appeared to be safe from attack, a young Cato was hot on the track to fulfil a promise he had made to prosecute anyone guilty under the new legislation.

Cato, or Marcus Porcius Cato Uticensis to give him his full name, was another rising star during this year, and he belonged firmly in the camp of traditionalists. His great-grandfather, Marcus Porcius Cato the Elder, had been such a staunch upholder of public morality that he even earned the *cognomen* 'Censorius', after his meticulous work in the office of censor. Cato the Younger had inherited these conservative values from his famous ancestor, but he also added some of his own, for he was a close follower of Stoic philosophy – a school of thought that provided its adherents with a very fixed code of conduct. He had been shocked by the level of open bribery in the summer's campaigning and together with Servius Sulpicius Rufus, who had been an honest but unlikely contender for the consulship, Cato launched his attack on one of the successful candidates: Lucius Licinius Murena.

Murena was, by all accounts, guilty as charged, but his prosecution put Cicero in an awkward position. For, even though he was friends with Sulpicius, and despite his own efforts to prevent bribery, Cicero felt compelled to defend Murena. Above all other concerns, no one knew what Catiline's next move would be, and there needed to be two consuls in place for the beginning of the year. If Murena was found guilty, there would have to be a re-election and that took too much time.

Another factor in Murena's favour was that he had some military experience and close personal ties to leading generals. Sulpicius, on the other hand, was a legal expert – and there was no question over who would be more valuable in repelling the armies of Catiline and Manlius. In a comic sequence of comparisons between the life of a soldier and that of a legal expert, Cicero poked fun at Sulpicius' claim to be the better candidate: 'You file a lawsuit; he draws up a whole legion. You make sure your clients are not caught off-guard; he ensures that cities and camps are not captured.' Cicero taunted: 'He knows how to keep off the enemy's forces; you know how to repel rainwater. He has been trained in extending boundaries, you in defining them.'[17]

At the same time, Cicero mocked Cato's commitment to Stoicism and presented the prosecutor as a zealot of an unrealistic philosophy. 'What a witty consul we have', Cato is said to have replied, and indeed Cicero's speech remains one of the funniest to have survived.[18] But underneath the humour lay a genuine fear: Catiline was still alive and Rome was not safe from attack. The jury too were convinced that the question of Murena's guilt or innocence was of secondary concern to the welfare of the state. Cicero had secured his client's acquittal by questionable means, but within weeks, if not days, the jury's trust in their consul paid off.

THE URBAN CONSPIRACY

Since Catiline's departure, the control of the urban conspiracy had passed to one of the praetors of the year, Publius Cornelius Lentulus Sura, who was planning slaughter and arson on a massive scale. Lentulus was a member of the nobility and even an ex-consul, but he was one of the many men who had been expelled from the senate in 70 BC. He was now working his way back up the ladder and aiming for the consulship again, yet his debts were accumulating as a result. His desperation may go some of the way towards accounting for his involvement in the conspiracy in the first place, but it may also help explain the critical blunder that he now made.

It happened that envoys from the Gallic tribe of the Allobroges were in Rome complaining, as usual, about the oppression of their governor. Lentulus saw a chance to enlist their help in the conspiracy: the disgruntled Gauls, he thought, could create a distraction by revolting in the province and thus divert the attention of both the senate and Rome's legions. And in an almost unbelievable display of their indiscretion, the conspirators revealed all their plans to the Allobroges. The conspiracy had been leaked, and after some deliberation the envoys decided it was in their best interests to tell their patron in Rome – who, in turn, passed the news on to Cicero.

The confirmation that a conspiracy was being hatched from within Rome was a remarkable coup for Cicero, but he needed more than the words of some foreign envoys to go on. And so Cicero instructed the Gauls to play along with Lentulus and secure what proof they could – signed letters or documents. This they achieved with alarming ease when Lentulus and two other conspirators, Cethegus and Statilius, naïvely handed over signed pledges containing the written details of the plot. They even gave the Gauls a guide, called Volturcius, to lead them to Catiline on their way home, and this guide also carried a letter written by Lentulus. He did not sign it but the words of encouragement spelled out his support for Catiline's conspiracy in no uncertain terms: 'You will find out who I am from the person I have sent to you', it read. 'Be sure to act like a man and take thought for how far you have advanced already. See to whatever you need, and make sure you take help from everyone who offers it, even the lowly [i.e. slaves].'[19]

The proof of the plot now rested firmly in the hands of the Allobroges, and on 2 December a trap was set to recover it. Cicero ordered two of the praetors, whom he trusted deeply, to stage an arrest. As Volturcius and the Gauls made their way across the Mulvian Bridge, which was less than two miles north of the city, armed soldiers sprung upon them from both ends. Apparently, the Gauls did not know what was going to happen that night. But they surrendered immediately, knowing that they did not need to put up a fight. Their surprise, which concealed their complicity, gives clear evidence of Cicero's mastery of the affair. For, seeing that he had been deserted, Volturcius surrendered too and was arrested. He proved to be a valuable prisoner, for he later turned informer to save himself – and he gave personal evidence against the conspirators.

In the early hours of 3 December, the prisoners, five in total, were summoned to Cicero's house, where they stayed until they were led before the senate later that same day. This time the meeting was held in the temple of Concord, which was surrounded by an armed force. Cicero led Lentulus in by his hand out of respect for his status as a praetor, while the rest followed under guard. Once there they had little choice but to confess their guilt: Volturcius and the Gauls provided damning evidence against them, the signed letters gave them away, and a mass of weapons found in Cethegus' home, all revealed their intentions. Finally the conspiracy was fully exposed.

CICERO: 'THE FATHER OF HIS COUNTRY'

The senate now realized beyond doubt its failure to heed Cicero's warnings. As the meeting drew to a close its grateful members bestowed exceptional honours upon their consul. A special thanksgiving was to be offered to the gods in Cicero's name – the first time this had ever been done for a civilian. The esteemed senator, Catulus, hailed Cicero the *pater patriae* ('the father of his country'); one member even suggested that Cicero should receive the prestigious civic crown, which was awarded for saving civilian lives. Cicero was overjoyed and he immediately addressed the crowds assembled outside to inform them of the day's news.

A version of his impromptu address was later published as the *Third Catilinarian* oration. It gives a blow-by-blow account of the conspiracy, details Cicero's discovery of the plot, and expounds the love the gods had shown for Rome. In addition, Cicero put the fear of fires, slave rebellions and plots involving Gauls into the minds of his terrified audience. Sallust tells us that the people had always supported and favoured Catiline; however, that evening, they changed their minds: 'They extolled Cicero to the skies, showing as much joy and delight as if they had been rescued from slavery.'[20]

The exhilaration of the day's events, however, was short-lived. For the pressing matter facing Cicero was how, as the consul of Rome, he intended to punish the conspirators; yet this was one conundrum that Roman law did not cover. As we have seen, Rome's prison was not a permanent place of confinement, and it was too small to detain all the men involved. And so, they were temporarily put into the custody of their peers in a state of house arrest. But on 4 December, when news came that an attempt to free Lentulus and Cethegus had been made by their supporters, it was obvious that something had to be done fast.

On 5 December, the senate convened to decide the fate of the conspirators once and for all, and Cicero put the question to the floor: 'I have decided to refer the matter to you, senators, as if it were still an open case so that you can pass your judgement on what has been done and how you think it should be punished.'[21] The dramatic details of this meeting were later published by Cicero as his *Fourth Catilinarian* speech, but we must treat his account with some caution: it was only published three years after the event, at a time when Cicero felt compelled to defend his actions. Nevertheless, in matters such as procedure, chronology and other points of information the speech represents broadly what happened on that fateful day; at the same time it gives us a fascinating glimpse into the workings of the senate at Rome.

In the first instance, as was customary, Cicero asked for the opinion of the consuls-elect, Silanus and Murena, who were the two men appointed to be consuls for the following year. Silanus spoke first and he voted for the 'extreme penalty' – by which he meant death. Murena spoke second and he agreed. After the consuls-elect, the former consuls spoke: there were fourteen of them, and they, too, unanimously opted for the death penalty. But then it was Caesar's time to speak, for he had been elected praetor for the next year, and he made a very different suggestion. The death penalty, in his eyes, would be a mistake. He alluded to the Sempronian law which stated that no Roman citizen should be put to death without first receiving a trial, either before the people or in the law courts. The conspirators, Caesar argued, should be put under house arrest for life, in various towns and communities across Italy.[22]

Caesar's solution was both impractical and illegal, but now there were two proposals before the senate, and no one could decide. Cicero interjected, knowing all too well how much time some senators could waste by filibustering, for he wanted a decision by the end of the day. He did not say so explicitly, but his call for severity made it obvious which of the two proposals he favoured:

> For I imagine this city, the light of the world and the citadel of every nation, suddenly collapsing beneath a single flame. I picture in my mind pitiful heaps of citizens, unburied, in a country that has itself been buried. Rolling before my eyes is the sight of Cethegus leaping in frenzy upon your corpses. And when I think of Lentulus ruling over us (as he confessed he hoped to on account of some prophecy), with Gabinius at his side in splendid robes of purple, and Catiline there with his army too, I shudder to my bones at the thought of mothers weeping, girls and boys fleeing, and vestal virgins being raped. It is because of these thoughts – so despicable and deplorable – that I am taking a strict and severe stance against those who want to see such atrocities happen.[23]

But all those who had spoken in favour of the death penalty began to change their mind: Silanus said that by the 'extreme penalty' he had meant prison all along. The question was – did the senate's ultimate decree override the basic right a civilian had to stand trial? This was essentially the problem that Caesar and Labienus had tried to raise in their prosecution of Rabirius at the beginning of the year. But it was now pitted against a more urgent problem, for a trial of the conspirators would only incur a dangerous delay while Catiline was still alive and fighting. The consuls alone were instructed to protect the state under the terms of the ultimate decree, but they could be held to account or prosecuted for their actions later. Furthermore, in the absence of Antonius, the responsibility for any action taken fell solely upon Cicero.

And so the debate continued. Even Cicero's brother Quintus, who like Caesar was one of the praetors-elect, was not convinced the death penalty was the best option; however, he and many others were doubtless anxious of the burden Cicero was prepared to shoulder. That is until Cato, the staunch upholder of tradition, spoke. Cato's words – recalling the severity of Roman tradition, and enlarging on the dangers pointed out by Cicero – put shame into the senior statesmen. When he sat down the senate broke into rounds of applause and everyone agreed: the conspirators must be executed.

Cato had won the day for Cicero, but not before a moment of farce provided some light relief from the sinister events under discussion. While Cato was delivering his powerful harangue, a messenger interrupted the senate meeting with a note for Caesar – it was a note, Cato believed, that implicated Caesar's involvement in the conspiracy, and he demanded his opponent to read it to the rest of the senators. But far from being a letter from one of the conspirators, it was a love letter sent from Cato's own half-sister Servilia – Caesar's long-term mistress. When Caesar casually passed it over for Cato to read, the latter threw it back at him with the words 'take it, you drunken fool!'[24] We do not know how Cicero reacted to this comic interlude, but fortunately it did not affect the rigour of Cato's speech.

The event also points to the fact that Caesar was not above suspicion, for he and Crassus had openly supported Catiline in the past. Indeed, the day before, Crassus had been named as one of the conspirators, and his subsequent absence from the senate was noticeable and suspicious. Caesar had, at least, attended the senatorial discussion; however, his comparative lenience towards the conspirators also seemed to point towards his complicity in the plot. That day, Caesar reportedly only escaped from the senate house with his life thanks to Cicero's intervention and protection. For amid all the finger-pointing, rumours and panic, Cicero stayed on the path where the evidence led. It had been an easy blow for Crassus' and Caesar's political opponents to take, but Cicero did not believe that they were involved. Catiline was desperate, defeated and broke; the same could not be said either of the rich Crassus or Caesar, who had just been made the chief priest of Rome (the *pontifex maximus*), as well as praetor for the forthcoming year.

For now, however, the decision had been made and Cicero wasted no time in implementing it. One by one the five conspirators were taken into the prison: a dingy, dark hole, according to Sallust, sunk twelve feet into the ground. It can still be visited today beneath the steps of the Capitoline hill. Each man was lowered into the hole, with a noose around his neck, where he met his death by strangulation. When Cicero emerged from the prison he announced just one word to the throngs of people awaiting news: '*vixere*' – it meant 'they have lived', and thus avoided the ominous mention of the word death.[25]

The sources that describe the events of that night are in all likelihood embellished, but they provide a captivating image of the mighty relief shared by the consul and his people. The euphoric crowd escorted Cicero through the streets of Rome hailing him as their saviour and chanting the words 'pater patriae' – he was the 'father of his country'. Women watched the scene from the rooftops, and the streets were awash with light from the lamps that flickered. For Cicero, it was the crowning achievement of his career; for the rest of his life he stood his ground and maintained that he had done the right thing.

As for Catiline, he met his end in battle in 62 BC. Sallust's description of his final moments, which is best left in the historian's words, paints the picture of a determined and ruthless fighter:

> When Catiline saw that his troops were routed, and that he only had a few men left, he remembered his birth and former status, and charged right into the thick of the enemy army – and there, fighting, he was fatally wounded. But when the battle was over, it was possible to see what determination and spirit had existed among Catiline's men. For almost every man had given his body and soul on the very spot he had held in battle . . . Yet Catiline was found a long way ahead of his men, buried among the enemy's corpses. Even then he was still breathing a little, and his face retained exactly the same look of bold arrogance as when he was alive.[26]

The conspiracy was over and the men who had tried to subvert the Roman constitution had either been executed in prison or killed in battle. This had been an eventful year for Cicero – and one that he may have predicted. For in the trial of Rabirius earlier in 63 BC, when Cicero deliberated how he would act, if he was faced with a crisis in his consulship, he had said: 'I would refer the matter to the senate, and I would exhort you to defend the republic' – meaning that he would request the passage of the ultimate decree. 'I myself would take up arms, and I, along with you, would take a stand against an armed opponent.'[27] And whether or not we agree with Cicero's actions, he lived up to the standards he had set for himself, and he did indeed save Rome.

8

High Hopes and Shattered Dreams (62–60 BC)

CICERO'S VISION

Everyone is here – men of every order, of every class, and every age; the forum is full, the temples around the forum are full, even the entrances and the grounds of this temple are full. For the first time since the foundation of Rome, a cause has arisen which unites everyone's agreement, one and the same – except only those men who realize they must die.

(Cicero, *Against Catiline* 4.14)

In the year of his consulship, Cicero had triumphed over populist attacks on the senate's authority, fought for and gained the senate's support against a revolutionary patrician, and saved the Republic from an attempted coup d'état. However, by the end of his consulship in 63 BC, he could claim another unique success. As the quotation above shows, men from all the ranks of society had gathered to support their consul and the senate. Only the conspirators were excluded from this harmony among the classes, and ultimately they paid the price with their lives.

In Cicero's understanding, such co-operation and unity, especially among the senatorial and equestrian orders, was vital for the future success of the Republic. For, he saw that, if the highest orders pooled their efforts and interests, they could rally against those who tried to destabilize the senate and its traditional authority. In the years that followed he increasingly called this union the 'concord of the orders', and Cicero's consulship, he believed, had witnessed the practical accomplishment of all his ambitions.

Now in 62 BC, Cicero's hopes for the future direction of the Republic were high. It is not impossible that he was already thinking about the political theory he later put down in writing. It was not a new idea, after all, but an amalgamation of Greek theory and Roman experience that formed the backbone of his famous work *On the Republic*. This treatise, written between 54 and 51 BC, harked back to Plato's *Republic* – one of the Greek philosophers whom Cicero had always admired. However, Cicero's version was set in Rome, and it represented his exposition of how he could see the Roman Republic working.

The mixed constitution – that famous blend of monarchy, aristocracy and democracy – lay at the heart of Cicero's political theory. However, he also saw that this constitution needed someone to guide it. To use one of Cicero's favourite metaphors, the 'ship of state' needed a helmsman, a director or, in some translations, an 'ideal statesman' to keep it on an even keel. Yet we do not know much about Cicero's ideal statesman, for most of the relevant chapter has not survived. Cicero may have had himself in mind – as has often been suggested. However, a look at the leading character, a military hero, implies that the self-confessed pacifist may have thought otherwise.

In Cicero's treatise, the central role was occupied by Scipio Aemilianus. This Scipio was the man responsible for Rome's final victory over Carthage in 146 BC. In sum, he was a man of great military strength, but his success was aided by his friend and political advisor: Gaius Laelius, later nicknamed *sapiens* ('the Wise'). While Cicero's thoughts and political leanings fluctuated over time, it is not hard to see who he had in mind for either role at present. In a letter sent in April 62 BC, he spelled it out explicitly: Pompey was the Scipio of his generation, and Cicero could play the part of his Laelius.[1]

In short, Cicero's plans for a working republican constitution in 62 BC included a unity of the upper classes, with himself and Pompey at the helm to guide their policy and practice. Sadly for Cicero, there were several fundamental flaws in his plan and his vision was soon to be shattered. First, not everyone had given their full support to his actions against the conspirators; second, Pompey was an unpredictable man; and finally, Cicero had underestimated the staunch resistance to change that was put up by the nobility's most recent champion, Cato.

CONDEMNATIONS AND CONGRATULATIONS: THE CONSULSHIP AND BEYOND

Cicero had been delighted by the votes of thanks he received from the senate after the suppression of the conspiracy. However, before the year was even over, it became clear that their support was not unanimous, when Quintus Metellus Nepos, one of the new tribunes for the year, took a mighty stand against the retiring consul. 'He tried to plot and plan his entire tribunate around my destruction', Cicero complained.[2] This was the first sign that all might not go according to Cicero's plan, and it started when Cicero arrived at the assembly on the last day of his consulship.

On 31 December 63 BC, Cicero planned to take the customary oath of the retiring magistrate and make his valedictory address to the people. But Nepos rebuffed him: a man who had executed Roman citizens without trial should not, he claimed, be allowed to speak to the Roman people. And so he deprived Cicero of the chance to deliver an oration before the people, allowing him only to take the oath: 'I swore the truest and finest oath in the loudest voice I could', Cicero later wrote.[3] All he should have said was that he had served the laws, but to the people's delight he added that he had saved Rome and the Republic.

With the exception of Nepos' hostility, however, Cicero's position at Rome seemed secure when he became a private citizen again on 1 January 62 BC. He was now a 'consular': that is, an ex-consul respected for his experience and opinion. All consulars were asked for their advice in the senate immediately after the consuls had spoken, but they were approached in order of priority. This 'pecking order' was set by the leading consul for January (for the two consuls took it in turns, month by month, to preside over meetings), and it remained the same throughout the year. It was a great honour to be 'the first asked' and this year the privilege fell upon Cicero. Furthermore, as an indication of the respect with which Cicero was now regarded in the senate, he had been placed ahead of its traditional leaders: Catulus, Lucullus and Hortensius could only speak, in turn, after Cicero.

Early in 62 BC, therefore, Cicero felt on top of the world, and he did not celebrate in silence. He drafted a letter – it was 'as long as a book' according to a later source – and sent it to Pompey in Asia.[4] It detailed the events leading up to and including Cicero's punishment of the conspirators, and we can imagine that Cicero let no opportunity pass to blow his own trumpet. The letter would certainly have emphasized both the danger and the drama he had faced. Pompey replied but not in terms that Cicero liked. Sadly these two letters are lost, but Cicero's following response survives to tell a part of the tale: 'Just so that you know,' Cicero wrote, 'there was something I missed in your letter. My achievements were such that I was rather expecting some form of congratulation from you – both because we are friends and for the sake of the state.'[5]

Like Cicero, we can only guess at the causes for Pompey's coolness towards him. It is possible that Pompey was jealous: he was the one who was used to saving the state. Maybe he had wanted to come back and defeat Catiline in the field, and thus save Rome and secure further personal glory. The tribune, Nepos, had even suggested recalling Pompey from the East for precisely this reason, but the opposition had grown so great against him that he had fled Rome with his tail between his legs.

Another reason may have been that Pompey was annoyed with Cicero. The previous year Cicero had made it possible for the general Lucullus, one of Pompey's arch-enemies, to celebrate a long-anticipated triumph in the city of Rome for his efforts against Mithridates. The triumph not only gave credit to Lucullus for his achievements in a war that Pompey was still fighting; it gave him great 'dignity' in the very Roman sense of the word.

A more likely reason lies in the fact that, in Pompey's eyes, Cicero had jumped on the bandwagon of his success only to serve his own ends. Early in his career, Cicero had won great popularity by allying himself with Rome's hero. Pompey, who had cleared the seas of pirates in just three months, and who had now defeated Mithridates, once towered over Rome. Cicero should have used his power of speech to keep him there. Instead, he was championing his own name, increasing his own dignity, and Pompey may have sensed a drop in his personal influence. The man who had publicly praised him now demanded his praise. Furthermore, the previous year's events had brought Cicero into an enviable position: the nobility had rallied behind him, yet they continually distrusted Pompey.

Pompey was not due to return to Rome until the end of 62 BC. Meanwhile, Cicero spent the rest of the year looking both forwards and backwards. Looking backwards he devoted a large part of the year to tying up the loose ends of the foiled conspiracy. Many others had been implicated and Cicero proceeded to give damning evidence against those guilty to secure their conviction. At the same time, he looked forwards to his life as a senior statesman. He needed a bigger house: a large villa was essential for a man who wanted to shine on the political stage. If we think back to the days of Cicero's own education, when he and his school friends sat in the crowded halls of Rome's leading politicians and lawyers, we may picture what Cicero himself envisaged. Cicero could offer legal advice, help his dependants and tutor the young. He saw a prominent role for himself in the Republic he had saved. For this he needed to be in the centre of Rome. The Palatine hill, Rome's most prestigious district on the fringe of Rome's busy forum, was where he set his heart – but it came at a cost.

CICERO: THE 'TYRANT' OF THE COURTS

While Cicero was busying himself giving evidence against those involved in the Catilinarian conspiracy, one man's name in particular came up for discussion: that of Publius Cornelius Sulla, the nephew of the former dictator. He was a disreputable man – tarnished, no doubt, by the stigma of his name. Yet this Sulla had grown tremendously rich off the back of his uncle's proscriptions, and there was no doubt that he had taken an active role. Years later, Cicero admitted as much. As he lamented civil war and the spear stained with the blood of a fellow citizen, Cicero named him explicitly as a culprit: 'Publius Sulla had brandished that spear when his kinsman was dictator.'[6]

The prosecution had evidently seized on Sulla's role in his uncle's reign of terror as evidence of his general depravity, much as we have seen Cicero do in his attacks on men like Verres and Catiline. Yet Cicero whitewashed these accusations: 'Even in the cruel and turbulent times of Sulla's victory, who could be found that was more lenient, more compassionate than Publius Sulla? How many lives he begged Sulla to spare! How many eminent and distinguished men – senators as well as equestrians – he saved by offering himself as surety for them!'[7] It was a gross misrepresentation of the truth, but Cicero needed to present his client's character in the best possible light.

Sulla's reputation and deeds had not improved over time, with the result that Cicero's decision to defend him certainly stirred some agitated rumours. Yet Sulla was a well-connected man and his friends, including the orator Hortensius, flocked to support him. Furthermore, there was no firm evidence to connect him to the conspiracy of 63 BC: 'When I was consul, I heard many rumours about the great dangers facing our Republic; I made many investigations; I learned many facts', Cicero told the jury. 'Yet no mention of Sulla, no information, no documents and no suspicion ever came my way', and his appearance for the defence meant that their victory was decisive.[8]

The prosecutor, Lucius Manlius Torquatus, knew that Cicero's authority had the power to make or break a case, and he launched a vehement attack. Cicero, he claimed, was a 'foreign tyrant', just like some of the earlier kings of Rome whose memory had become so hated by the Roman populace.[9] His point was that Cicero was establishing a tyranny over Rome's courts: by his very appearance, for or against a man, Cicero could determine who was acquitted, and who was condemned.

The charge of acting like a king or a tyrant was part of the stock-in-trade of Roman political slander, but this dose of abuse had a nasty aftertaste for Cicero. Nepos had already shown that not everyone approved of Cicero's handling of the conspiracy. And now Torquatus' remark also hit a raw nerve, for Cicero felt compelled to defend his motives for speaking in Sulla's defence in the long introduction to his speech. He felt obliged to defend him, and he wanted to prove his leniency towards those implicated unjustly, Cicero claimed. However, it did not take long for the rumour mill to start running. For the acquittal of the very rich Publius Sulla was all too conspicuously followed by Cicero's purchase of a very expensive house, right where he wanted one, on the Palatine hill: it almost overlooked the whole of Rome.

At the cost of three and a half million sesterces, Cicero's house did not come cheap. It was almost as expensive as running an entire legion, made up of around five thousand men, for a whole year. For a new man like Cicero, it was an extravagant purchase, and there was no denying that Sulla had given Cicero a hefty sum towards his house: a 'loan' of two million sesterces. Cicero, at least, was able to laugh at himself: 'I realize that I now have so much debt, that I should be willing to join any conspiracy going, if only anyone would have me', he joked to a friend.[10] But irregular financial dealings were just the kind of ammunition that Cicero's enemies needed to trigger hostile feelings against him.

The view from the Palatine hill today: the brick building at the right
of the photograph is the senate house (Photograph © Hannah Swithinbank).

By January 61 BC, tales connected to another loan were beginning to call
Cicero's integrity further into question. This time it was a loan that had been
agreed with his former colleague in the consulship, Antonius, who was now
in the province of Macedonia. Yet it seems Antonius had set no limits on the
amount of extortion he or his comrades could commit, and rumour had it that
he was extorting money on Cicero's behalf too. Cicero was flabbergasted. The
man spreading the rumours was Atticus' client and accountant, and he was with
Antonius in Macedonia. 'If you can manage it,' Cicero urged, 'get that wretch out
of the country.'[11]

Financial assistance in return for past favours was not unusual in the give-
and-take culture of Cicero's day. Indeed, the high levels of debt and expenditure
remind us of how important it was to keep up with appearances, for money
enabled men to buy some share of the dignity they desired. Yet it is enough to say
that Cicero's financial dealings with both Sulla and Antonius were short-sighted.
In the case of Sulla, Cicero could be accused of accepting bribes to save conspirators. Or, by accepting money from Antonius, he could be criticized for complicity
in a corrupt governor's extortions. Neither of the charges was demonstrably true,
but Cicero needed to stay mindful of his reputation.

At the beginning of 62 BC Cicero had felt indispensable but he was wrong. The
opposition of Nepos, the taunts against him in the trial of Sulla, and the jealousy

that his extravagant purchase produced, all pointed towards one hard reality: Cicero's position was far from secure, and the events of the next few years were to show him just how much he had to lose.

POMPEY'S RETURN AND A SCANDAL AT ROME

The political events of 62 BC passed relatively smoothly as Rome awaited the imminent return of Pompey from the East. But all this soon changed. By the end of 61 BC, Cicero's 'concord' between the senatorial and equestrian orders was falling apart; worse still, as the year 60 BC drew to a close, the senate was divided and rivalries were tense. Within these two years, Pompey had returned, a great scandal rocked Rome and Cato emerged as the leader of the conservative nobility. From this time on, we hear a lot about events at Rome from Cicero's correspondence, because Atticus had left Italy and was staying on his estate in Epirus (in north-west Greece). Indeed, a letter written to Atticus on 1 January 61 BC does well to give us a flavour of the times ahead:

> People think that Pompey is now very friendly towards me. His decision to divorce Mucia is strongly approved. I imagine you have heard about Publius Clodius, the son of Appius: he was caught at the house of Caesar, dressed as a woman, while the sacrificial rites for the people were being made. He only survived and escaped because a slave-girl helped him. The whole affair really is a shocking scandal.[12]

To begin with the relationship between Pompey and Cicero, it was not as simple as outward appearances suggested. While people thought that Pompey appeared to be friendly towards him, Cicero was very unsure about the terms of their friendship. As we saw earlier, Pompey's first letters to Cicero had been distinctly cool. By the end of the month, Cicero was none the wiser. Pompey seemed fond of him and, on the surface at least, was happy to praise Cicero; however, underneath he was jealous, or so Cicero thought. Cicero's view, as we see from his letters, was that Pompey was awkward and complex: there was no substance to his political thought – he was dishonest, timid and disingenuous.

In February 61 BC, Cicero reported that Pompey's first public appearance had fallen flat. He had said nothing to give any hope, encouragement or pleasure. Yet Pompey had returned to a very different Rome to the one he had left, and he was still trying to find his political footing. He wanted a union with the senatorial élite, but they would not have him. When Pompey divorced his third wife, Mucia, he was making one in a series of political statements. Her brothers-in-law were prominent populist politicians and, by divorcing Mucia, Pompey was symbolic-ally making a clean break from his former political leanings. He wanted to marry Cato's niece – a marriage with a noble household – but Cato refused the offer.

The senate's distrust of Pompey was probably misguided at this point. Many had feared that he might march on Rome and establish a military rule in the wake of the Catilinarian conspiracy and current crises. However, it does not seem to have been within Pompey's nature to seek a position akin to that of either a Sulla or a Marius. Arriving back at Italy, he simply disbanded his army outside the city, as the law required, and entered Rome. He demanded only what was needed to complete the war: land for his soldiers and the senate's ratification of the settlements he had made in the East. But Pompey would have to wait his turn. For Rome was alive with rumours of a sacrilege, and it took the senate the best part of six months to agree on how best to proceed against the culprit: Publius Claudius Pulcher – or 'Clodius', as he preferred to call himself (the popular version of his name).

The notorious event was the scandal that occurred at the festival of *Bona Dea* (the 'Good Goddess') – an annual event held every December for women only. The rites that were being performed were meant to protect Rome, and they were being conducted by Caesar's wife in Caesar's house; the vestal virgins were there, as were most women of high birth. Yet, as we can see from Cicero's letter, Clodius had infiltrated the rites dressed as a woman. He ran away when his disguise failed, but it was too late. That a man had broken into this women-only festival was a matter of great concern, and many of the senate's leaders, and above all Hortensius, now pressed hard for a trial severe enough to match the crime.

The chance to discredit Caesar was an added bonus, for, according to a rumour that may have spread later, Clodius was having an affair with Caesar's wife, Pompeia. For his part, Caesar did not admit his wife's guilt but divorced her anyway on the grounds that 'my wife must be above suspicion' – or so he reportedly said, alluding to his position as Rome's *pontifex maximus*.[13] But it was a clever move: by refusing to pass judgement, Caesar was able to remain on the right side of Clodius, whom he may have seen as a potential 'friend' in politics.

The continued call for Clodius' trial became a showcase of political muscle over what was, in reality, probably little more than a prank. Clodius was like many of Rome's younger generation, who were all criticized by the elder members of society for being frivolous, carefree, rich and wanton. Cicero took a hard line to begin with, thinking that it would be a good chance to teach the young men at Rome a much-needed lesson in morality. But he soon realized the potential danger in allowing events to escalate: Clodius held some sway among the younger crowd, and his use of gangs was worrying. However, the influential voices calling for his punishment got their way and the trial went ahead.

The trial of Clodius took place under extraordinary circumstances in the spring of 61 BC, when a special court for dealing with sacrilege was appointed. The defence team rested their argument on the claim that Clodius had been away from Rome at the time of the festival. Unfortunately for Cicero, however, he had been an eyewitness; he had seen Clodius in Rome on the day in question, and it was enough to break his alibi – even though Cicero later claimed to have 'drawn in his horns' on this particular occasion. It looked as though a verdict of guilty was sealed, but a scandalous amount of bribery ensured Clodius' release: thirty-one voted for acquittal against twenty-five who maintained his guilt. Crassus, Cicero implied, had paid for the lot. As for the jury: 'There has never been a more disgraceful bunch of men in a low-grade music hall!'[14]

For Cicero, although he did not realize it yet, the result was nothing short of disastrous. While he had not altogether approved of the nobility's persistent hounding of Clodius, Cicero had given evidence against a man who was now free and very dangerous. To make matters worse, Cicero openly (and perhaps foolishly) taunted Clodius in the senate. Cicero described the event to Atticus in a letter, but the essence of what they said is best paraphrased in dialogue form. After several insults hurled between the two men, the final blow was delivered by Cicero, and it played on words associated with 'credit' (in terms of trust) and 'credit' (in terms of payment):

CLODIUS: Tell us about this house you've bought.
CICERO: Anyone would think you were saying 'I have bought a jury'.
CLODIUS: The jury didn't give *you* credit when you were a sworn witness.
CICERO: Actually, twenty-five of them did give *me* credit but thirty-one of them gave *you* none, for they had received their payment in advance![15]

It was a brilliant demonstration of Cicero's quick wit, and a defeated Clodius sank back into his seat. He may have been silenced for now but that was not the last Cicero heard from him. In the years to come, as we shall see, Clodius' bitter hostility proved catastrophic for Cicero on a personal level. At the same time, and as an immediate consequence, the acquittal of Clodius made a dent in Cicero's political dreams of concord among the classes.

DISCORD AND DISCONTENT

Something needed to be done to prevent such bribery taking place in the courts again, for the laws dealing with the acceptance of bribes were severely limited. Back in 70 BC, when the jury-panels were first divided between the senatorial and equestrian orders, the law had not been extended properly to include the new equestrian jurors. It meant that only senators who accepted bribes could be prosecuted, and now the senate proposed to correct that anomaly so that the equestrians could be investigated too. But their timing made it look as if the senate blamed the equestrians entirely for Clodius' acquittal (when everyone knew that the bribery had been arranged and paid for by senators). Cicero blocked the investigation in the interests of maintaining his harmony among the upper classes, but this was just the beginning of the discord that developed between the two orders.

By 5 December 61 BC, two years exactly since the execution of the conspirators and his moments of glory, Cicero saw that his dreams for a unity between the senate and the equestrians were looking positively unlikely: 'Those of us who are here in Rome live in a Republic that is weak, sad and unstable', he wrote to Atticus. 'I suppose you have heard that our friends, the equestrians, have almost entirely split from the senate.'[16] The final break came when the equestrians approached the senate with a favour. But it was a shameful request that requires some explanation before we consider Cicero's response to it.

As we have seen, without a civil service, Rome's equestrians performed many of the day-to-day activities we would expect a public body to perform. The system of tax collection, which was handled by tax-farming companies, was one of these tasks. If the tax system was correctly managed, it could bring great personal profit, but if poorly managed, the tax farmers would operate at a great loss. For it was like the 'futures market' of the ancient world: the tax farmers offered a lump sum based on how much tax they thought they would be able to collect. Anything they made in excess was theirs to keep and, consequently, anything they lost was their burden to bear.

Now, in 61 BC, the equestrians who managed the tax-farming companies had been too hasty in offering a deposit which was far beyond what they could feasibly make back. And, spurred on by Crassus, they asked for the senate to renegotiate the terms of their contracts. Unsurprisingly, there were many, led by Cato, who refused point-blank to yield to such barefaced cheek. And when their request was finally denied in 60 BC, it was a major blow both to the relationship between the two orders and to Crassus' pride.

Crassus had lost face in front of the equestrians whom he had supported, and he was not the sort of man to take humiliation lightly. But Pompey was also facing similar frustrations with the senate, which was still being steered by Cato's unflinching conservatism. Pompey had been back at Rome for more than a year, and he still needed to complete the administrative side of his war. His soldiers needed land on which they could retire. And his settlements – the promises he had made to the Eastern kings in return for their co-operation – still needed ratification. His demands were legitimate, but there were many in the senate who thought Pompey only had his eyes on his own interests and another special command.

For his part, Cicero was more supportive of Pompey and Crassus than most – and it was all in the name of the *concordia ordinum*. He thought the equestrians' demand was greedy, but he thought that the loss was a small one to make if it kept the equestrians on the side of the senate. Some of the provisions in the land bill supported by Pompey, he thought, could do with being deleted; however,

Cicero was otherwise flexible and agreed both with the need to release land that was property of the state and for the need to accrue more. As for Cato: 'He has an excellent mind and the topmost integrity,' Cicero wrote, 'but he can harm the state occasionally; for he speaks as if he lives in Plato's *Republic* rather than in the gutters of Rome.'[17]

Cato represented the extreme of republican ideals – an extremity which Cicero realized could be divisive in politics. Yet Cicero's dreams for a harmony of the orders were rooted in the same republican ideal, and this was rapidly becoming outdated. While Cicero believed that a unity of the upper classes could revive the republican institutions, he failed to take account of two major developments within Rome's political climate. First, not everyone believed in the ability of the senate's leaders to initiate and conduct economic policies that were beneficial for all; furthermore, these senators had given no real reason why the equestrians or the rest of the population should follow their lead. Second, not even the senate was unanimous about the value of the republican institutions; there were many who placed self-interest and their own factions ahead of the old system.

In short, what Pompey and Crassus both needed was a strong voice to back their interests, but Cicero was not the kind of man to provide this for them. However, there was a man who could – Caesar, and in the last half of 60 BC, the three men dealt a formidable blow to the heart of the republican institutions, when they formed the alliance now known as the 'first triumvirate' (for reasons which will become clearer in the next chapter).

It all started when Caesar's ambitions, too, were thwarted by Cato and the senate, when he returned from his governorship of Further Spain in the June of 60 BC. Caesar wanted a triumph for his achievements there, but he also had his heart set on the consulship for 59 BC – and the senate made him choose between the two. If he wanted the triumph he had to wait *outside* the city *with* his army; however, if he wanted to run for the consulship, he had to be *inside* the city *without* his army. Despite the fact the senate had made exceptions in the past for men facing a similar dilemma, they refused to bow to Caesar now. It was either one or the other: Caesar went for the consulship and he won it.[18]

Caesar's success at the polls put him in a position of power to give Pompey and Crassus everything they wanted the following year – so long as they all co-operated. Between them, they planned to be a trio of men (a 'triumvirate'), all working to help each other. It was a big secret for now, but this decision spelled doom for Cicero's hopes, both for his own career and for the Republic. During the years 62–60 BC, Cicero's alliance with Pompey had failed to materialize, the harmony among the orders – if it ever truly existed – had crumbled and Cicero had made an implacable foe out of Clodius. Now, the formation of the triumvirate, although he did not know it yet, meant that the years ahead were turbulent and testing times, not just for Cicero but for the whole of Rome.

9

Enemies, Exile and Return (59–57 BC)

THE 'FIRST TRIUMVIRATE': POMPEY, CAESAR AND CRASSUS

During Caesar's consulship [i.e. 59 BC], a partnership of power was formed between Caesar, Crassus and Pompey, which brought destruction to the city, the whole world and even, at different times, to the three men. Pompey's reason for following the plan was that many people were still objecting to his settlements in the overseas provinces; he hoped that these could finally be ratified now that Caesar was consul. For his part, Caesar realized that he could increase his own influence by giving Pompey his way. Caesar also saw that he could strengthen his own position by making Pompey bear the brunt of the unpopularity caused by the alliance. As for Crassus, he had never managed to reach a position of influence on his own; but with the help of Pompey's prestige and Caesar's influence he saw a chance to gain one.

(Velleius Paterculus, *The History of Rome* 2.44)

There is something almost unique about the year 59 BC in the place of classical history. Everyone who has commented on it, whether they were living at the time, a decade, a century or even two millennia later, agrees – the partnership called the 'first triumvirate' was nothing short of a catastrophe.

For Cicero, if the years 62–60 BC had witnessed the end to his hopes for harmony among the orders, the years 59–57 BC saw an end to everything he cherished. Within this time, the republican government collapsed, Cicero broke with the political powers at Rome and he was forced into a bitter and humiliating exile. Cicero's vision had rested on achieving unity within the senate, but his dreams were dashed by the opposing and divisive forces of personal ambition versus senatorial conservatism.

In 59 BC, the men looking out for their own interests – Pompey, Caesar and Crassus – finally pooled their resources, so that they had the popularity, power and the money between them to achieve their ends. Caesar had the official power and from the minute he entered the consulship he set to work. First, he passed a land bill to provide settlements and farms for Pompey's veterans; then a second bill ratified Pompey's arrangements in the East. A third measure saw to it that the tax farmers of Asia had their contracts reduced by a third, as Crassus had wanted. And after helping his friends, Caesar looked next to his own interests. The senate had allocated him a very low-key province for the following year: the 'woods and paths of Italy'. Yet Caesar wanted a province that offered glory and wealth; he wanted the provinces of Gaul and Illyricum for five years with three legions – and he got them.

Exactly when all these secret arrangements between the three men took place is unknown. The compact between them even came as something of a surprise to Cicero, who was always an astute political observer otherwise. But it all became very obvious by May 59 BC, when Pompey used his traditional method of announcing his intentions and married Caesar's daughter Julia: 'We must expect the worst,' Cicero told Atticus, 'it is clear that he is preparing to take absolute power. What else can this sudden marriage alliance signify?'[1]

It has often been said that the years after Cicero's consulship were the years of his political failure. As we shall see, he *could* have joined the three men in their political domination, yet he chose the path of futile resistance. However, when we consider the ultimate fate of the other three protagonists of this particular drama, it seems that Cicero did well not to strike an alliance with them.

In chronological order, Crassus met his death in 53 BC, commanding Rome's army in one of its most crushing defeats: the battle of Carrhae against Parthia. Upon his death, or so the story went, the Parthians poured molten gold down his throat in mockery of his love for money. In 48 BC Pompey was decapitated as he landed on the shores of Egypt, but by men he considered his friends, not enemies. As for Caesar, his assassination is notorious. His body was pierced through with the stab wounds inflicted by friends and enemies alike. The only thing dignified about it was the fact that he managed to fold his toga over himself neatly before he fell to the ground.

Cicero could not, of course, read into the future. However, history had shown that radical populist reformers almost always met with violent opposition from those who wanted to retain the *status quo*. Cicero could well anticipate that the triumvirs' breach of the constitution would lead to the destructive effects listed by Velleius Paterculus above – and Cicero himself lived to witness them all. And so, despite the embarrassments and distress that resulted from his decision not to join the triumvirs, it is perhaps unfair to criticize Cicero's political strategy in these years. For *his* death, as we have seen, is often regarded as his finest hour; the same cannot be said of Pompey, Caesar or Crassus.

CHANGED CIRCUMSTANCES:
CICERO AND THE POLITICAL CLIMATE AT ROME

In order to understand the decisions Cicero made, however, we need to go back to the year 60 BC. In this year, a huge and obvious transformation was taking place in Roman political life. To begin with, the aristocrats who had always championed the élite's authority were no longer steering the senate's opinion. By May 60 BC, Catulus had died and Cicero felt that he was taking a lonely walk along the 'optimate road'; he had no companions or supporters, but he believed his commitment to the senate remained the right path.[2] For Hortensius and Lucullus were increasingly retiring into a life of luxury, looking after their prized fish: 'Our leading men think they have reached the summit of the stars if they can get the bearded mullets in their fishponds to eat out of their hands!' Cicero complained to Atticus.[3] All that was left was Cato. True, he was a man of integrity; but he was guiding the senate down a route of vain obstinacy.

In several letters to Atticus during this year, Cicero expressed his plans to exercise a more moderate way of political life: to be as committed as the Republic required him to be, but to remain cautious and careful. The honest men were weak, the malevolent were unfair and the unpatriotic rabble was full of hatred, he complained. His judgement was probably fairly accurate, but Cicero would have done well to remember it more. In the letters of 60 BC, we witness the beginnings of the highs and lows to which Cicero's mood could swing.

That was in March, yet less than three months later, in June, Cicero was boasting that Pompey was his fan and advocate, he claimed to be teaching Clodius some manners, and he even entertained hopes of making Caesar a better citizen too. Cicero was a natural optimist; he admitted as much in a letter to Atticus. However, the reality was that Cicero only succeeded in alienating himself further and further from the major political players.[4]

That Cicero suspected the rumbles of an impending storm may be gauged both from what he said to Atticus in his letters and from what he did. Clodius had not forgotten Cicero's disservice to him over the *Bona Dea* trial, and Cicero was anxious over his next move. A patrician by birth, Clodius wanted to be adopted into a plebeian family. If he could manage this, he could become a tribune of the plebs (from which his patrician ancestry otherwise excluded him). He would be in a position of power to make or break legislation: 'If Pretty Miss Pulcher (*Pulcherella*) pushes his madness any further, I shall be calling on you to come back very loudly', Cicero warned Atticus, referring to Clodius by the nickname he had conjured up for his opponent.[5] But, jokes aside, he was right to be afraid: within two years, as we shall see, Clodius managed both to become tribune and to force Cicero into exile.

As for what Cicero did, he started a propaganda campaign to glorify his consulship of 63 BC. Cicero maintained that he published the speeches of that year because the younger students were desperate to read them. In addition, in their published form, the speeches helped him in his pursuit for glory and lasting fame; they put him on a par with the Greek orator and statesman Demosthenes, who Cicero emulated in both capacities. But on top of the speeches, he also composed an account of his consulship in Greek, another in Latin, and he even wrote an epic poem – in three long books – on the subject, 'so that no form of singing my own praises will be passed over in silence!' Cicero joked to Atticus.[6] Whether it was linked to his fear of Clodius' animosity, his political isolation or to a mixture of reasons, Cicero evidently felt the need to justify and elevate his achievements as consul.

The published speeches, including the four against Catiline, remain the most valuable source of our information for the events of 63 BC. However, the poem, which only survives in fragments, has often been seen as something of a mistake on Cicero's part. In particular, there were two lines of Cicero's poem which came under heavy attack from his critics. The first – 'How fortunate the state of Rome, which under my consulship was grown' – was simply offensive both to standards of decorum and to literary taste. However, the second line seemed to suggest that Cicero the statesman rated his own successes above those of the military-minded Pompey: 'Let arms to the toga cede, a soldier's laurels to glory concede.' In other words, a civilian's toga and fame were more important than the soldiers' weapons and triumphs.[7]

It is unfortunate that our assessment of the poem as a whole is largely guided by these two lines. Both sentences are difficult to translate effectively into English, but it is easy to see how much bait Cicero had fed to his enemies. The soldier's laurels refer to the crown of bay leaves that a soldier wore around his head when he celebrated a mighty victory. Pompey had celebrated one such triumph just the year before, in 61 BC – and there were some who claimed that Cicero had managed to offend Pompey as a result.

Cicero's boasts in 60 BC, coupled with his self-promotion, only added to the irritation he had caused Pompey when he sought his congratulations after the Catilinarian conspiracy. Five years later, Cicero strongly denied the accusation when Lucius Calpurnius Piso taunted him in the senate: 'You scoundrel!' Cicero replied, 'Do you hope to suggest that Pompey became my enemy because of *that* line of verse?'[8] But even if the word 'enemy' was too harsh a term, it is extremely likely that Cicero's continuous bragging was proving too much – not just for Pompey but also for many of his peers in the senate.

At the beginning of 59 BC, however, Cicero still had one important associate. This man knew from experience that Cicero's way with words could amount to the power of life or death – it was Caesar. As we have seen, he had returned from Spain in 60 BC, and it was towards the end of this year that he set in motion his plan to unite Pompey and Crassus. But he also had a fourth member in mind: Cicero, whose persuasive talents would have been an invaluable asset to the trio. He did not spell his plans out to Cicero explicitly, but hindsight helps us understand a passing reference to an event Cicero mentions in one of his letters. For early in January 59 BC, Cicero wrote to Atticus to tell him of a visit he had received: 'Cornelius came to my house, I mean Cornelius Balbus, Caesar's friend. He said that Caesar is planning to follow mine and Pompey's advice in all matters, and that he is going to see to it that Pompey and Crassus are brought together.'[9]

Caesar's friend, Balbus, was testing the waters. He made no direct mention of a political alliance but Cicero could see that some kind of union was on the table. It had its advantages. Reconciliation would bring a more intimate alliance with Pompey, as well as with Caesar; it also brought a resolution to his old enmities with Crassus, and guaranteed peace with the crowds and tranquillity in his old age. Yet there was something stopping him, he explained to Atticus – it was the finale of the poem *On His Consulship* he had written:

> The paths, which from the first flourish of youth you did pursue
> The paths, which you sought with courage and mind as consul too,
> Follow them always; foster your fame and the praises of good men.[10]

And Cicero believed it: the path that upheld tradition and senatorial authority was the only path to follow. He turned down Caesar's offer, and even when he started to realize the impact it had on his own political career, Cicero never regretted his decision: 'It will never even enter my mind to envy Crassus or regret the fact that I have stayed true to myself', he promised Atticus a few months later.[11]

From April to June 59 BC, Cicero kept a cautious eye on events at Rome despite claiming to be sick of politics. He was away from the city during these months, travelling around his various villas. We find him watching the waves and studying geography at his villa in Antium (modern Anzio); at Formiae he waited for letters from Atticus, who seems to have visited him the following month at his home in Arpinum. When Cicero did return to Rome in June 59 BC, the news was not good: 'As for the present state of affairs,' he told Atticus, 'everyone groans with one voice but no one says a word to make it better.'[12] For Cicero, however, it only got worse.

The formation of the triumvirate was devastating for Cicero. He had never been on friendly terms with Crassus. He had now also offended Pompey and rejected Caesar's offer of an alliance. But a word should be said about the term 'triumvirate'. It is used only by historians after the event, and is misleading insofar as it suggests something permanent and official – which it was not. The term follows from that of the more official pact, the so-called 'second triumvirate', agreed by Antony, Octavian and Lepidus in 43 BC. A contemporary writer, Varro, had a better name for the union between Pompey, Caesar and Crassus: 'the three-headed monster'.[13] Varro's description conjures up images of the mythological, snarling three-headed dog that guarded the underworld, Cerberus. And, like Cerberus, this dog's bite was as bad as its bark.

CLODIUS' REVENGE

For a long time, Clodius had been seeking his revenge on Cicero. Cicero had testified against him over the *Bona Dea* scandal and attacked him verbally in the senate. If Clodius could fulfil his ambition to become a tribune of the plebs, the power of that office would provide him with the means to gain the vengeance he desired. Yet it was not an easy task. As mentioned above, Clodius would have to be adopted into a plebeian family if he was to represent the plebeians' interests. He had already tried and failed to be adopted the year before. But, in 59 BC, with the help of both Pompey and Caesar, he managed it.

Pompey's growing detachment from Cicero has been charted, but we may ask why Caesar suddenly turned coat on Cicero too. The rejection of an alliance with him was one thing; however, the final straw allegedly came when Cicero delivered a speech in defence of his former colleague, Antonius, a notoriously corrupt man. We do not know exactly which of his many crimes Antonius was being prosecuted for – maybe extortion, violence or treason – but the charge related to his period as governor in Macedonia. Cicero was reluctant to defend him due to rumours he had been taking his share of Antonius' ill-gotten gains. However, in his speech, Cicero sidestepped the topic of his guilt and bewailed the current crisis instead. Antonius had, after all, worked with Cicero to save the very constitution that was now in the destructive hands of the triumvirs. And the occasion of his defence offered Cicero the chance to pour scorn upon the men now threatening the Republic.

The defence of Antonius was not Cicero's wisest move. To begin with, the defence was unsuccessful; furthermore, Cicero aggravated the 'regime' in the process. Caesar was the *pontifex maximus*, while Pompey was one of the augurs, whose duty it was to look for signs and omens before any public business could be conducted. Between them, they had the religious and political authority to process Clodius' transition into a plebeian family. And within just three hours of Cicero's speech for Antonius, Caesar sanctioned his adoption and Pompey helped him – in doing so, they unleashed a monster who had a terrible vendetta to settle against Cicero.

Clodius' adoption took place in March 59 BC, and shortly afterwards he was elected to be one of Rome's ten tribunes for the following year – just as he had hoped. As the situation grew worse at Rome, Cicero repeated his worry that he might need Atticus' help: 'Be ready to come flying if I call!' he begged.[14] But Clodius was not his only worry. Pompey, Caesar and Crassus had taken full control by now; no one else could do anything. Cicero decided to retire from political life to watch, as he phrased it, the inevitable 'shipwreck from *terra firma*.'[15]

At this point, we may well wonder who and where was Caesar's colleague in the consulship for 59 BC. There were, after all, supposed to be two men in power to prevent precisely the kind of control that the year had witnessed so far. The other consul was Marcus Calpurnius Bibulus, and leading members of the senate had rallied together to get him elected the year before. Even the upright Cato had contributed to a pool of funds that were used to bribe the voters extensively, for they had hoped that he would be an effective check against Caesar's ambitions. However, that was before the compact of the three men had become obvious, and there was little Bibulus could do to stop Caesar at present.

From the time of April onwards, Bibulus stayed at home 'watching the skies', presumably for anomalies in the weather or the flight paths of birds which were meant to prevent any public business taking place.[16] On these grounds, he could later invalidate all of Caesar's legislation, which had not only disregarded the sacred period declared by Bibulus, but which had also been passed through by force. For his part, Bibulus won great popularity from the many who detested the regime, but it came at a cost. On one occasion, his official attendants (the lictors) were assaulted, their *fasces* were broken, and Bibulus himself had a bucket of manure hurled over his head. This year was a hazardous one for those who took a stand against the triumvirs.[17]

The senate's strategy, however, did not help Cicero; as we have seen, he had felt abandoned by its leaders for a long time. Even so, he still expected them to defend him the following year, when Cicero was sure that he would be prosecuted by Clodius for executing five of the Catilinarian conspirators without a trial. Cicero had, after all, been acting under the senate's ultimate decree, and he had asked for their opinion and their support. And so, it would be in their interest to unite in his defence, just as they had joined in support of Gaius Rabirius (the aged senator we met on trial for treason in Chapter 7). For any prosecution against Cicero's actions in the wake of the conspiracy would be an attack on the senate's authority; so, there was every reason to believe they would be there for him.

Cicero, as we shall see, had underestimated the extent of Clodius' hatred, but Caesar was not so naïve. Perhaps regretting his part in Clodius' adoption, from mid 59 BC onwards, he sought to help Cicero in various ways. Caesar offered him a place on his staff in Gaul so that he could escape Clodius' daggers, but Cicero wanted to stay in Rome. His brother Quintus was due to return from a spell as the provincial governor of Asia, where his behaviour had caused some grounds for complaint. Among other things, he had punished some provincials with the favourite method of penalizing patricides: he had thrown them in the sack. There were strong rumours that Quintus was going to be prosecuted, and Cicero wanted to be in the city to help his brother.

Other factors had given Cicero the hope to stay in Rome. Pompey had continually vowed to protect Cicero: Clodius would only harm Cicero over his *dead body*, were his words. Besides, Cicero had continued his work in the courts and his house was always crowded with visitors; he felt well liked and in a position of influence. At the same time the triumvirs' popularity was at an all-time low. It even looked as if the triumvirate was beginning to fall apart at the seams. Cicero, at times, expressed some fear that his hopes were groundless; yet he had decided to remain in the city, and to take his chance against Clodius. He even started to imagine the trial and the arguments he would use in his defence. In June 59 BC, Cicero admitted it: he was 'eager to fight'.[18]

In August, however, it all went sour when rumours starting circulating about a planned assassination attempt on Pompey's life. An informer called Vettius came forward and denounced a number of men for their involvement, including an 'eloquent ex-consul', who had been inciting the would-be assassins – or so he claimed. And although he did not mention Cicero by name, it was obvious to everyone whom Vettius meant.[19] Furthermore, it drove a nasty wedge between Cicero and Pompey, who was one of the only men who could protect him against Clodius.

It is impossible to believe that Cicero was involved: his feelings towards Pompey and his reaction to the event are all contained in his private letters. As to whether there was any substance to the rest of the accusations, we simply cannot tell, for Vettius was mysteriously found dead before there could be a judicial investigation. It has often been suggested, as Cicero believed, that Caesar stage-managed the whole bizarre event; and if so, it worked. An insecure and terrified Pompey fled back into the arms of Caesar, where he intended to stay. He did not even emerge to save Cicero from Clodius, as he had promised he would. Indeed, far from helping him, Plutarch alleges that Pompey even slipped out the back door of his own house because he was too ashamed to face Cicero in the days leading up to his exile.

For when Clodius finally took his revenge, it was worse than Cicero could ever have anticipated: he did not intend to prosecute Cicero before a jury in the law courts, where there was every chance he would escape conviction. Instead, he proposed a law that stated that 'any man who had ever executed a Roman citizen without trial should be forbidden fire and water'.[20] This was the Roman phrase for sending a man into exile, and even though it did not stipulate him in person, Clodius' proposal had Cicero's name written all over it; should the bill be passed as law, this was exactly what Cicero would have to do.

However, it should be noted that Cicero was only a part, and not the whole, of Clodius' plans for his year in office, which revolved around his desire to create a popular following. For Clodius had witnessed the revolutionary activities of Catiline, and his eyes had been opened to a source of political power that, as yet, had not been exploited to its full potential – the urban mob. Many politicians had obviously appealed to the interests of the plebs in the past, but they had not done so directly and exclusively. Indeed, this had arguably been Catiline's mistake, for, in the wake of the conspiracy, the people had been convinced to abandon him and champion Cicero instead. And so, while hatred and bitterness towards Cicero certainly spurred Clodius on, the orator's worrying influence must also have played a very large part in his destruction.

Clodius' first move was to make sure that he had the backing of both the common people and the consuls before he made his attack on Cicero. To start, he passed a series of very popular measures including, for the first time ever, free grain hand-outs for the masses. Then he enticed the consuls for the year: Lucius Calpurnius Piso and Aulus Gabinius. To these men he offered great rewards in return for their support. After their year in office, thanks to Clodius, they were to receive special commands in the rich provinces of Macedonia and Cilicia. Their hands were tied by their own greed, and Cicero never forgave them for that.

Clodius was strategically getting rid of anyone and everyone who was likely to oppose him in his year of office. Cato, whose ever-predictable obstinacy would have been useful to Cicero, was removed from Rome by a clever manoeuvre: Clodius proposed that Cato should be granted extra powers to organize Cyprus as a Roman province. Cato had always made a point of objecting to such extraordinary commands, and so it was highly ironic that he was now given one. Despite the terrible effects this had on Cicero's predicament, it was an ingenious plan.

Further obstacles that Clodius foresaw were removed by less subtle methods: bribery and violence were set to work against the men who would have stood up to defend Cicero. His supporters among the equestrian rank were frightened off by the sight of weapons, and all they could do was show their sympathy by wearing clothes of mourning. Cicero, too, changed his clothes and he allowed his hair to grow long and dishevelled; however, Clodius and his men simply revelled in Cicero's demise, and they jeered at him and pelted him with mud. When a group of senators also voted to adopt the mourning style to lend support to Cicero's case, the consuls forbade them. According to Plutarch, several senators burst out of the senate house tearing their tunics and shouting aloud in the streets. These scenes may have been embroidered by later writers, but they are not impossible: such dramatics were a recognized means of gaining sympathy for oneself in ancient Rome, but sadly this time they did not work.[21]

Realizing the futility of his efforts, Cicero fled Rome the evening before a vote was taken on Clodius' bill. On 20 March 58 BC the bill was passed and it became law. On the same day, a second bill was passed – this bill did name Cicero explicitly. It officially exiled him and Cicero's property was confiscated. His beautiful, big house on the Palatine was even knocked down and destroyed. To make things worse, the second bill also stated that Cicero had to be about four hundred miles away from Italy – even Sicily, which may have offered Cicero some comfort and friendship, was considered too close.

INTO EXILE AND BACK

Written from Brundisium: 29 April 58 BC

From Tullius to his dear Terentia and Tullia and little Cicero

I am writing to you less often than I can because, although every stroke of time is miserable for me, whenever I either write to you or read your letters I am so overwhelmed by my tears that I cannot bear it. If only I had been less eager to save my life! For sure, I would have had very little or nothing to be sorry about in my lifetime. But if Fortune has saved me so that I may hope of one day recovering some small shred of well-being, then I have made less of a mistake; but if these present evils are fixed, then, yes, I want to see you, my love, as soon as possible and to die in your arms . . .

I think I should put it like this: if there is any hope of my return, you must make it stronger and help in the campaign; but if, as I fear, it is all over, then come to me in any way you can. Just know this: if I have you, I shall not feel so utterly destroyed. But what will become of my little Tullia? You must see to that; I have no idea what to suggest. Except that, whatever happens, the poor girl's marriage and reputation must be looked after. And what will my little Cicero do? Let him forever stay wrapped in your embrace. I cannot write any more now; misery prevents me . . .[22]

As he wrote this letter to the wife he had left behind, Cicero was at Brundisium (Brindisi, on the heel of Italy). From there he was preparing to set sail across the Adriatic and leave his country; for all he knew and feared, he might never return. We can perhaps share in Cicero's relief that many of his friends risked their lives to help him. One of these was a man called Marcus Laenius Flaccus: 'I hope that one day I shall be able to show him my gratitude,' Cicero wrote in the same letter, 'I shall forever be grateful.' But these thoughts did little to console him, for he also wrote to Atticus: 'The fact that you are calling on me to live is the only thing stopping me from laying hands on myself.'[23]

It is the letters from his exile that have prompted some of the strongest emotions among the scholars who study them. In these letters, Cicero wants to die, he bursts into tears, he blames himself, he blames others more, and he even blames Atticus. Time and time again, Cicero says that all is lost and no hope remains. The letters from this period of Cicero's life are neither an easy nor an enjoyable read. Cicero continually worries that he has let his family down and he fears for their safety too; the preceding extracts provide a small flavour of their highly charged contents. Little did Cicero know that on 5 August 57 BC – in less than eighteen months' time – he would be back in Brundisium celebrating a triumphant return.

Until then, he spent six months in Thessalonica (Salonika in Macedonia) followed by nine months in Dyrrachium (Durazzo) on the Adriatic coast. He had a miserable time.

To put the raw emotions of the letters into context, we must consider what exile meant to a Roman. It was the worst punishment a man like Cicero could be forced to endure. He had gone from being the 'father of his country' to an outlaw. He had lost the country for which he had so long fought. He was not even counted as a citizen. When we consider how much Cicero hated to be away from Rome, perhaps, as he claims, death would have been an easier sentence. Admittedly, Cicero had chosen to leave Rome before the bill had been passed; yet it is hard to imagine what else he could have done. It seems unfair to judge Cicero on the basis of his desperate letters. He was, as he admitted to Quintus, 'the image of a breathing corpse'. He was no longer the man Quintus had known.[24]

Cicero had not been in exile long when the attempts to gain his recall started, but these met with violence. For as long as he was a tribune, Clodius managed to veto any calls for Cicero's return; furthermore, there was nothing anyone could do to counter the hired thugs and gangs that Clodius kept by his side. Rome, we should remember, did not have anything like a police force. Caesar was out of the country, for he had taken up his command in Gaul. And Pompey's insecurity and fear of being disliked had, by now, turned into a full-scale paranoia of assassination. He pushed hard behind the scenes on Cicero's behalf initially, but Pompey was scared and so he retired to his various houses in the country for the rest of the year.

At the beginning of 57 BC, the situation looked more promising and the efforts to reinstate Cicero continued. Clodius' term as tribune had expired, and eight of the ten new tribunes for 57 BC were on Cicero's side. One of the consuls too, Publius Lentulus Cornelius Spinther, was in Pompey's pocket – and Pompey was now desperate to get Cicero back. But the violence and bloodshed continued to hamper a vote being taken on his recall. On one occasion, Quintus was seriously injured. Clodius' men had hunted him down in the forum and left him for dead; the only thing that kept him alive was the hope of Cicero's return. On that day, Cicero later embellished, 'the corpses of citizens crammed the river Tiber, the sewers were clogged, the blood that had been shed in the forum had to be soaked up with sponges'.[25]

In the end, the only way to counter Clodius was to meet force with force. Two of the tribunes working for Pompey, Publius Sestius and Titus Annius Milo, decided to raise their own gangs. Milo even went so far as to prepare a squad of gladiators for the purpose; these were the depths to which Roman political life had fallen. At a heavily guarded meeting of the senate in July 57 BC, four hundred and seventeen senators finally assembled to vote on a decree. This decree contained the senate's suggestion that the magistrates propose a bill for Cicero's recall, and it met with almost unanimous favour. There was only one man who voted against it: Clodius.

Now all Cicero needed was the vote of the people, and a date was set for an assembly meeting to achieve this: 4 August 57 BC. A powerful array of Rome's leading politicians, including Pompey, all proclaimed the same thing – everyone wanted Cicero back. Furthermore, a number of measures had been taken to make sure that the bill went through. First, the senate declared that anyone hindering the vote would be declared a public enemy. Second, the people were assembled by centuries rather than by tribes. This guaranteed a favourable pool of voters, for the centuriate assembly gave far more leverage to the senatorial and equestrian élite than it did to Rome's poorer citizens (whom Clodius could easily have bribed or induced to vote against it). Finally, Milo's gladiators kept a tight rein on proceedings. We do not know whether Clodius was there or whether he voted, but by now he must have seen that resistance was futile.

The minute the bill was passed into law, Cicero wasted no time. He had been waiting for this news. He set sail immediately and was back in Brundisium the very next day. His beloved daughter Tullia was there to meet him – it happened to be her birthday. The recent death of her husband Piso (in unknown circumstances), who had worked tirelessly for Cicero's recall, surely meant that the sight of her father was especially welcome.[26] They were happy to be re-united. Terentia met them *en route* with their young son Marcus. And together the Cicero family headed back towards Rome – to start their second life together.

As Cicero made the journey from Brundisium to Rome, men flocked to congratulate him from every quarter. Atticus could not be in Rome to meet Cicero: the sight of his dear friend, Cicero later wrote, would be his crowning joy. But, otherwise, everyone who was anyone gathered to greet him. As soon as he could, Cicero sent Atticus a letter: 'The steps of the temples were swarming with people who welcomed me with such great applause', he told him. 'The same-sized crowd and the same applause followed me right up to the Capitol.'[27] And as he stood in the forum, back in Rome, Cicero absorbed the spectacular sight before him. He was back where he belonged.

10

Cicero and the Triumvirs (57–53 BC)

STARTING A SECOND LIFE

I would need an eternity to proclaim and recall all the services that many men have performed on my behalf. On this day, however, I have resolved to give thanks, by name, to all the magistrates who helped and to one man, in particular, who acted as a private citizen [i.e. Pompey]. He approached the municipalities and colonies with calls for my safety; he humbly implored the Roman people; he gave his weighty opinion, and you followed it: you all restored my dignity.

(Cicero, *On His Return to the Senate* 31)

Cicero had returned like a triumphant hero, and Rome seemed to love him again. In a letter, sent to Atticus on 10 September 57 BC, Cicero remarked that coming back from exile was 'like the beginning of a second life'.[1] Admittedly, he had returned to great financial difficulties, and there are hints that all was not well between Cicero and Terentia after the difficult eighteen months apart. However, Cicero had achieved what he thought would be impossible: his public prestige, status in the senate and his influence were all as strong as ever before. Cicero was delighted.

However, there was a problem. Cicero's house on the Palatine had been burned down, and his villas in Tusculum and Formiae had been ransacked and looted. All his silver, together with his furniture and works of art, had gone. The grand columns that once adorned the courtyard of his Palatine house had been removed: one of the other consuls had allegedly given them as a gift to his mother-in-law. Even the trees surrounding his Tusculan villa had been given a new home.[2]

To make things worse, Clodius had established a religious shrine to 'Liberty' on the Palatine hill, on the exact site where Cicero's house had once stood. Cicero, he claimed, had been a tyrant: he had executed Roman citizens without a trial. His banishment from Rome was like that of the legendary kings of Rome. Everything that Cicero had done for his family and country was now worthless. From the minute Cicero returned, his main concern was to get them back.

First, however, he delivered a speech in the senate. It was a speech of thanks to those who had worked hardest for his recall. One startling piece of information shows that Cicero wanted to name everyone who had helped him: of all the speeches that Cicero ever delivered in his long career, this is the only time that we know he relied on a script. As we can see in the passage quoted above, he felt very much in Pompey's debt. At the same time, he bitterly attacked those who had done the least to help him: Lucius Calpurnius Piso and Aulus Gabinius, the consuls of 58 BC. They had let Clodius' offers of lucrative provincial commands blind them to any thoughts for Cicero's safety. Cicero had not expected anything better of Gabinius, he claimed: 'For who could hope for anything good to come from a man who, from the first flourish of youth, has openly indulged in every form of sexual excess?'[3] Against Gabinius, Cicero paraded all the stock forms of abuse: charges of sexual perversion, extravagance, drunkenness – and to these he now added Catilinarian sympathies. However, we can detect a note of genuine disappointment in his tirade against Piso:

> As for you, compassionate man that you are, you traded me: I was your connection by marriage; the man whom you trusted to be the primary guard over your tribe at your election; the man whose opinion you said you would ask for in third place throughout the year of your consulship. Yet you handed me over, bound up, to the enemies of the Republic. When Piso and Tullia fell to your knees, you spoke in the most arrogant and cruel tones: you repelled *my* son-in-law, who was *your* own flesh and blood, and *my* daughter, who was *your* connection by marriage.[4]

Piso should have helped Cicero. There is no sign here of the humour that Cicero often used to deliver his damning attacks on his opponents. These are the words of a bitterly saddened and hostile man: a friend turned foe.

There were other men Cicero blamed: Hortensius was foremost among them. When Clodius had first engineered his plans against Cicero, Hortensius and other leading senators had been the ones to advise Cicero to leave Rome. Their false show of friendship had been something of a preoccupation in Cicero's letters to Atticus during his exile. Cicero passed over them in the course of this speech, but they would have known that Cicero felt let down by them too. Later, Cicero did not veil his resentment towards his peers when he made a similar speech of thanks to the people:

> At that time, I realized that among that body of men – the very body of which I was considered a leading figure – some were deserting me, and some were even betraying my cause, either because they were jealous of me or because they feared for themselves.[5]

It is important to understand how Cicero viewed the men around him both during and after his exile. For only then can we begin to understand the decisions he made as political circumstances continued to change around him.

It was Pompey to whom Cicero felt obliged. This may come as a surprise;

Pompey had, after all, acquiesced in Cicero's downfall by allowing Clodius' adoption into a plebeian family. Cicero had further felt deceived and disappointed by Pompey's alliance with Caesar and Crassus. But there was no denying that he had pulled his influence in the campaign for Cicero's recall. Besides, Cicero had once held high hopes for Pompey, and so it was perhaps natural that he chose to ally himself with the great general once more. Indeed, he spoke up for Pompey just days after his return. When everyone surely expected Cicero to stand back from public affairs, demure, he threw himself straight back into the fray.

Things at Rome had deteriorated rapidly in the time that Cicero had been away. The triumvirate, which was probably never intended as a permanent alliance, was on shaky grounds. Pompey and Crassus had always distrusted each other, but now they each championed a different gang leader: Crassus backed Clodius, while Pompey was often associated with Milo – and the clashes between their respective gangs only exaggerated the tensions that existed between the two triumvirs. Meanwhile Caesar was in Gaul, and he was winning mighty acclaim. Pompey was growing increasingly jealous of Caesar, and he wanted a great campaign of his own: he needed to live up to his name again.

Clodius had unwittingly provided the means for Pompey to get his wish – his next big command. For, thanks to Clodius' free grain dole, it happened that Rome was suffering from a severe food shortage, and there were problems in the production, price and distribution of grain. Pompey, Cicero now argued, should be placed at the head of a special commission to deal with all of Rome's grain supplies, in a command that would stretch five years. And the senate accepted Cicero's motion. It was only 7 September 57 BC, and Cicero had been back in Rome for just three days. The people, too, were delighted. They responded by chanting out Cicero's name; this was their 'silly new fashion' of showing approval, Cicero later commented – perhaps showing how rowdy the mob had become under Clodius' leadership.[6]

For the next few months, however, Cicero was preoccupied with the problem of his restoration. The fact that a shrine to Liberty had been built on the site of his former house on the Palatine meant that Cicero's land was now a sacred spot, and that, in Roman thinking, was an act that could not, or rather should not, be reversed. To get his house back, Cicero first had to win the backing of the pontifical college, the prestigious board of fifteen men who administered and supervised Rome's state religion.

If Cicero was to get his land back, the pontifical college had to decide that Clodius' dedication to Liberty could be annulled without causing sacrilege. In short, they needed to be persuaded that the site had not been properly consecrated. The speech that Cicero delivered, *On His House*, survives among the published works and, in Cicero's eyes, it was a masterpiece: his grief and the great interests at stake both gave his speech 'a certain force of eloquence', he believed.[7]

And the result was that the board of priests finally agreed to make restoration to Cicero – much to Clodius' displeasure.

Cicero's restoration was essentially complete, but his exile and return had left Cicero's finances in disarray. For, although the pontifical college had decided in Cicero's favour, their assessment of his losses had been made 'ungenerously' – or so Cicero and many others felt. He received only two million sesterces for the house on the Palatine (which had cost him three and a half million, just a few years before). They valued the damages to his Tusculan villa at half a million sesterces, and his estate at Formiae was reckoned at just a quarter of a million. As for why they had been so miserly, Cicero explained: 'Those men, my dear Atticus – you know exactly who I mean [referring to Hortensius and his circle] – the very men who scorched my wings, do not want them to grow back.'[8]

This attitude is typical of Cicero. Throughout his life, he only thought of his 'enemies' as falling into two categories: either those who were dishonest or those who were jealous of him. It is possible that Cicero took politics too personally some times. He was loyal and supportive to his friends, and he expected the same in return. However, true friendships, according to Cicero's model, were very difficult to sustain in the public and political life of Rome – as Cicero later admitted in his treatise *On Friendship*.[9] Rather, they were temporary alliances. And if further proof of this was needed, the most notorious of these alliances – that between Pompey, Caesar and Crassus – demonstrates just how impermanent and disastrous they could be. For, when Cicero returned to Rome, the triumvirate was in crisis.

TENSIONS AMONG THE TRIUMVIRS

For a long time on the streets of Rome, the rival gangs of Clodius and Milo had highlighted a very real tension between Pompey and Crassus: Milo used his troops in support of Pompey's policies, while Clodius was supported by Crassus. However, the hostility between the two gang leaders was also paraded in the law courts, with each man wanting to prosecute the other on charges of violence. Fortunately for Clodius, he had secured his election to the aedileship for 56 BC, which meant that he could not be prosecuted. Yet he could still prosecute Milo, and at the preliminary hearing in February 56 BC, Pompey rose to speak in *his* gang leader's defence. But Crassus was also there, and it was clear that he was not on Milo's side.

The fights between Clodius and Milo, however, were only a part of the tensions brewing between Pompey and Crassus. At the time of the hearing, there was another political issue burning in the background: the 'Egyptian problem', which revolved around who should be given the command to restore the Egyptian king,

Ptolemy, to his throne (for he had been driven out of Alexandria by his citizens several months before). The command in question had a long convoluted history in Roman politics, but it was one that would bring great glory, wealth and influence to anyone who obtained it. Unsurprisingly, there were several contenders, and Pompey and Crassus were among them. Indeed, their rivalry for the post provided the occasion for a sudden outburst of violence on the day of Milo's hearing.

When Pompey rose to speak in Milo's defence he was met with uproar from Clodius' side. Pompey, somehow, managed to finish his speech. However, when Clodius rose, he met with a similar commotion from Milo's men. He went 'deadly pale' according to Cicero in a letter he wrote describing the event to his brother Quintus. And rather than finish his speech, Clodius began shouting out questions to his gangs in the crowd:

> 'Who is starving the poor to death?' he asked – they replied 'Pompey!'
> 'Who wants to go to Egypt?' he asked – and again they replied 'Pompey!'
> 'Who do *you* want to go?' – to which, they replied 'Crassus!'[10]

The fracas continued as Clodius' gangs started spitting at Milo's supporters, and when fighting broke out, Clodius was even flung from the *rostra*. Without a police force to temper the riots, the danger must have been electric. Cicero decided to escape for fear of what might happen, and Pompey too went home while the senate convened to discuss what had just happened.

The whole event gives us a lively impression of how public affairs were conducted in Rome, as well as the levels of violence within the stormy political climate. It also signifies Pompey's growing unpopularity with the plebeian masses, which were steered by Clodius in support of Crassus. For Cicero, however, such open demonstrations of conflict gave fresh hope that the triumvirate was on the point of collapse. Pompey, who still harboured morbid fears of assassination plots, was moving closer and closer to Cicero. If only he could convince Pompey to abandon his union with Caesar and Crassus, Cicero saw that there was a chance to restore the constitution. Indeed, at the end of the month, Cicero felt bold enough to repeat his hopes and fears for the Republic in Pompey's presence.

The occasion was the trial of Sestius, one of the tribunes who (like Milo) had hired gangs to counter those of Clodius. He had been active in Cicero's recall campaign, and now Cicero rose to defend him against the charge of having used armed violence. The speech has become famous for the ideals which Cicero expounds. In particular, Cicero claimed that there was a need for 'tranquility with dignity' (*otium cum dignitate*): a slogan that meant something like peace for the people and honour for the senate. This was what all the *optimates* desired, he argued – using the term that he had normally only ever applied to the wealthy ruling class. But he also broadened his definition of who the *optimates* were.

They were not just the 'best men' from within the senate; the *optimates* were the honourable men of every class. His view is wildly exaggerated, but Cicero had clearly been doing a lot of thinking.[11]

In the event, Sestius was unanimously acquitted. But not before Cicero had severely attacked one of the prosecution's witnesses, Publius Vatinius, who was also one of Caesar's right-hand men. As tribune of the plebs in 59 BC, Vatinius had been the prime mover of Caesar's legislation, including the bill which gave Caesar a five-year command over Gaul. It was a 'criminal act' to give Caesar so much power, Cicero boldly claimed. And although Cicero made a show of dissociating Caesar from Vatinius, his compliments of the triumvir betrayed a veiled criticism.[12]

It was the first time Cicero had attacked Caesar since his return. In April, he went even further and actively challenged one of Caesar's bills: the agrarian law, which redistributed the fertile plains in the Campanian region to veteran soldiers. The bill had been unpopular when Caesar first forced it through. But, now, Cicero succeeded in putting it on the agenda for discussion in the senate on 15 May 56 BC – and there were many senators who would also have liked to see this particular law reconsidered and revoked.

Reflecting on this occasion, Cicero saw it as a high point in his activity against the triumviral alliance. His hopes to separate the three men were at an all-time high. An attack on Caesar, he thought, was an attack on the 'citadel of that alliance'. Pompey had shown no offence at the pro-republican/anti-triumviral remarks, or so he told Cicero.[13] Yet Pompey was being his usual non-committal and disingenuous self. Cicero knew that Pompey was on his way to Sardinia (he was going to monitor the ongoing grain situation); what Pompey did not tell Cicero was that he was planning to meet Caesar and Crassus on his way there.

The meeting between Pompey, Caesar and Crassus has become known as the 'conference of Luca' (modern-day Lucca, near Florence). It was here, in April 56 BC, that the three renewed their alliance; and according to the new terms, each man came out stronger than before. To begin with, Pompey and Crassus were reconciled. It was agreed that they were to hold another joint consulship the following year, in 55 BC. This also entitled them to profitable commands the year after that, in 54 BC. Crassus accepted the fatal Parthian campaign. Pompey, on the other hand, accepted a five-year post in Spain, which he planned to govern through legates so that he could stay at Rome. To coincide with the commands of Pompey and Crassus, Caesar's governorship in Gaul was renewed for a further five years.

A later source claims that over two hundred senators were present at Luca to lend their support to the negotiations. The exact numbers are questionable, but the trio clearly felt confident that they could get everything they wanted. Opposition could be countered by violence, if and when necessary. On the other hand, men like Cicero and Clodius, who had aggravated the alliance, had to be checked. They had to know their place.

In hindsight, Cicero should have seen the warning signs; namely, that, as in 60 BC, Pompey's alliance with Cicero had not given the former everything he desired. In reality, it was frequently difficult to know what Pompey wanted, as Cicero often complained in his letters. True, Cicero had managed to get the command of Rome's grain supply passed in Pompey's favour. However, it is likely that Pompey wanted it on far more generous terms. (Another tribune had gone so far as to suggest that Pompey should be given a fleet, an army and supreme command over all the provinces, but Cicero had not supported this particular proposal.) Next, Pompey had wanted the Egyptian command, but that had also fallen out of the picture. The triumvirate may have looked as though it was about to cave in; however, Pompey still had much to gain from an alliance with Caesar and Crassus. Furthermore, they still had a lot to gain from Pompey.

Caesar had many opponents in the senate, and the security of his position depended heavily on Pompey's support. At any time, Pompey could have pulled the rug from under Caesar's feet, leaving him on very dangerous grounds. Pompey had also shown Crassus that he could match him, blow for blow, in mustering forces at Rome. He was surely the one in the strongest position – but only just. For Caesar was accumulating wealth and glory all the time he was in Gaul. It is possible, as has been suggested, that Pompey even used Cicero to assert his superiority. Pompey may have let Cicero deliver his tirades against Caesar simply to highlight the weakness of the latter's position. Of course, it is impossible to know if, or to what extent, Pompey was taking advantage of Cicero in this way. But one thing is sure: when Pompey decided it was time for Cicero to stop, Cicero stopped.

Pompey did make his way to Sardinia after the conference at Luca. There he saw Quintus, who was overseeing and regulating the grain supply as a member of Pompey's staff. 'Ah!' Pompey is reported to have said, 'Just the man I want – perfect timing. If you do not deal with your brother Marcus soon, you will have to pay me that surety you offered on his behalf.'[14] Quintus had evidently offered some sort of guarantee that Cicero would behave himself. To make doubly sure that Cicero got the message, Pompey sent him a letter telling him to drop the matter of Caesar's legislation, which was scheduled for discussion in the senate on 15 May. Cicero did as he was told and the matter was promptly forgotten.

Cicero had no choice: after the conference of Luca, he had to support the triumvirate. The political distinction and independence he had enjoyed since his recall from exile was over. As a sign of his submission, Cicero openly declared his new support in a puzzling document he refers to as his 'palinode' – possibly a letter, speech or a poetic retraction of his previous attacks on Caesar. For once, he had not sent a copy of it for Atticus to read: 'I did not have a spare one,' Cicero explained, 'besides (and, note, I have been chewing around what needs to be swallowed for too long now), I did feel that my "palinode" was rather shameful. But goodbye to principles, integrity and honest conduct!'[15]

For the next few years, Cicero defended anyone the triumvirs told him to defend, and supported any motion they asked him to support. 'Am I to be a common soldier,' Cicero asked only a year later, 'having refused to be a general?'[16] He did not need Atticus to answer. His 'second life' at the summit of Roman political life had been rudely cut short. Cicero did more than admit defeat to the triumvirs; he became their advocate and orator.

WEIGHING UP THE LOSSES: CICERO'S DECISION

In June 56 BC, less than two months after the reunion of the triumvirs had struck him silent, Cicero wrote to Atticus:

> Let this be an end to it. Since the men who are powerless refuse to like me, I shall have to see to it that I am welcomed by the powerful. You will say 'I told you so!' I know that is what you wanted me to do – what a prize ass I have been![17]

This private letter shows the rationalized conclusion of a man who realizes he has much to lose. By Cicero's own admission, he had been 'a prize ass' for always supporting men who had let him down in the past – men, he believed, who were simply jealous of his success. And there was, as Cicero realized, no middle path in politics. Cicero neatly expressed his dilemma to Atticus: He had either to continue on the traditional but powerless road – the optimate way, as he had once called it – with men who did not like him; however, this road had already led him into exile once. Or he had to embark on a new alliance with men who were willing and able to protect him and his family. It was one or the other, and Cicero chose the alliance, as Atticus had been urging him to do for some time.

It is easy to find fault with Cicero for the political decisions he took in these years, especially when we consider the honourable resistance with which he initially refused a share in the triumvirate. It is further difficult to understand why he became an outspoken supporter of the three men when he had made his decision to submit to them. But Cicero was not the kind of man to stay silent. Furthermore, he was surely right, a decade later, to claim that silence would always be seen as hostility on his part: silence, from a man who always spoke his mind, could have been interpreted as repressed disapproval of the 'regime'.[18]

Having sided with the triumvirs, Cicero had no choice but to speak for them. Yet a further factor has often been neglected in considering the choice that Cicero had to make: his family. Thanks to recent scholarship in the area, it is now possible to imagine what the women in Cicero's life, Terentia and Tullia, must have suffered during his absence from Rome. To this, we can add considerations of what was expected of a young man, and where his father's exile left Marcus.

Under the second bill that Clodius passed – the interdict banning Cicero from fire and water – Cicero had become an outlaw. He was no longer a Roman citizen, and Terentia was no longer legally married to him according to Roman law. Cicero's children would no longer be under his power. Tullia was now twenty years old and married, but Marcus was only seven. 'As long as you are safe,' Cicero told Quintus, 'at least they will not be fatherless.' 'Please watch over Terentia too', he begged his brother.[19] For, although Terentia could continue to behave as if she were married, there was no legal substance behind her decision. Cicero's loss of position was a major blow for all the family.

The legal aspect scratches only the surface of what Cicero's family must have experienced. There are many questions to which we can only guess the answers, but they are worth asking. Where were Terentia and her children when their Palatine home was burned down? And where did they live afterwards? Tullia, we can assume, would have been at home with her husband. Terentia and Marcus might have taken refuge with her half-sister, Fabia, in the sanctity of the house of the vestal virgins. Yet it must have been a frightening and traumatic time. What was their financial position like? Tullia could be supported by her husband, while he was alive. Cicero was more worried about his young son's future prospects: 'As for what you write, my Terentia, about your plans to sell some property, what, I beg you (the wretch that I am!), is to happen? And if the same fate presses on us both, what will become of our poor boy? I cannot write any more, so strong are my tears.'[20] If the efforts for Cicero's recall failed, it is clear that Terentia intended to follow him into exile. Any property she owned, Cicero felt, should be preserved for their children's future security. In this way, when he grew up, young Marcus could still hope to embark on a political career himself.

Finally, we may ask, how did society treat Cicero's family and what was their daily life like? Their friends, as one would expect, rallied around them. Cicero's letters to Atticus relay Terentia's gratitude towards him. Yet his enemies could be bitter. Terentia and Tullia wore the appearance of mourning – black robes and dishevelled hair – to elicit sympathy for their family's suffering. This must have been a humiliating experience for women, who had been the wife and daughter of Rome's consul, their country's saviour, only a few years before. Some women were doubtless sympathetic; others, like Clodia – the sister of Clodius – seem to have relished in their fall. Clodius, too, summoned Terentia and interrogated her. Cicero does not tell us the details, but he wept when he read about it: 'Ah, light of my life, my beloved, everyone everywhere used to go to you for help, but now *you* are the one who is tormented, cast down in tears and mourning – and it is all my fault, because I saved others only to destroy us!'[21]

After his submission to the triumvirs, when Cicero's opponents sneered at him for no longer speaking out with his former freedom, Cicero argued that his loss in 58 BC had caused him to consider his own and his family's welfare.[22] As always, it is difficult to assess the motives behind any comments Cicero makes, especially when they are made in public, and in a law-court speech. But a hint that Cicero may be telling the truth can be found, buried, in the wealth of evidence that his personal letters to Atticus provide: Cicero had kept quiet at a trial when he could have spoken – 'my little girl,' he explained, 'was afraid it might annoy Clodius.'[23]

In short, we may not approve of Cicero's decision. Nor, indeed, may we respect the fact that he went on to defend men at the triumvirs' command. But Cicero had made his decision and, for as long as he could bear to, he stuck to it with resolute steadfastness.

LEVISSIME TRANSFUGA: 'A MOST FICKLE DESERTER'

Cicero's complete submission to the triumvirs was apparent to his peers almost immediately, for before the middle of June 56 BC Cicero made a startling speech in favour of Caesar. There were many who were trying to strip Caesar of his command in Gaul. Only a few months before, Cicero had called the bill giving Caesar this command a 'criminal act', yet now he was arguing *against* the proposal that sought to remove the province from Caesar's control: 'You have conferred many exceptional honours upon Caesar, and nearly all of them were unique', he told an audience of senators. 'Insofar that he has earned them, you have shown gratitude, but, also, because he is most committed to this order, you have shown a godlike wisdom.'[24]

It is possible, as many scholars believe, this speech is the shameful 'palinode' that Cicero regretted. But worse was to come, as a string of high-profile defence cases were passed Cicero's way. In 56 BC, he defended Lucius Cornelius Balbus, a close friend and confidant of both Pompey and Caesar. He successfully defended a man he disliked: Titus Munatius Plancus Bursa – if we can trust Plutarch, Cicero later admitted Bursa's guilt in a fit of rage. By the summer of 54 BC, Cicero was jumping from one case to the next: 'I am defending Messius, . . . then I get ready for Drusus, from him to Scaurus.'[25] All these men, and more besides, were associated with the triumvirs. But, then, there was Cicero's defence of Vatinius, also in the summer of 54 BC. Just two years before, in the trial of Sestius, Cicero had torn Vatinius to shreds. They had never got on. Cicero did not want to defend him, but pressure was mounting from both Pompey and Caesar.

Cicero evidently felt the need to justify his actions in these years; not just for defending Vatinius, but for his whole line of conduct in supporting the triumvirs. Indeed, it was at this time that he famously tried to convince a respected historian – Lucius Lucceius – to write a glorified account of his consulship, exile and return: Cicero, it seems, needed to bolster his public image again. For, aside from oratory, he co-operated with the triumvirs in other ways. In 55 BC, Pompey opened Rome's first ever permanent theatre. The spectacle was a sight to behold: six hundred mules appeared in the dramatic performance of *Clytemnestra* (the wife of Agamemnon, who murdered him when he returned from the Trojan war). In another play, *The Trojan Horse,* three thousand expensive wine-bowls were paraded to represent the spoils of Troy after their legendary defeat. On top of these performances, there were athletic games, wild-beast hunts and gladiatorial shows.

Cicero detested such events: 'Magnificent sights – no one can deny it,' he admitted, 'but what delight can a man of culture have in watching a puny man being torn to shreds by the mightiest of beasts, or in seeing a noble beast pierced through by a hunting spear?'[26] But Cicero was there to be seen. Not everyone would have approved of the theatre. Actors and gladiators were low-class: they represented sexual licence, deviance and perversion. A permanent arena in which to stage such events did not sit easily with everyone. 'Pompey was criticized by his elders,' the Roman historian Tacitus later wrote, 'for it was feared that people would become lazy, spending days on end in the theatre.'[27] The younger Cato would most certainly have disapproved too. But Cicero's visual presence was required, and he obliged.

Caesar too found other uses for Cicero. In the summer of 54 BC, Caesar was planning a great building programme. This kind of project was both a great service to the community and a sure means of immortalizing one's name. Caesar wanted to increase the forum. He planned to make the area around the field of Mars more functional and attractive: it would have marble booths surrounded by a high colonnade, a mile long, to provide shade for the voting populace. 'We, Caesar's friends (I mean Oppius and myself), have not minded spending sixty million sesterces on the project,' Cicero told Atticus, '. . . We shall achieve something very glorious.'[28]

Yet it seems that Caesar and Cicero had not just reconciled old differences for practical ends; their friendship may have been genuinely felt. Their shared literary pursuits bound them closer: Caesar had written a book on Latin grammar, which he dedicated to Cicero; in turn, Cicero wrote an epic poem on Caesar's campaigns in Britannia. As much as Cicero despaired at Caesar's political methods at times, he also seems to have admired him as a man of culture. Cicero also loved to feel appreciated, and Caesar did value him.

Cicero's decision to side with the triumvirs had undoubtedly been forced upon him, but what kept him there was the security of his position among them. However, before too long the demands made of Cicero became intolerable. He had already defended Vatinius, a man whom he had scathingly criticized in public before. But now Gabinius, who had deserted Cicero in his hour of need

Marble portrait of Julius Caesar (© The Trustees of the British Museum).

and traded his safety for a lucrative province, returned from Cilicia. Moreover, he returned to a whole catalogue of criminal accusations. In October 54 BC, Cicero narrowly avoided having to defend Gabinius at a first trial, but Pompey had urged and convinced him to stand as a witness for the defence. Shortly afterwards, a letter to Quintus gives us a stark glimpse into Cicero's mind. For, by the beginning of November 54 BC, his despair had plummeted to new depths – he was being forced into defending Gabinius in another trial, which he eventually did. His agony is best left in Cicero's words:

> I am tormented, my sweetest brother, tormented: there is no government; there are no law courts. At this stage of my life, when my influence in the senate should be flourishing, I am either being thrown into legal work or occupying myself with private study. And so, that motto, which I have loved since I was a boy – 'Far to excel, surpassing all the rest' – has been shattered. I have been unable to attack some of my enemies, others I have even had to defend. I am neither free in what I think, nor in whom I choose to hate.[29]

In other letters from the same period, Cicero could bear life more philosophically; after all, his predicament now was better than it had been while he was in exile. 'I do not remember the height from which I have fallen,' he could write to

Atticus, 'but the depth from which I have risen'.[30] However, some of his contemporaries were not so generous in their assessment. A famous pamphlet, wrongly attributed to the Roman writer Sallust, survives to tell the tale, and it gives some flavour of the taunts Cicero faced.

Old jokes about the poem *On His Consulship* he had written emerged, as well as accusations that Cicero aspired to be a king: he was 'Arpinum's answer to Romulus', the author claimed. According to this evaluation, Cicero was also a turncoat and a traitor:

> You laud the power of the men you used to call tyrants. Those whom, in days past, you regarded as the 'best men', you now call frenzied madmen. You defend Vatinius, yet you think ill of Sestius. In the most petulant words, you lay into Bibulus, but you lay the praise on thick for Caesar. The man that you hated the most, you praise the most. You stand with one set of feelings about the Republic, and you sit with another. These men you insult, and those you hate, you most fickle deserter, you do not pitch your loyalty in any camp.[31]

In the light of everything we know about Cicero's principles, political thought and personality, there is no denying that his submission to the triumvirs was a momentous reversal of all that he stood for. But, fortunately, this blip in Cicero's career – his alliance with the triumvirs – did not need to last long. For two events soon brought a natural end to the triumvirate.

The first was the death of Julia during childbirth in 54 BC. She had been Caesar's only child and Pompey's beloved wife. Both men had been incredibly fond of her, and it may even have been Julia's influence that had helped them reconcile their differences in the past. Had she lived, Julia could have served to mediate between the two men. However, with that tie broken, a strong chain binding the two dynasts had been severely weakened – for the baby also died, just a few days afterwards.

A year later, in 53 BC, the death of Crassus in the Parthian campaign meant that the three men were down to two. For some time, Pompey and Caesar managed to work together. But it is a point of some significance that, when Caesar later tried to renew the alliance with another marriage offer, Pompey refused to remarry into Caesar's family. Pompey's commitment to Caesar was no longer bound by any formality. As usual, he liked to bide his time and review his options.

For Cicero, the death of Crassus brought an unexpected advantage. For Crassus' son had died fighting alongside his father, and his death opened up a prestigious vacancy on the board of augurs – it was a position for which Cicero had long hankered, and now he got it. It was Hortensius who sponsored Cicero – evidence, perhaps, that Cicero had not completely alienated himself from the senatorial élite. And maybe the last three years had not been as much of a *faux pas* as they seem.[32]

We may still wonder whether Cicero had been right to submit to the triumvirs after the conference of Luca. On the negative side: he had lost the freedom to make his own political decisions, he had earned the contempt of some of his peers and he had felt increasingly disparaged at the state of the Republic. But, more positively, he had not made any lasting enemies beyond what was usual in the turning tides of Roman politics. Furthermore, he had been saved from the ongoing wrath of Clodius.

In these years too, Cicero had retreated more and more into his literary studies, providing Rome with a canon of literature to rival the Greeks. This was Cicero engaging in politics and persuasion from a very different angle: he wrote theoretical works on them. First, there came the *Republic*, which, as we have seen, explored his ideas for a working political constitution. Then there was *On the Orator*, a dialogue which sought to explain the qualities a good speaker should possess. He also began a work called *The Laws*, the sequel to the *Republic*, in which Cicero examined the legal codes that the ideal state should possess – although this was only published some years later, maybe even after Cicero's death.

The publication of all these works was a political act in itself, but his studies may also have had a very discernible political result. These works, it has been argued, reminded Cicero of everything he stood for: 'Thanks to such work, Cicero finally overcame his depression of spirits; in it, he found the means to pull himself together and to stand upright again.'[33] And, indeed, Cicero did not have to wait long to show off his new-found strength, for the opportunity emerged in 52 BC, when he had to defend his friend Milo against a charge of murder. Yet the victim of this murder was Clodius, and this was one topic on which Cicero had a lot to say.

11

Cicero, Clodius and Milo (52 BC)

CONTINUING HOSTILITIES: CICERO AND CLODIUS

Publius Clodius, a man of noble birth, eloquent and reckless, recognized no limit either in speech or in deed . . . This man waged a bitter hatred against Marcus Cicero – for what friendship could there be between men so different?

(Velleius Paterculus, *History of Rome* 2.45)

The name of Clodius has loomed large over the last three chapters as, indeed, it did over Cicero's life for almost a decade. In 61 BC, Cicero had earned Clodius' enmity, when he testified against him in the *Bona Dea* scandal. From that time on, Clodius hounded and threatened Cicero. He drove Cicero into exile. He fought every fight he could to prevent his recall. But his animosity did not stop there, it continued until Clodius' dying day: 18 January 52 BC. This was the day on which the 'Battle of Bovillae' – or so Cicero called it – occurred: a fight to the death between Clodius and his long-term rival, Milo. Before we examine the death of Clodius and the trial for his murder, it is time to review Clodius' political career and his continued attacks on Cicero.

It is difficult to know exactly what kind of man Clodius was. According to Cicero, in a bitter attack after the death of his enemy, he was:

A man whose punishment the senate had often demanded in order to expiate for his religious breaches. A man who committed the unspeakable crime of incest with his sister (Lucius Lucullus swore on oath that he had found this out for certain after holding an investigation). A man who used gangs of armed slaves to drive out a citizen: a citizen who, in the eyes of the people and all the nations, was judged to be a saviour – both of the city and the lives of her citizens. A man who parcelled out kingdoms, or stole them, and divided up the whole world for whoever's benefit he pleased. A man who committed endless slaughters in the forum, and who used armed force to blockade an exceptionally courageous and famous citizen in his home. He was a man who saw no sin in either his criminal deeds or his lustful escapades.[1]

Even allowing for some rhetorical amplification, it has to be admitted that

Cicero's accusations *do* ring true. Clodius had, after all, profaned the sacred rites of the *Bona Dea* festival. From his point of view, it may have been no more than a silly prank, yet it was a breach of religious sanctity that had been of great concern to some of Rome's elders. The charges of incest – which were normally just a routine part of the abuse that Romans hurled at each other – seem credible, if the investigation of Lucullus is anything to go by. The sister in question was the youngest of three (all called Clodia); Lucullus had been her husband, but he divorced her in 66 BC on the grounds of her adultery. At the same time, it is beyond doubt that Clodius drove Cicero out of Rome, blockaded Pompey in his home or that he parcelled out provincial commands to men like Gabinius and Piso in 58 BC. (Clodius had also taken the highly unusual step of making a man, called Brogitarus, the king of Galatia in Asia Minor – the only time this had ever been done by a tribune of the plebs, and not the senate). As for the slaughter, force and weapons rife among Clodius' men – no one could deny it. Clodius was, in the words of a modern biographer, 'an arrogant, reckless, well-connected, and good-looking terrorist.'[2]

During his tribunate, Clodius had passed a number of measures, including Cato's annexation of Cyprus, Cicero's banishment and the free grain dole that he provided. However, he also passed a law that allowed the plebs to associate in colleges (*collegia*) – the local associations and trade unions. They had held this right once before the time of Clodius' legislation, but the senate had stopped the colleges, fearing that they were the breeding grounds of seditious plots. Yet Clodius not only legalized the old *collegia*, he even recognized new ones. And their re-establishment gave Clodius direct access and huge sway over all their members, ex-slaves and gladiators among them. He could use these colleges for his own political ends, but they also provided a 'front' for his recruitment of gangs. It was organized violence on a scale Rome had never witnessed before – and it explains how Clodius could terrorize the streets of Rome and hound all those who stood in his way.

In 57 BC, when all efforts were blazing to recall Cicero, Clodius had put up a fight for as long as it seemed viable. Eventually, checked by the counter-gangs of the tribunes Milo and Sestius (who were working in Pompey's favour to help Cicero), Clodius could do nothing to prevent Cicero's return. But that does not mean that Clodius had given up altogether – far from it. Just two days after Cicero's return, Clodius showed that he still meant trouble. When debates were taking place on the shortage of grain in the city, Clodius worked up the crowd. It was Cicero's fault, he urged them: throngs of people were in Rome for Cicero's return – and that was why there was so little food. Cicero was perhaps not that alarmed. He managed to win the crowds over by securing the grain command for Pompey. But he still felt it was worth telling Atticus about this event, in the same letter that he announced his triumphant return to Rome.[3]

Yet it must have pained Clodius to see Cicero's house being restored to him. Indeed, when the work began to rebuild Cicero's house on the Palatine, Clodius moved in with the demolition gangs. Cicero gives a lively account in a letter to Atticus on 23 November 57 BC. On 3 November, Clodius' gang drove the workmen from the site; they knocked down a whole portico that was being rebuilt; they threw stones at Quintus' neighbouring property, and then set it on fire. On 11 November, Clodius' men chased Cicero down the Sacred Way – the main street of Rome. Stones and swords were flying, and Cicero had to take refuge in a friend's house. On 12 November, they turned their hostility back towards Milo. They tried to storm and set fire to his house; their swords were drawn – and in full daylight. This was a private letter – Cicero did not need to lie to Atticus.

Clodius' attacks on Cicero continued into 56 BC – but they took different forms. For a series of dangerous portents had occurred: a large rumble (probably an earthquake) had been heard in the suburbs, and it meant something was seriously wrong. The senate turned to the soothsayers. These were the Etruscan priests – famous for their pointed hats – who were called to interpret the meanings behind unusual events. Their answer (vague as ever) was that there had been a series of human transgressions, and holy grounds had been profaned. In truth, the validity of such signs, omens and soothsaying had been questioned for some time in intellectual circles. But their potential political leverage was beyond doubt. Clodius argued it was Cicero's fault – his house should not have been rebuilt over the site of the shrine. Cicero, for his part, could not resist turning the tables when he was called to reply to the soothsayers: the profanation referred, among other things, to Clodius' scandalous intrusion of the *Bona Dea* festival.

In the face of these persistent attacks, Milo gave Cicero a guard for his house. And Cicero retaliated against Clodius with the full force of his oratory. His speech *On the Replies of the Soothsayers* does deal with the charge against his house; but it also includes a full exposé of Clodius' scandalous career and debauched life. Cicero did not stop at attacking Clodius; his family, too, came under scrutiny. When Marcus Caelius Rufus, Cicero's former protégé and friend, was brought into court on a charge of violence, Cicero took great delight in the fact that a certain Clodia was behind the prosecution. She was, as her name shows, the sister of Clodius (the second of the three women, who was also accused of having an incestuous relationship with her brother). She had once had an affair with the young Caelius, but was now trumping up charges – or so Cicero claimed – in revenge for his cruel rejection of her advances.

Critics of Cicero, ancient and modern, have long admired Cicero's speech *For Caelius* for its devastating wit and biting humour. A famous example of this comes about halfway through the speech, when Cicero decided to recall Clodia's illustrious ancestors. What would they think of Clodia today? – Cicero invited the audience to ask. And, as if picking an example off the top of his head, he selected Appius Claudius Caecus ('The Blind') – he would be the least shocked of all Clodia's ancestors, for he would not be able to see her. This man had been the censor of Rome in 312 BC. He had built the first stretch of the famous road, the Appian Way, which led from Rome to Capua. And he had also been behind the construction of Rome's first water channel, the Appian Aqueduct. We can only imagine the laughter in court as Cicero, impersonating the dead man, boomed his damning condemnation:

> Was it for this reason that I brought water into the city – so that you might use it in your incestuous rituals? Was it for this reason that I built a road – so that you might cavort on it, escorted by a string of other women's husbands?[4]

Yet, behind the laughter, serious political tumults were rumbling in the background. The speech was delivered just days before the renewal of the triumvirate between Pompey, Caesar and Crassus in 56 BC. This, as we have seen, put a check on the careers and conflicts of Clodius, Cicero and Milo in the short term. The hostilities between the men continued – Clodius on one side, Cicero and Milo on the other. But further civil unrest was stirring, and more pressing emergencies dominate what we know of events in subsequent years.

In the time between the formation of the triumvirate and Clodius' death, every attempt to hold elections was stalled by violence or other tactics of obstruction, perpetrated by the various candidates and their supporters. The result was that, for three years in a row, there were no consuls in place when January came. And things were only going to get worse during 53 BC, as it emerged that Milo was seeking the consulship, and Clodius the praetorship – both men wanting to hold office in 52 BC. Again the attempts to hold elections were disastrous, and neither consuls nor praetors had been elected by the time the year 52 BC opened. Political violence had reached an all-time high, and the situation was escalating out of control.

'THE BATTLE OF BOVILLAE'[5]

On 18 January 52 BC, in the early afternoon, Milo and Clodius happened to pass one another on the Appian Way – they were about twelve miles outside of Rome at the time, on the road near Bovillae. Milo was heading to his home town, Lanuvium. He was the dictator there, and he was due to appoint a priest the following day. Clodius, on the other hand, was returning from Aricia, where he had been addressing the town council. Clodius was travelling on horseback with an escort of around thirty armed slaves. This was customary – to protect against bandits on the way through the Italian countryside. But Milo had a much larger train of slaves and gladiators to protect himself and his wife, who was travelling with him. Clodius and Milo appear to have passed each other without incident. But two of Milo's slaves – who were trailing at the back of the line – picked a fight with Clodius' gang.

The fight turned into a full-scale brawl – a brawl which resulted in Clodius' death. This was a watershed moment in Cicero's life. The fear and humiliation, to which he had been so publicly subjected, was lifted. In a letter to Atticus over a year later, Cicero still referred to the date as if it were a major historical event, like the foundation of Rome: 'We arrived at Ephesus on 22 July,' he told his friend, '559 days after the Battle of Bovillae.'[6]

However, what may have started as an accidental encounter between Milo and Clodius resulted in murder. As Clodius turned round to see what was happening, one of Milo's men pierced his shoulder with a hunting spear. Clodius' men carried him to a nearby tavern. But Milo ordered his gang leader, Marcus Saufeius, to turn Clodius out of the tavern and kill him. By this point, all of Clodius' slaves had either been killed or seriously injured. And so Clodius was dragged out of the tavern, murdered, and his body was left in the middle of the road – by an ironic twist of fate, it all took place by the site of a shrine to the *Bona Dea*.

If these events read like a story, it is because that is what they are – but this is not Cicero's version of what happened. Instead these are the 'facts' behind the case – or so a later scholar, called Quintus Asconius Pedianus, knew them. Asconius was writing only a century later, in the time of Nero (AD 54–68), but there seems no reason to doubt him. His commentary on Cicero's speech *In Defence of Milo* survives today. And it opens our eyes very wide to the fact that events did not always happen the way Cicero makes them seem.

Cicero's account of Clodius' death, delivered in the course of his defence of Milo, differs in key points of information from that of Asconius. Cicero claimed that the incident took place nearer nightfall, and by a house that Clodius owned along the Appian Way. Both details were altered to point the finger of suspicion at Clodius, who – in Cicero's version – had set a trap for Milo. They suggest that Clodius had prepared to ambush Milo near his home, and that he had no intention of returning to Rome after the murder. But, before we look at the speech Cicero delivered in defence of his friend, let us pick up the trail of Asconius' account and follow it to the time the case came to court.

When they had left Clodius' body on the road, Milo and his gang continued on their way to Lanuvium. But a passing senator discovered the corpse on the road, picked it up and sent it to Clodius' wife – a lady called Fulvia (who went on to marry Mark Antony several years later). The body arrived shortly after nightfall, whereupon Fulvia displayed it to a large crowd of onlookers. On 19 January, two Clodian tribunes encouraged an angry mob to take the naked corpse, bruised and battered as it was, to the *rostra*. From there, it was taken into the senate house where they cremated it on the spur of the moment. The senate house went up in flames as a result of their actions, but the mob did not stop there. They made their way to Milo's house (for there was no doubt about who had committed the crime). They were about to attack it, but they were driven off by a barrage of arrows. Rome had descended into chaos. The crowd seized the *fasces* – the bundle of rods emblematic of *imperium* – and called upon Pompey's name repeatedly. They were yelling for him to take power and restore some form of order.

These details provide a glimpse of the violence and effrontery of the Clodian mob – an important point to remember when we examine how Cicero performed on the day of the trial. Rome was in the midst of massive social and political unrest. All this time Milo stayed away from the city. But, according to Asconius, the general indignation soon turned more against the Clodians, for burning down the senate house, than it did against Milo's faction. Buoyed on by this, Milo returned to Rome, where he even continued his campaign for the consulship, for the elections had still not taken place. Instead, Rome was being ruled by a series of short-term appointments; these men collectively were called *interreges* (dating back to the time when Rome had had kings). But there was only one *interrex* at a time, and each man held office for just five days. Considering the scale of the crisis facing Rome, this was no longer a suitable arrangement.

Shortly afterwards, the senate passed its ultimate decree, unusually, however – since there were no consuls – it called upon the *interrex*, the tribunes of the plebs and Pompey, all 'to see to it that the state came to no harm'. In addition, Pompey was asked to raise troops throughout Italy. But there was also mounting pressure for Pompey to be made a dictator. The senate were as hesitant as ever about giving Pompey too much control – but they reached an unusual compromise: Pompey was made sole consul for the year. The motion was made by Bibulus (formerly one of Pompey's opponents), and it was unanimously supported. Plutarch adds that even Cato agreed: any government was better than no government – he is reported to have said. The matter was decided, and Pompey immediately set about the task of restoring order to the city.[7]

THE DEFENCE OF MILO

If Clodius' supporters were to be pacified, Milo needed to be brought to trial. To this end, Pompey immediately passed a new law on violence. It was called 'the Pompeian law on violence', and it was specifically tailored to deal with Clodius' murder, as well as the events subsequent to it. He also passed a second law, to deal with electoral bribery: 'the Pompeian law on electoral malpractice'. And trials under each law would follow a special procedure. Witnesses were to be heard before, instead of after, the speeches. The speeches for both the prosecution and defence had to be delivered on the same day. The prosecution were given two hours for their speech, while the defence had three hours to present its side of the case. In addition – to the upset of many – character references were banned.

The briefs against Milo came flooding in. First of all, he was to be tried under the Pompeian law on violence – on the charge of murdering Clodius. Second, he was condemned for the use of bribery in his consulship campaign, under the Pompeian law on electoral malpractice. And, should either of these fail, a third charge was brought against him under the Licinian law on political associations – again, for malpractice in his electoral campaign. But there would be no need for the last two in order to secure Milo's exile. It was inconceivable that he would be acquitted of Clodius' murder – even with Cicero as an advocate.

On 4 April 52 BC, Milo's trial came to court. Prior to the speeches, the evidence was heard for three days, and the emotions were heated. On the first day, a witness for the prosecution tried to stir up feeling against Milo – by exaggerating the brutality of Clodius' murder. When Marcus Marcellus (Cicero's assistant in the trial) was cross-examining this witness, he was so intimidated by the uproar of Clodius' supporters that he was forced to take refuge with the presiding magistrate. In fear of further violence, Cicero and Marcellus asked that armed troops attend the rest of the trial. And for the rest of the trial Pompey's soldiers packed the forum.

As guards surrounded the court, more witnesses were heard. Inhabitants of Bovillae testified to the murder of the innkeeper, who had also been killed when Clodius was dragged out of the tavern. The priestesses of a nearby cult told how an anonymous woman had come to them, at Milo's bidding, to discharge a vow for Clodius' murder. The climax of the prosecution's presentation of its witnesses occurred when two other women took the stand: Clodius' mother-in-law, Sempronia, and his wife, Fulvia.

The final appeal was emotional, and designed to counter any pleas for sympathy that the defence might make. Although, unusually, Cicero tells us, Milo refused to wear the traditional mourning garb of the defendant. Milo was too proud for that. Cicero, on the other hand, excelled at this art. In his own speech, as he recalled the services Milo had performed in recalling him from exile, and considering the fate awaiting his client, Cicero had to stop himself: 'Let that be an end to it: for I can no longer speak for tears, and Milo has forbidden the use of tears in his defence.'[8]

Asconius does not tell us anything about the witnesses produced by the defence, but we know from Cicero that Marcus Favonius gave evidence in Milo's favour. For Favonius reported something he had heard from Clodius just three days before the incident on the Appian Way – Clodius had said that *Milo* would be dead *within three days*. This was key to the line of defence that Cicero took. For, as we shall see, the question put to the jury revolved around who had set an ambush for whom – had Clodius set a trap for Milo, or had Milo set a trap for

Clodius? Rumours were flying around, and the supporters of Clodius and Milo each had their own stories to tell.

On the fourth day, there was a break while preparations were made for the main hearing of the speeches. But one of the tribunes, Titus Munatius Plancus Bursa, who had been involved in events since he first instigated the people to cremate Clodius' body, used the day to whip up further frenzy. He addressed Clodius' supporters, urging them to come to the trial the next day – it was up to them to see to it that Milo did not escape justice. And so, on the fifth and final day, all the shops in Rome were shut, soldiers patrolled the forum and the speeches for both the prosecution and defence were heard. It was now 8 April 52 BC.

Three advocates spoke for the prosecution – Appius Claudius Pulcher (the oldest of Clodius' three nephews), a young Mark Antony and Publius Valerius Nepos. They spoke in the two hours allotted to them, and they hinged their prosecution on the argument that Milo had plotted Clodius' death. Asconius, of course, tells us explicitly that the meeting on the Appian Way was a chance encounter. But the laws on violence in ancient Rome stipulated the need for the prosecution to prove *intent*. The prosecution could have focused solely on events after Clodius had been dragged from the tavern. But, instead, they decided to argue that the whole thing had been a set up from the beginning. One imagines they saw a great argument from probability in the making: Clodius only had thirty men, Milo had nearer three hundred.

According to a complex system of rhetorical theory that had developed in the second century BC, Cicero had four options on what line of defence to take. He had to find the 'issue' of the case. It was all about choosing which one question to ask: (i) Did Milo actually kill Clodius? (ii) Was Clodius' death the result of murder or homicide? (iii) If Clodius *was* murdered, was his death justified by the circumstances? (iv) Was the legal process employed in the prosecution of Milo fair? This last issue was ineffectual: Pompey's law on violence had been specifically created to deal with the trial, and Cicero could only make a passing dig. (The process was not unjust – but there was no real need to pass another new law to deal with Milo, he remarked.) Nor could Cicero dare to deny the murder outright: ample witnesses had testified to Milo's part in the killing.

This left Cicero with two main options: he could argue that it was self-defence, not an intentional killing. Or he could argue that Clodius' murder was justified by the nature of the times. Opinion was divided as to how Cicero should proceed. According to Asconius, some thought that the best line of defence would be to argue that Clodius' death was in the public interest, and thus justified. Yet it is hard to see how this would have helped settle tensions at Rome, given that Clodius had so much support among the plebeian mob. For his part, Cicero preferred the issue of definition: it was not murder, he claimed, because Milo was forced to defend his life.

All that remains, gentlemen, and the only thing that you should ask is this: which of the two men set the trap for the other. So that you can place the arguments into perspective more easily, please listen carefully, while I tell you briefly what happened.[9]

In Cicero's version, as we have seen, events took a very different spin. They were also highly distorted by arguments from probability. True, Milo had a bigger retinue, but who would be more likely to have murder in mind: the man travelling unencumbered on horseback (Clodius), or the man travelling in a carriage with his wife (Milo). It was Clodius that set the trap for Milo, he claimed: Clodius and his men jumped on their victim, after laying in ambush in Clodius' house. Not missing a trick, however, Cicero also claimed that *even if* Milo *had* planned to kill Clodius, the killing of Clodius was a great benefit to the Republic. In short, Cicero combined two powerful – but completely incompatible – arguments. As one modern scholar has pointed out, Cicero was 'attempting to have his cake and eat it'.[10]

Cicero's strategy was bold, but his performance on the day was far less than its usual best. In the published oration, Cicero admits his own fear. And even though he may be drawing attention to his fear to score a rhetorical point (the rowdiness of the Clodians, or to capture the good will of his audience), there is ample evidence to suggest that the circumstances were highly irregular. Ancient sources disagree about how much of the speech he even delivered. Plutarch says that his body shook and his voice choked when he saw the soldiers. Cassius Dio goes further, adding that Cicero only managed to stutter a few words before giving up. Yet we know that a transcript of what Cicero said on the day was written down and circulated without his permission – so he must have spoken. And so, Asconius' account is probably closer to the truth: Cicero did deliver his speech, but he did so without his 'usual steadiness'.[11]

In the event, the jury did not believe that either Clodius or Milo had set a trap for the other; but they did believe that Clodius had been put to death on Milo's orders. The speech that Cicero later wrote down and published is the copy that survives today. It is a shame that the pirate version does not survive so that we can compare them – for Milo could apparently tell the difference. When Cicero later sent him a copy of the published speech, Milo is reported to have been glad that Cicero did not deliver *that* exact version. Otherwise he would never have got the chance to taste the wonderful mullets in Massilia (Marseilles), where he was now living in exile.[12] For Milo was indeed found guilty. But his friendliness towards Cicero would suggest he realized that there was nothing else Cicero could have done: the fact that Cicero managed to deliver a speech in those circumstances at all must surely be to his credit.

AFTER MILO: CICERO, POMPEY AND THE SENATE

The speech Cicero delivered, *For Milo*, has often been viewed as one of Cicero's best published orations; but his success was not just a literary one. For we should see in this trial the re-emergence of the independence that Cicero thought he had lost. Pompey was in a position of great power, yet Cicero was not defending Milo to please *him*. Milo and Pompey had been politically detached for some time. Furthermore, now that Clodius was dead, it was surely expedient and to Pompey's favour that the other gang leader, Milo, should no longer be in Rome. Pompey appears to have wanted Milo's conviction, which means that it was upon Cicero's own will that he undertook the defence. And it was the first speech he had delivered in the law courts as a free agent since the collapse of the triumvirate.

For the rest of 52 BC, further trials did occur as a response to the violence that had been perpetrated by the two rival gangs. But what is interesting is that the Clodian side suffered most under these legal processes, and public opinion had clearly turned. Cicero continued to work on the side of Milo's faction. He successfully defended Milo's gang leader, Saufeius, on two separate occasions. On the other hand, Clodius' gang leader, who had instigated the cremation of Clodius' corpse in the senate house, was convicted by a massive forty-six votes to five.

During these events, Cicero even undertook the second (and only other prosecution) of his entire career. As soon as the tribunate of Bursa expired, Cicero prosecuted him for his inflammatory role in the aftermath of Clodius' murder. Pompey, who had been on the side of the Clodians throughout, even tried to break his own new law to help Bursa. The anecdote is too good not to repeat it. According to Plutarch, when Pompey stood up to provide a character reference for Bursa (which was now an illegal thing to do), Cato – who was one of the jurors – made a point of putting his hands over his ears, to demonstrate his refusal to listen.[13] Plancus too was convicted and went into exile. They may only have been small triumphs, but Cicero was not on the sideline in these events. He had the freedom again – to choose whom he hated and in whose interests he spoke. Bursa had been one of the men he had been compelled to defend under the triumvirate, but this time Cicero got the outcome he wanted.

Another major implication of the whole Milo affair must not be overlooked: it had brought Pompey over to the side of the senate's traditional leaders. When the crisis reached boiling point, the only man able to step in and take an authoritative grip on the situation was Pompey. According to Plutarch, Pompey once boasted that every official position had come to him sooner than he had expected – but that he had also laid it down sooner than others expected.[14] And once more, he proved that he was happy to take power when needed; however, he also demonstrated that he was just as happy to hand it back – or, at least, share it. For in mid 52 BC, Pompey appointed a co-consul to help him guide the senate for the rest of the year.

The man Pompey chose as a colleague was not just any conservative senator; rather, he was impressively aristocratic both in his reputation and in his very long name – Quintus Caecilius Metellus Pius Scipio Nasica. Furthermore, this man was also Pompey's new father-in-law, a fact which signified Pompey's increasingly intimate alliance with the senatorial élite. Unfortunately, we have so few letters from this period that it is difficult to know how Cicero viewed these developments, or what his predictions for Pompey were. However, his new marriage marked a major transition in Pompey's political career; simultaneously, it symbolized the break in his coalition with Caesar. We can only imagine that Cicero was relieved at the breakdown in their partnership of power; however, although he did not realize it yet, Pompey's alliance with the leading senators was to have a profound impact on Cicero's world in the coming decade.

Before this happened, however, one of the measures that Pompey passed had an immediate effect on the direction of Cicero's life. It was 'the Pompeian law on provincial commands', and its main purpose was to check both the obscene levels of electoral bribery and subsequent extortion in the provinces. Its aim was simple but potentially effective. For years, high-ranking Romans had been bribing their way to the top of the political ladder. Funding an election campaign was no small undertaking, but the candidates knew full well that – should they be successful – they could more than make up for their losses in their provincial year that followed. Pompey's law sought to remedy this situation by imposing a five-year waiting period between office and province. Candidates would be far less ready to spend, and creditors far less ready to lend, money that could not be recovered quickly.

Although bribery and extortion were precisely the kinds of crime that Cicero wanted to see stopped, Pompey's legislation brought bad news to Cicero. Pompey ordered all the senators who had not previously held a provincial command to be dispatched immediately to perform the customary year in office. Their rotation would fill the gap needed to create a five-year waiting period. The result was that now Cicero had to take the command he had never wanted; he was being forced to leave his beloved Rome again. It was tantamount to a second exile in his eyes – and even further away. Cicero was allotted Cicilia: the large south-eastern coastal stretch of Asia Minor (modern Turkey), extending over and including Cyprus. And there he stayed from the summer of 51 to the summer of 50 BC.

The year 52 BC had witnessed a dramatic resurgence in Cicero's oratory and his political independence. His major enemy was dead, and the senate had united with Pompey. In theory, it should have been the start of another era – one without a triumvirate, or any of the other obstacles to a free and functioning constitution. Yet his defence for Milo was the last major law-court speech Cicero ever delivered in the courts as he knew them. For, by the time he returned, Rome was on the brink of a disastrous civil war – it was a civil war from which the Republic never fully recovered.

12

Away from Rome: Governor of Cilicia (51–50 BC)

THE CILICIAN COMMAND

Written from Laodicea: 3 August 51 BC

From Cicero to Atticus, greetings

I arrived at Laodicea on 31 July. From this day you must begin your year's calculation. Nothing could have been more longed for or dearer than my arrival. But it is incredible how much this whole business bores me, for it gives no adequate playing field for my mind to run on, or for the industry which you have come to know well, and it has disrupted the work that is my pride. Indeed – here am I giving my legal opinions in Laodicea while Aulus Plotius gives his in Rome! And while our friend [Pompey] has his huge army, I have a nominal force of two emaciated legions! And at the end of the day, these are not the sort of things I long for; it's the world, the forum, Rome, my house, and all of you that I want. But I'll endure it as much as I can – provided it's only for a year. If it is extended, I give up. But that can be resisted very easily so long as you are in Rome.

(Cicero, *To Atticus* 108/5.15.1)

The posting to Cilicia could not have come at a worse time for Cicero. When he left, the split between Pompey and Caesar was beginning to crack; by the time he returned, it was an irreparable divide. He was desperate to make sure that the post would not be extended beyond its annual tenure. For, on top of the twelve months in office, it was a six-month round trip just to get there and back. Cicero would be away from Rome for eighteen months.

Cicero left Rome on 1 May 51 BC, and we can trace his journey to Cilicia from the letters he sent to Atticus on every step of the way. *En route* Cicero spent three days with Pompey, who was 'most prepared to fight back against the dangers we fear'.[1] The impending danger was Caesar, and no one was blind to the trouble brewing between the two men. Cicero was probably already weighing up in his mind which man he would support if their breach came to civil war. Yet, despite his growing attachment towards Caesar in recent years, there was no real possibility that Cicero would ever support populist politics that were detrimental to the senate's authority; especially not now that its leaders had placed Pompey at the helm.

One problem for Cicero was that he had accepted a huge loan from Caesar four years previously – a loan of eight hundred thousand sesterces. Cicero did not want to be in Caesar's debt upon his return. As he left for his province, Cicero continually asked Atticus to make arrangements for the loan to be paid off in his absence. In the event, the loan was not repaid until days before civil war broke out on Cicero's return. Yet Cicero's anxiety over this unfortunate debt forms a dominant theme in many of the letters from this period.

Even as he made the journey, Cicero's spirits were not high. He had not yet reached the province when he wrote to Atticus from Athens, complaining:

> Even here and now, in fact, I bear it on the surface – well, at least I think I do – with the calmest of expressions. But deep down inside, I am torn apart, so much so that every day I either say or do something angrily, or rudely, or – in every way – stupidly, absurdly, arrogantly: there are many examples. I won't give you any, not to hide them from you, but because they are difficult to put into words. And so you will admire my self-control when we return home safely; so many opportunities are being given to me to practise this one virtue.[2]

Cicero's display of the self-control, mentioned above, reminds us of the excessive extortion committed by governors in recent years. This was one topic that Cicero had had a lot to say about in the past, especially in his prosecution of Verres. For a governor of a province had a very considerable degree of freedom in how he managed affairs. There were no permanent members of staff, apart from the garrison troops, and each new governor brought out the men he needed with him. An entourage of reliable men could be a pillar of strength to a moderate governor. On the other hand, under a less scrupulous or a weak leader, their behaviour could wreak havoc.

When Cicero left for his province, he was accompanied by a number of men, including Quintus, who was a general under his brother's command. Their two young boys also travelled with them to gain a taste of military life (although they did not actually join their fathers on campaigns). Another important member of Cicero's entourage was a young man called Tiro. He had formerly been Cicero's slave, but he had just recently been given his freedom. Cicero trusted him as much as he trusted anyone else, and he cared for his former slave deeply. Tiro was like a member of the family, and he greatly assisted Cicero in his secretarial and administrative duties. Other members of staff he either met on the way or when he got to the province.

Now, in Cilicia – as Cicero admitted to Atticus – he had to practise what he had preached. And Cicero surely had one eye on the fact that Atticus (and others) would disseminate the reports of his exemplary behaviour. In all his letters to Atticus, Cicero does not just stress his own propriety; the good conduct of his men also forms a key part of his self-presentation as a governor. But it would be unfair to say that Cicero was solely concerned about his own reputation. It is clear that he also had the provincials' well-being in mind too. And Cilicia fared much better under Cicero's governorship than ever before. Cicero, for his part, vowed to govern the Cilicians with justice, abstinence and clemency; however, these ideals seem to have escaped Cicero's oppressive and cruel predecessor entirely. He was Appius Claudius Pulcher, the brother of Cicero's former enemy, Clodius.

On reaching Cilicia, Cicero told Atticus of his first impressions: 'The wounds inflicted by Appius are open and cannot be hidden.'[3] These 'wounds' primarily resulted from the high levels of debt in the province. The communities moaned and groaned, Cicero told Atticus, after spending just two weeks travelling around Cilicia. They could not pay the high poll taxes that Appius had imposed. Indeed, his exactions, Cicero complained, were 'monstrous – like those of some wild beast, not a human being'.[4] The result was that Cicero made it his main administrative duty to curb the financial ruin facing the provincials.

Cicero targeted debt with a two-pronged attack. On the one hand, he refused to levy money from the provincials in return for his own maintenance and services. Counter to the self-glorifying practices of many governors, Cicero forbade statues, temples and commemorative chariots to be 'donated' in his honour. And the refusal of these customary duties meant that the outgoings of the natives were dramatically curtailed. On the other hand, Cicero investigated the causes of debt and proposed effective solutions. Many of Cilicia's own magistrates, he discovered, had been profiteering from the public purse. Without openly blaming and shaming these magistrates, Cicero nevertheless managed to get the guilty parties to repay the money back into the treasury. Everything helped towards lightening Cilicia's financial burdens.

In addition, Cicero proposed a very simple but successful solution to relieving debt across all levels of society. He capped the annual level of interest at twelve per cent, and he used this agreement to encourage the provincials to make their loan repayments on time. For Cicero set the repayment date sufficiently far in advance to provide ample time for the debtors to gather the money. If debts were not settled by the agreed time, the creditors could revert to the original (often highly extortionate) contract agreement. The result: the debtors were repaying their loans at a reasonable rate, and the creditors were happy to get the money back: 'They *all* think they are my friends,' Cicero proudly boasted to Atticus, 'and each man thinks he is my best friend.'[5]

To begin with, Cicero's actions in reversing his predecessor's decisions raised some eyebrows among hostile circles. Appius initially resented Cicero, for he and his friends regarded Cicero's careful administration as a deliberate slight on Appius' own – far less scrupulous – performance. But despite his disapproval of everything Appius had done, Cicero made every effort to remain on good terms with him personally. Cicero's complaints about his predecessor were for Atticus' eyes only. For Cicero's letters to Appius strike a very different tone: they profess friendship, coupled with promises to protect his good reputation should there be any threat of prosecution in the future.

Cicero's affability towards Appius was a strategic move, for he was a well-connected and influential man. One of Appius' daughters was married to Pompey's son; another daughter had married the noble Marcus Junius Brutus (Caesar's future assassin). Cicero did not want to offend any of the circles in which Appius moved; let alone suffer the hostility of another member of the Claudius family. In time, Appius was reconciled towards Cicero and even began to return Cicero's friendly gestures. And so, it was a cause of some embarrassment to Cicero that his domestic and political concerns collided later the next year.

The timing of Cicero's departure from Rome had not just been bad for Cicero politically; there were domestic matters that also required his attention. A chief concern for Cicero was finding a new husband for Tullia. Her first husband, Piso, had died shortly before Cicero's return from exile. She had been married again since then – to a young man called Furius Crassipes – but the match had not worked well, and they had since divorced. It was not ideal for a young woman to be left unmarried for too long, especially when she was childless. But Cicero had been forced to leave this particular arrangement to his friends, wife and daughter, who was now nearly twenty-seven years old – and doubtless had her own views on whom she wanted to marry. The search for a suitable match forms another major theme in Cicero's letters, and it reminds us of the huge overlap between personal and political affairs.

For back in Rome, the marriage market had produced a suitor who was agreeable in the eyes of Terentia and Tullia: a man of patrician stock, called Publius Cornelius Dolabella. The embarrassment for Cicero arose from the fact that Dolabella was an up-and-coming young man, eager to undertake a spectacular prosecution – as many aspiring politicians did. But he had his sights set on no other than Appius, whom he prosecuted for treason. Cicero's shock could not be concealed from Atticus: 'While *I* am here in my province furnishing Appius with all manner of compliments, suddenly I find myself becoming the father-in-law to his prosecutor!'[6]

The whole affair left Cicero in an awkward position, and he quickly dispatched a grovelling letter of apology to Appius. It was the most difficult case he had ever had to plead, Cicero claimed. He was doubtless exaggerating, but the whole incident sheds a humorous light on the ways in which the narrow circles of Rome's leading members either co-operated or clashed. In the end, Appius was acquitted and he bore no resentment to Cicero. It stands as a remarkable testament to Cicero's own ability to win friends and influence people. But it also alerts us to the fact that a politician at Rome was never 'off duty' – even when he was thousands of miles away.

CICERO *IMPERATOR* ('COMMANDER')

The task of administering a province effectively and judiciously came very naturally to Cicero. His common sense, feelings of duty, diplomacy and tireless energy all combined to serve him as well abroad as they did at Rome. However, he was more apprehensive about the other responsibilities that such a command brought. For the months spanning July to December were spent on military campaigns. And the East remained a volatile part of the world. It was, after all, only two years since Crassus' disastrous campaign, and no one knew what move the anti-Roman Parthians intended to make.

Cicero only had two legions at his disposal. In a good year, this would have given him around twelve thousand men. But the ranks were short in numbers, and Cicero could only complain at the senate's reluctance to send further assistance. Fortunately, however, help was on hand from King Deiotarus of nearby Galatia, who sent Cicero extra troops. These men were efficiently armed according to the Roman model, and they effectively doubled Cicero's manpower. With this help, and under the strategic guidance that his officers could provide, Cicero's military leadership was remarkably successful for a self-pronounced pacifist.

To begin with, it looked like the Parthians were advancing against the neighbouring province of Syria, where Bibulus was supposed to be governor. (Bibulus, however, was late in arriving and had not taken up his post yet.) Fortunately, the Parthians retreated, but Cicero launched an attack on the hostile tribes of the Amanus Mountains, which separated Cilicia from Syria. These men were the *Eleuthorocilicians* (the 'Free Cilicians'), and they had never surrendered to Rome. One of Cicero's officers, Pomptinus, clearly did the majority of the fighting against these tribes; but it was Cicero who was hailed as *imperator* by his men. This was no small accomplishment; it meant that Cicero had earned recognition as a 'commander' of a military expedition. It also meant that Cicero was entitled to claim the hugely prized reward of a triumphal procession – if the senate agreed. Bibulus on the other hand, who had finally arrived in Syria, had less luck with the enemy. When he too tried to claim some of the success, he lost his entire first cohort of men (about six hundred men).[7]

The campaigning season continued and it ended well for Cicero. He had launched a second attack against one of the towns of these restless tribes: the town of Pindenissum. As he wrote the details in a letter to Atticus, Cicero imagined his response:

> Early on the Saturnalia, Pindenissum surrendered – almost eight weeks after we began our attack on them. 'What on earth? Who are these Pindenissites?' you will say: 'I've never heard of them'. Well, there's nothing I can do about that – I can't make Cilicia as famous as Aetolia or Macedonia, can I?[8]

But it was a major achievement, even if it cannot be compared in scale with some of the more pressing military campaigns in Cicero's times. We can even detect a hint of excitement as Cicero relates how he marched on the town, encircled it with a moat, erected ramparts and attacked it with artillery, archers and siege towers.

The Saturnalia was an annual Roman festival that took place around 17 December. This year's celebrations were particularly merry, for Cicero gave all the plunder to his men and officers. All, that is, except for the captives. They were sold off, as was usual, and the profit went to the Roman treasury. Even as Cicero wrote the above letter to Atticus, he had already made well over one hundred thousand sesterces for his country.

In every area of his provincial administration, Cicero, never one to be modest, felt that he achieved beyond his expectations. But there can be no doubt that he wanted more than just praise from his lifelong friend. Numerous letters to influential senators, including a long one to Cato, make it plain that Cicero had in mind a formal thanksgiving festival (a *supplicatio*) from the senate – a necessary precursor, if he was to obtain a triumphal procession upon his return. In truth, Cicero was light-hearted about his military accomplishments. As he wrote a letter to Atticus from his camp, pitched on a site called Issus – where Alexander the Great had once fought a spectacular battle – he could poke fun at his own, relatively modest, claims to the title of *imperator*.

Yet this was Cicero playing the political game from a different angle. To be awarded a thanksgiving or, even better, a triumph brought great personal prestige. Perhaps this was something that Cicero felt was still missing from his career, and it may have gone some way towards healing the injustice of his exile. Many senators agreed that a thanksgiving should be awarded to Cicero, but there was one predictable voice of opposition. For, when the senate debated the matter, Cato was one of the only members to vote against the motion: 'What is worth far more than any triumph,' he later explained, 'is for the senate to judge that a province has been protected by its governor's mild and upright conduct, rather than by the force of an army or the good-will of the gods.'[9]

In the light of the recognition Cicero felt was his due, it is easy to understand his frustration with Cato. Furthermore, we might have sympathized more with Cato's stance towards 'empty honours' had he not gone on to propose an extended thanksgiving for his brother-in-law Bibulus (whose efforts in Syria had, by Cicero's account, been nothing short of disastrous). The event goes some way towards confirming Cicero's general perception of Cato as a man of integrity, but an often unrealistic one. For Cato certainly stood by his principles to the point of obstinacy, when it suited him; however, he could also change his tone to suit the tune of his intimates, when it suited them.

Cicero responded to Cato politely, but deep down he was furious: 'I cannot and will not tolerate such things', he told Atticus. However, there was another man who was delighted at Cato's spiteful treatment of Cicero: 'Caesar jumped for joy at Cato's most ungrateful disservice towards me', Cicero confided in Atticus.[10] As we shall see, this was the first in a series of moves that Caesar made to detach Cicero from the senatorial leaders in the months that followed, for the slippery slide towards civil war had been picking up pace for some time back in Rome – Pompey and the conservatives on one side, Caesar and his supporters on the other. By the time Cicero returned, the madness had reached a point of no return.

EVENTS AT ROME

When the day finally came for Cicero to leave his province, he wasted no time. He had been counting down to this date, 30 July 50 BC, ever since he first set foot in Cilicia. Yet Cicero has often been criticized for acting irresponsibly; for his successor had not arrived to take over the command. Furthermore, by Cicero's own admission, he had left affairs in the hands of a rather junior quaestor: he was just 'a boy, and perhaps a rather silly one, who lacks seriousness and self-control', he told Atticus.[11] To a degree, then, it certainly seems that Cicero placed his own interests ahead of the province's safety. However, the Parthians had remained at bay, and there was no immediate threat from invasion to hinder him. Nor was he obliged to remain in Cilicia beyond the stated term of his office. And Cicero doubtless saw it as mismanagement on the senate's part, for they had failed to appoint a replacement in time.

Moreover, Cicero had pressing reasons for wanting to get back to Italy. For the entire time he had been away, Cicero had kept a careful eye on events at Rome. His watchdog had been a young man called Marcus Caelius Rufus – and Caelius' letters survive to give us a highly entertaining narrative as events drifted more and more towards civil war. He may not have appreciated the full severity of the situation at Rome when he left Cilicia, but Cicero knew that his place was at the hub of activity and not at the borders of the empire.

As he made his return journey, Cicero begged Caelius to bring him fully up to date on affairs. One such letter reached his hands just a few months later, and it contained the news he had been dreading:

Written from Rome: September 50 BC

Caelius to Cicero, greetings . . .

On the topic of high politics, I have often written that I do not see peace lasting for another year; and the nearer the conflict comes (which it will do), the clearer the danger appears. The issue to be fought out by those in power is this: Pompey has decided that he will not let Caesar become consul, unless he hands over his army and provinces first; but Caesar is convinced that he cannot be safe if he leaves his army. Caesar, however, has put forward the suggestion that they *both* hand over their armies. So this is the depth to which their love affair, that hateful union, has fallen: it is not just slander exchanged behind one another's backs, open warfare is breaking out. And nor, for my part, do I know what plan to hatch, and I have no doubt that this exact decision will trouble you too: for ties of friendship and obligations bind me to Caesar's men. On the other side, I love the cause, but I hate the men.[12]

Caelius' letter recalled the troubles that were evidently brewing when Cicero left Rome in May 51 BC. This is not the place for a detailed examination of the reasons for the civil war, or to ask who was to blame, and whether it could have been avoided. However, a brief overview is necessary if we are to understand the political turbulence behind the events of this year, as well as the news that Caelius' letter brought Cicero. For the issue in question hinged on the legislation which Pompey had passed in 52 BC, and Cicero was anxious that he would be called to express his opinion on these matters when he returned to the senate.

When Pompey had passed his laws two years earlier, it was known to all that Caesar's campaigns in Gaul were approaching their end. His term of office was due to expire on 1 March 50 BC. And the moment he lay down his official command, Caesar became a private citizen. It offered a tremendous window of opportunity for Caesar's enemies in the senate; for without the immunity that an official post brought its holder, Caesar could be prosecuted. There were plenty of men ready in the senate to launch into an attack, and it gave them the chance to end Caesar's political career once and for all. That is why Caesar was convinced he could not be safe if he left his army. He had to be able to assume the consulship straight away to protect himself.

According to the traditional system, Caesar was more or less covered. Although his office expired on 1 March 50 BC, there would not actually be anyone ready to replace him until the end of 49 BC. This was because the provincial posts were always allocated a year in advance, and Pompey had postponed discussion on the matter of Caesar's replacement until the end of his command. Even then, Caesar's replacement would not realistically arrive in Gaul until the end of the year, and so Caesar could then safely enter into the consulship for the year 48 BC, without a break in his career. Here Pompey's legislation came in, and initially it looked as though he intended to help Caesar.

The current law stipulated that a candidate for the consulship had to nominate himself in person. This had been the cause of Caesar's problems back in 59 BC, when he had chosen the consulship over a triumph. However, Pompey used the tribunes to pass a bill dispensing with this regulation – as a special case for Caesar only, when the time should arise. This meant that Caesar could nominate himself *in absentia*: that is, he could run his campaign even if he was not in Rome to present himself as a candidate, as the law normally required. Caesar did not need to lay down his command, but he could come back from Gaul in January 48 BC. Providing his electoral campaign was successful (which it would be), he could then enter into a position of consular power immediately, without the much-dreaded lapse in his official roles.

However, Pompey soon backtracked, and his subsequent legislation left Caesar in a difficult position for two main reasons. These were the two issues Cicero did not want to discuss, as we shall see. First, Pompey passed a contradictory law which prohibited candidacy *in absentia*. This clearly undermined and complicated the special exemption his earlier law had made for Caesar. Second, Pompey's law on the provincial commands, which staffed the provinces with men who had not held their governorships at the appointed time, had made it possible for Caesar to be replaced as soon as his term of office expired. Caesar still hoped to prolong his command until he could assume his second consulship. However, he had many enemies who were determined to prevent this constitutional breach from taking place.

By the time Caelius' letter reached Cicero, the anticipated moment of 1 March 50 BC had long passed, and Caesar had not yet been recalled from Gaul. For Caesar's position at Rome was continually defended by the blocking tactics of one tribune in particular – Gaius Scribonius Curio. So far, Curio had successfully vetoed any proposals to strip Caesar of his command. However, a new date had since been put on the agenda: 13 November 50 BC.

Pompey was now on the side of Caesar's enemies, and he was working to deprive his former friend of his official power. As for Curio, he continued to work as Caesar's representative, and it was Curio who made the proposal that both dynasts hand over their armies at the same time. What this would achieve is impossible to tell, for Caesar would still be open for prosecution. But it clearly pitched the battle as a personal struggle between Pompey and Caesar – and it was time for men to start choosing sides.

The letter Cicero received thus spelled out the immediacy of civil war. Armed with this knowledge, he continued his journey. But as Cicero reached Athens he was in turmoil. Both Caesar and Pompey had written to him – each requesting his support. As always, he turned immediately to Atticus for advice, and a few extracts from his letter do well to capture his mood and thoughts:

Written from Athens: 16 October 50 BC

Cicero to Atticus, greetings . . .

Now there looms ahead – as you point out and I see – a great struggle between Pompey and Caesar. Both men count me on their side, unless one of them happens to be pretending . . . Moreover, I received letters from them each at the same time as I received yours; both letters were the sort that made it seem that neither man values anyone in the world more than myself.

But what I am to do? I don't mean in the last resort (for if it comes to war, I am clear that defeat with one camp is better than victory with the other), but what do I do about the matters that need to be settled when I get back – making sure that Caesar should not be allowed to put his name forward for the consulship *in absentia*, and making sure that he does dismiss his army. 'SPEAK, MARCUS TULLIUS' [the presiding magistrate will say]. What am I to reply? 'Please, wait a minute, while I check with Atticus?'

I am greatly in favour of lingering over the matter of a triumph, which will give me a very legitimate reason for staying outside the city bounds. All the same, they will make every effort to elicit my formal opinion. You will probably laugh when I say this, but how I wish I was back in my province already![13]

Here we have Cicero's 'unofficial' decision and stance on the matter. There was no doubt in his mind that the better cause – referred to by its adherents as the 'republican' cause – was represented by Pompey, Cato and their circles. And Cicero would follow the honourable path, even though he knew the Caesarian side was far stronger. For as long as he could, Cicero communicated with both Pompey and Caesar, in the hope that he could strike an agreement between the two men. And so, when Cicero arrived back in Italy late in November 50 BC, he followed the strategy he had set out in his letter to Atticus – he stayed out of Rome.

Cicero's term as a provincial commander had been successful. He alleviated debt in the province, administered justice fairly, and even earned himself the title of *imperator*. However, in the eighteen months that Cicero had been away, Caesar and Pompey had embarked on a power struggle which offered no return. Men were already choosing sides, but here Cicero's provincial command gave him an advantage. While Cicero retained his army and proconsular power (his *imperium*), he was forbidden by law from entering the city.

Waiting for a triumph gave Cicero the perfect excuse: it meant that he could remain out of the senate, and he did not have to be seen to join a side. And for as long as there was at least a glimmer of hope that a compromise might be reached, Cicero's outward independence was vital. For Cicero was one of the only men in a position to mediate between the dynasts. And from the moment he landed in Italy, until long after the war had started, Cicero worked tirelessly to promote peace – but it was to no avail.

13

Away from Rome Again: Civil War (49–47 BC)

THE 'MADHOUSE OF MEN'

I arrived too late; I was alone; people thought that I was ignorant about the facts of the dispute – I had fallen into a madhouse of men who were thirsting for war.

(Cicero, *To Friends* 150/4.1.1)

On 4 January 49 BC, Cicero finally reached Rome. His triumph had been granted, which meant he and his troops could not enter the city, but he had been in Italy for over a month. All this time, Cicero had been near enough to witness the turmoil unfolding at first hand; furthermore, he could still attend the crisis talks held at Pompey's villa in the suburbs. The men, he later said, were 'thirsting for war'. This was the moment many Romans had been expecting for some time now, for the campaign to recall Caesar from Gaul had been carried on ever since 51 BC. In September 50 BC, Caelius had remarked to Cicero that war seemed inevitable, and he was right.

In the December before Cicero's return to Rome, events accelerated at an unstoppable speed. Initially it was only a dominant faction, and by no means the majority of men, who wanted war. For, on 1 December 50 BC, the tribune Curio finally asked the senate to vote on his proposal that both Pompey and Caesar should surrender their provincial commands at the same time. And they voted overwhelmingly in favour of his compromise deal: three hundred and seventy senators supported Curio's motion, with only twenty-two voting against it. But, the twenty-two die-hard conservatives were powerful, and the vote was vetoed by another tribune, who was acting in their favour.

According to the Greek historian Appian, the consul dismissed the meeting in a rage, uttering the words 'enjoy your victory and have Caesar for a master'.[1] But worse was yet to come when the same consul unofficially gave Pompey control of two legions and urged him to recruit more troops, for his acceptance of this command was one of the final steps in the slide towards civil war. As Pompey left Rome to gather his forces, Cicero watched the panic and hostility spread across Italy:

I fear for the Republic more and more each day. For the 'good men' (the *boni*) – as they are reckoned – are not united. How many Roman equestrians and senators I have seen cursing both the general conduct of affairs and this trip of Pompey's – they use the most bitter words. Peace is what we need. A victory in war brings a whole host of evils and a tyrant for sure.[2]

However, the tide of feeling among the senators changed when a letter from Caesar was read out to them on 1 January 49 BC. Its message was 'bitter' and 'menacing' according to Cicero; in this letter, Caesar threatened to come down from Gaul and take revenge for himself and his country if Pompey did not surrender his command, as Curio's proposal had suggested.[3] Panic and alarm spread fast. A sweeping majority in the senate now responded by voting that Caesar should either surrender his army by a certain date or that he should be declared a public enemy. But two of the new tribunes for the year were determined not to let this happen: Mark Antony and Quintus Cassius Longinus.

Antony and Cassius had entered office less than a month before, and they had made it plain that they intended to continue Curio's pro-Caesarian policies. Yet this time the senate were not going to tolerate the vetoes of Caesarian tribunes, and the two men were strongly advised to leave for their own safety. And so, on 7 January 49 BC, Antony and Cassius left Rome. Curio joined them – as did Cicero's young friend Caelius, who had decided to switch to the stronger side. From Rome they headed north to meet Caesar, who was already preparing his forces for the attack.

War had not been openly declared, but the Caesarian faction felt they had no other option. Unless Caesar gave up his command, he was to be a public enemy in the eyes of the law – and Caesar was not going to back down. Furthermore, a chilling request was also made by the senate back at Rome: the consuls, praetors, tribunes, and those proconsuls who were near the city (i.e. Pompey), should 'see to it that the state came to no harm'. It was the old recourse to the senate's ultimate decree. This was the 'madhouse' to which Cicero had returned just three days earlier, and the men who had been 'thirsting for war' now got it.

CHOOSING SIDES: CICERO'S DECISION

On 11 January 49 BC, Caesar arrived at the river Rubicon; this river was not just the boundary between Gaul and Italy: it marked the divide between a province and Italy. If Caesar crossed it without laying down his command, and if he brought armed soldiers into Italy, it meant war. But this is exactly what he did, at the same time shouting the words which have become famous: *alea iacta est* ('the die is cast').[4] And as Caesar – famous for his speed – marched through the country, the towns of Italy fell to him one by one. As he made his way down the

Adriatic coast, with his mighty troops, the inhabitants did not even put up a fight.

On 17 January 49 BC, as the reports of Caesar's progress reached Rome, Pompey decided to evacuate his supporters from Italy. This had the advantage of avoiding bloodshed in the heart of the city itself, but the real reason was that Pompey and the senate did not have sufficient troops at hand to fight off Caesar. An alarmed senate decided to flee – but the decision was not unanimous. Many men were torn between the two sides.

On the one hand there was Pompey, ostensibly fighting for the cause of the Republic and the authority of the senate. On the other, there was Caesar, who argued that he was fighting for his *dignitas*, his public standing and career. Some men pitched their camp where their personal loyalties lay; others fought for principle; a large number threw their lot in with the stronger side, the Caesarians, with a view to their own safety and livelihood.

The war had the power to divide friends and family. Many of Cicero's friends went over to Caesar. His friend and correspondent Caelius had already defected to the Caesarians; his son-in-law Dolabella, too, had long been a supporter of Caesar. For a horrible moment even the younger Quintus, Cicero's nephew, went over to the Caesarian faction, but his father soon rebuked him for his betrayal. Yet Quintus was probably typical of many young men thinking of their future paths – men like Caelius, who had certainly decided that the outcome of the war was more important than the cause.

Cicero has often been criticized for his hesitation in the months that followed, and it has been suggested that his mind was torn over which side to join. But this is not entirely accurate. There was no doubt where Cicero's loyalties lay: his heart rested with the side that championed the Republic. As we have seen, in his letter to Atticus, he had already declared his allegiance to the Pompeian side unofficially. In a letter dated to 21 January 49 BC, he blamed Caesar for the war – he was acting more like Hannibal than a Roman general. He hated Caesar's cause: 'He says he is doing all this for the sake of his *dignitas*, but where is dignity without a sense of honour?'[5]

However, Cicero had more than a few criticisms to spare for Pompey too. He knew that Pompey had been, and surely would be again, as willing to transcend the rules as Caesar. When all was said and done, he had to admit that 'both men have sought after personal domination, not the happiness and welfare of the community'.[6] The result was that neither side inspired Cicero to join the fight, and his thoughts are neatly encapsulated in his famous slogan, coined in the March of 49 BC: 'I know whom to flee, but I know not whom to follow.'[7]

By this time, Pompey had left Rome to join his legions. The consuls, magistrates and other senators had rushed after him – in their haste, they forgot to take the money from the treasury. Rome was undefended and her wealth was left at Caesar's disposal. And so, for all the times that Cicero has appeared self-centred, we have to admire his decision to place his principles ahead of personal gain and glory. The Pompeian side appeared to be a disaster: 'As for what Pompey is doing, I don't think even *he* knows; none of us certainly do,' Cicero told Atticus, '. . . It is all fear and bewilderment.'[8]

Fortunately for Cicero, while the rest of the senators deliberated about which way to turn, he was given a job to do. Cicero still held his *imperium* and legions from Cilicia, and now he was asked to supervise Campania and the coastal area. It was a small responsibility, but that was as much as he wanted; in the event, he performed the role half-heartedly, if at all. But, crucially, this post gave him another excuse to stay away from Rome, and another reason to remain inactive in the war. It meant he could base himself at his villa in Formiae, where Terentia and a pregnant Tullia joined him in February. Furthermore, he could continue working for peace, should there be any last hope left. And Cicero believed there was, for as long as Pompey remained in Italy there was still always a chance, and Cicero had a valid reason to hesitate.

But any hope for peace was soon dashed. On 17 March 49 BC, Pompey set sail across the Adriatic and joined the forces awaiting him in Dyrrachium (Durazzo), a port on the north-west coast of Greece. He had another army stationed in Spain. Cicero had been agonizing over this moment for a long time: what would he do – stay or go? Pompey, for his part, had constantly urged Cicero to join him, while Caesar was bidding him to stay.

Up until this point, there had been much to tempt Cicero onto the Caesarian side, for many of Cicero's friends, including his son-in-law, had opted to follow the rising star. Caesar, too, flattered Cicero and tried to entice him back to Rome. Even among his busy campaigns, Caesar found the time to write to Cicero personally: 'What I especially ask of you,' Caesar begged, 'since I trust I shall arrive at Rome soon, is that I shall see you there, and that I shall be able to make use of your advice, influence, dignity, and help in all matters.'[9]

At the same time, there was much to tempt Cicero away from the Pompeian side: Pompey (who had been seriously ill) was a shadow of his former self, the plans were in disarray and the men had been hungry for war from the start. And inside, although he knew where his heart lay, Cicero was in turmoil. He swung back and forth, this way and that; he wrote to Atticus continually – he complained, moaned and criticized. In a long letter sent to Atticus on 18 March 49 BC, he expressed all the hopes, fears and uncertainties that had plagued him from the start: 'I think I have been out of my mind from the beginning' – he explained.[10] Because the moment Pompey left, the feelings of remorse and guilt overcame Cicero. For all his hesitation, he knew where he should be, and finally the republican cause – the 'right and honourable' cause – took him to Greece.[11]

CICERO AND THE CIVIL WAR

It was not until June, however, that Cicero actually left Italy. Caesar had continually courted him since his return; on 28 March 49 BC he even visited Cicero at his villa in Formiae. Caesar wanted him to attend a meeting of the senate at Rome, but Cicero remained steadfast. Cicero narrated the whole meeting in a letter to Atticus. The conversation and Cicero's reaction are best relived through his own words, and they are worth quoting at length:

> First, my speech was such that Caesar was respectful rather than grateful towards me; secondly, I stood by my decision not to go to Rome. Whatever in the past made us think he was an accommodating man, surely led us astray – I have never seen him less so. He said that my judgement was a condemnation of him; that everyone else would be slower to come to his side, if I did not come. I replied that it was different in their case. When we had spoken much, he said: 'Come then and work for peace.' 'At my own discretion?' I asked. 'Who am I to lay down guidelines for you?' he answered. 'Very well,' I said, 'I shall state that an expedition to Spain is not in the senate's interests, and that an army should not be transported to Greece, and then,' I added, 'I shall have much to say on Pompey's behalf.' At which, he replied, 'Those are not the kind of things I want said.' 'That's exactly what I thought,' I retorted, 'which is why I don't want to be present. Either I must speak on those lines or stay away; for there are many other things I would have to say if I were there.' His final words were: 'at least think about it' – as if he was looking for a way out of the conversation. I thought it best not to refuse. And that is how we left it. So I trust Caesar is not happy with me. But I was really happy with myself – and I have not had that feeling for quite some time now.[12]

Cicero's decision was out in the open, yet he was in no rush to leave. First, he wanted to conduct his son's coming of age ceremony in Arpinum; then he wanted to go on a tour of his villas, which he did not expect to see again. By the end of April, the only thing holding him up was the weather, he said.[13] His anxieties, doubts and fears did not leave Cicero in these months, but on 7 June 49 BC, Cicero was finally on his way; he was heading straight for Pompey's camp. Quintus and their two sons, now young men, went with him, as did the soldiers from his two Cilician legions.

For the events that follow in the civil war, we have Caesar's own comprehensive (albeit one-sided) account – a commentary in three books detailing events from the Rubicon to the decisive battle at Pharsalus in Thessaly. It helps us fill in what Cicero must have witnessed or heard, for his letters are limited beyond this point. The difficulty and the danger of sending letters to friends or relatives in Italy dramatically hindered his normally voluminous correspondence. And the possibility that letters would be intercepted and read meant that Cicero could not speak in his usually frank manner to Atticus.

The third book of Caesar's *Civil War* takes us to Greece, and it tells how Caesar (for he always refers to himself in the third person) battled against Pompey – first outside Dyrrachium and then Pharsalus. The first battle saw a victory for the Pompeians. For by the time Cicero arrived in Greece, the republican cause was not in the shambolic state that it had been at the beginning of the war. Now they had assembled troops and money from the East – even Cicero was able to make a large contribution from the money he had deposited in Greece following his Cilician command.

Both sides had their weaknesses and strengths, and the outcome of the war was far from predictable. However, elated by their initial success, Pompey decided to risk a decisive battle at Pharsalus in Thessaly – but this decision was a mistake. Although Pompey's forces outnumbered Caesar's by almost two to one, on 9 August 48 BC, Caesar's troops battled courageously and brilliantly defeated the Pompeians.

Pompey himself escaped to Egypt, but there he met his death at the hands of his former friends. The Egyptians turned against him in a bid to curry favour with Caesar, the victor in the civil war. Some time later, when Caesar too arrived in Egypt in pursuit of his enemy, the Egyptians presented him with an unusual welcome gift: the head of Pompey, pickled and stored in a box. As for the republican troops that survived, they scattered across the globe – Africa, Spain and Greece – where the war was carried on for another three years with varying degrees of success and failure.

We do not know what part Cicero was playing during these events, but some letters do help us vaguely piece together his thoughts and movements. To start, he probably made his way to Thessalonica, where the senate had regrouped. However, for the most part he was encamped in Dyrrachium, where bad health detained him. And finally, we find him in Patrae, on the gulf of Corinth, from where he finally decided to sail back to Italy. However, Plutarch's account does give us some further information, and it is to this source, coupled with Cicero's remarks after the event, that we must turn.

In short, Cicero's contribution to the war can be summed up as pretty ineffective (except for the loan and troops he contributed to the cause). It seems that everyone was glad to see him initially – everyone, that is, except Cato, who told Cicero he would have been more useful retaining his stance of neutrality in Italy. But, despite the fact that he had now declared his allegiance openly to the Pompeian camp, Cicero appears to have continued his campaign for peace. This is entirely plausible, if we can believe Caesar's claim that he was still hoping for a peaceful reconciliation; for *his* stories of the campaigns against Pompey are interlaced with reports of his own peace-making attempts.

In a letter sent to Atticus on 15 July 48 BC, Cicero confirms that he was avoiding any responsibilities. Indeed, Cicero's later reflections make it clear that he was disgusted by what he saw: the men were cruel and barbaric, and there was talk of further proscriptions. It is equally likely, therefore, that Cicero was every bit as annoying as Plutarch's account suggests he was. For his desire for peace, his disaffection for his comrades, and his biting tongue allegedly all got the better of him; he went around the camp gloomily, making inappropriate jokes. He did nothing to help morale, for example, when the troops' spirits were raised at the sight of seven eagles in Pompey's camp – a highly pleasing omen. 'That would be wonderful,' Cicero retorted, 'if we were at war against jackdaws.'[14]

Yet, crucially, we do know that Cicero was not on the battlefield at Pharsalus. He had remained ill at Dyrrachium, where Cato was in command of a number of cohorts. And, when the news of the defeat and Pompey's initial flight reached the camp, Cicero wanted no more part in the war. Cato asked Cicero to take command of the forces, but he refused. Pompey's son was furious: he drew his sword and would have run Cicero through with it, had Cato not intervened. But Cicero's mind was made up. First he sailed to Patrae, where a letter came his way that changed Cicero's direction again. For Dolabella was still with Caesar – and Caesar, it seemed, wanted Cicero to return to Italy.

And so, with a speed he later regretted, Cicero made the journey back to the port at Brundisium in Italy. His son and his attendants all went with him, but his brother and nephew did not: 'Quintus was particularly hostile towards me at Patrae', Cicero lamented to Atticus. 'His son joined him there from Corcyra [Corfu]. Then they left with the rest, I imagine.'[15] The brothers' argument may have been about money, politics, the decision to follow Pompey, other causes of resentment or a combination of reasons – but one thing is certain: it was a rift that, as we shall see, had a traumatic effect on Cicero.

Many other men went their separate ways after Pharsalus, and the war raged in different parts of the empire until 45 BC – Spain, Africa and Greece among them. Cicero's part had been minor in the event, and his decision to join the Pompeian cause was, by all other standards, late. But he had displayed the strength of mind to resist Caesar; this is precisely where others failed. For the reservations and regrets that seem characteristic of Cicero were doubtless shared by many at the time. Cicero's friend Caelius certainly found himself in a desperate situation in the February of 48 BC: 'It is not that I have lost confidence in Caesar's cause,' he wrote to Cicero, 'but, believe me, I would rather die than look at these people.'[16]

It is a sign of the times that men on either side of the cause could complain about their comrades' behaviour. To end the story of Caelius, he was later murdered in an overhasty attempt to rise against the Caesarian faction at Rome. Thousands of other men also lost their lives: the death toll for Pharsalus alone was said to have been upwards of fifteen thousand men, but only two hundred of those were Caesarians.[17] The 'madhouse of men' had paid a heavy price for the war they wanted.

And so, although Cicero did not prosper, he did not fail either. There were further conflicts and casualties in the years that followed Pharsalus. But Cicero's own traumas in the aftermath were of a very different nature: domestic disputes, death and divorce all added to the pressures upon Cicero, as he waited to see how Caesar would treat him upon his return.

AN UNHAPPY HOMECOMING

During the civil war, Cicero had been to Thessalonica, Dyrrachium and, in late October 48 BC, he finally arrived back at Brundisium. The chilling parallel to be drawn with his period in exile, when he had stayed in all these places, cannot have escaped him. But this time, there was no triumphant return, and neither Terentia nor Tullia were at the port town to greet him. Furthermore, Cicero had to wait for an official 'pardon' from Caesar, who was determined to review the case of every man, individually and personally, before allowing former Pompeian supporters to return to Italy. He was stuck at the port, where Cicero was forced to wait miserably, but he did not regret leaving the camp, he told Atticus:

> I have never regretted leaving the war. There was such cruelty among our men, such an affinity with barbarian races; so much so that they were drawing up a proscription list which included not just names – but whole classes. Universal opinion had already decided that the possessions of each and every one of you should be the reward for a victory. I say *you* explicitly, Atticus; for there were only the cruellest of intentions towards you personally. And so I shall never regret my decision, but I do regret the course I took: I wish I had retreated into some town or other until I was actually summoned.[18]

In the meantime, Cicero and Marcus probably rented a house in Brundisium. To make their presence less obvious, Cicero told his official attendants (his 'lictors') to dress and mingle as the everyday crowd. Cicero was still a proconsul of Rome and he still held military authority; this was not the time for him and his men to be drawing attention to themselves. As Cicero wrote the above letter to Atticus in the November of 48 BC, the town was encircled by Caesar's armed troops. He was trapped. Atticus suggested that they should make their way out under the cover of the night, but Cicero did not dare the attempt.

News came of Pompey's death in November, and Cicero was surely sad at the death of his former friend: 'I knew him to be an honest, decent and upright man', he wrote to Atticus.[19] But the death of Pompey had further consequences for Cicero. For Caesar, hot on his enemy's heels, had followed him all the way to Egypt. It was only when Caesar arrived that he learned about Pompey's fate. However, Caesar also arrived to find Alexandria in a state of great civil unrest: Cleopatra and her brother (who was also her co-regent and husband, according to Egyptian custom) had proved unable to share power. And now Caesar launched another campaign, the Alexandrian war, which detained him in Egypt until late 47 BC.

Back in Italy, Cicero found the wait agonizing. The uncertainty made it worse, for Pompey's supporters had been mustering strength again, while Caesar's absence from Rome only caused worry and gossip. It was rumoured that Caesar was having an affair with the Egyptian queen Cleopatra, and his communications with Rome were scant. No one knew how the Alexandrian war was progressing, but it seemed that either Caesar could not or did not want to come back from Egypt. As the civil war continued without Caesar, there was always the horrific possibility that the fortunes of war would swing in the republicans' favour. If this happened, Cicero, who had extricated himself from their cause, was in deep trouble.

To intensify Cicero's plight, serious domestic problems plagued Cicero: he was 'exhausted by the pain of the greatest grief', he told Atticus in one of his many letters from this period.[20] And these troubles are worth surveying in brief before we pick up the thread of Cicero's journey, for private and political anxieties often shared a common dimension, as Cicero's quarrel with Quintus demonstrates. However, this was more than a minor argument: it was a betrayal and a devastating divide.

At the outbreak of the civil war, for reasons that are nowhere made explicit, Quintus Cicero vowed to follow whomever his brother favoured. The result was, as we have seen, that the two brothers and their sons followed the cause of Pompey and the Republic. However, Quintus and his son had since fled to Caesar's camp – thus causing the hostile exchange of words as they parted at Patrae. But the two Quinti did worse than just change sides. To safeguard their acceptance in the Caesarian faction, they blamed Cicero for their initial alliance with the Pompeians, and now they launched a vicious attack against him.

Cicero's brother was unmistakably a petulant man, but as the reports of his slanderous abuse and vile language reached Cicero, it was more than he could take. Atticus had been on the receiving end of Quintus' temper several years before: 'You know the style; perhaps you have even experienced it', Cicero wrote. 'It has all been turned on me.'[21] His nephew was equally, if not more, vicious. But what made the betrayal even worse was that Cicero had already sent a magnanimous letter to Caesar on behalf of the two men, exonerating them for their part in the war. Their spite towards Cicero all seemed horribly unnecessary, and the rift took several years to heal.

A deep crack had also started to show in Cicero's marriage to Terentia, but this damage was irreparable. Signs of stress on their marriage can be traced back as early as 57 BC, following Cicero's loss of position and the financial difficulties during and after his exile. But Cicero's trust for Terentia had further been tested throughout the period of his Cilician command and the civil war. During these years (51–48 BC), Terentia had been left in charge, and there were several inexplicable irregularities in their financial affairs. Worse was to come when Terentia set about making a new will, for the couple clearly had different ideas about what was best for their children's welfare. The details are not the sort of material that Cicero could entrust to a letter, so it is difficult to know the precise problems. Nor do we know the whole picture behind the breakdown of their marriage: finances, stress, disappointment and more could have added to the couple's estrangement. Yet the reasons were serious, and the couple divorced early in 46 BC – after over thirty years of marriage.

Before their divorce happened, however, there was the more worrying problem of Tullia: both her health and her marriage were in a miserable state. Shortly before Cicero had left for Greece in June 49 BC, Tullia had given birth prematurely. The child did not survive, and nor does her physical condition seem to have recovered fully. But her situation was not helped by the neglect she suffered at the hands of her husband. Cicero had not been completely displeased at the match Terentia and Tullia struck with Dolabella in his absence, but he had expressed his concerns early on – as had Atticus, in a series of letters exchanged between them in August 50 BC. Dolabella was clearly charming and slightly younger than Tullia; however, he was also rather radical – both in his political behaviour and apparently in his sexual conduct. The possibility of a divorce had been raised the previous year, but that was at the height of the war, when Dolabella's connection with Caesar seemed vital for the family's long-term safety. Now, in 47 BC, the situation was more urgent.

In Caesar's absence from Rome, Dolabella's political activity had taken a highly worrying turn. He had given up his patrician status and made the transition into a plebeian family. His aim, which he achieved, was to be a tribune of the plebs for the year 47 BC. In this capacity, Dolabella promised the cancellation of debts, instigated armed violence in the streets of Rome, and even (to Cicero's horror) proposed to erect an honorific statue of Clodius – his father-in-law's great enemy in days past. Dolabella's behaviour was that of an extreme populist, with the result that he was becoming more of a political liability than an insurance of Tullia's safety. In the June of that year, Tullia made the long journey to Brundisium to be with her father, where she seems to have stayed until at least August. For a short time, Tullia and Dolabella were reunited, but the divorce finally went through in 46 BC – even though Tullia was pregnant with her estranged husband's child at the time.

All of these private disputes added to, or were inextricably tangled up in, the political climate, the war and the uncertainties of Cicero's situation. But the narrow confines of Brundisium meant there was little Cicero could do but brood, or ask for Atticus' help. It was a great relief when Caesar finally returned from Egypt in September 47 BC. Cicero was among the men who went to greet him on his arrival, and he evidently received Caesar's official pardon. According to Plutarch, when Caesar saw Cicero, he jumped down from his carriage to meet him. He treated Cicero warmly, gave him his full attention and they walked a few hundred yards together, talking all the time in private conversation.[22] And very soon Cicero was back on the road to Rome, but his journey back into politics was to take a much slower, more arduous route.

The Roman road leading to the forum (Photograph © Hannah Swithinbank).

14

Cicero and Caesar (46–44 BC)

ORATORY AND POLITICS UNDER CAESAR

The long silence, senators, which I have kept all this time – not from fear, but from a combination of grief and reticence – has been brought to an end on this day; at the same time, today has brought me back to my former practice of speaking about what I hope for and what I think. For such great humanity, such unusual and unheard of clemency, and such exceptional moderation in a man who holds supreme power over everything, and finally such incredible and almost godlike wisdom – these are all impossible for me to pass over in silence.

(Cicero, *For Marcellus* 1)

A whole year after his return to Rome, in September 46 BC, Cicero finally spoke in the open again; it was almost seven years since he had delivered his last speech, *For Milo*, at the end of 52 BC. Not only had the Cilician command and the civil war kept Cicero out of public affairs, but the Rome to which Cicero had returned was a very different city to the one he had left. To begin with, many of the familiar faces had either died or were still fighting in the civil war. In addition, there was no place for independent political or oratorical activity – decisions were no longer left to the senate, and nor were there any significant trials taking place. Instead, everything was conducted either by Caesar directly or by his two agents, Oppius and Balbus.

Following his pardon and the permission to return to Rome, Cicero had no choice but to accept the reality of Caesar's control; however, at first he only attended the senate to be seen and not heard. Otherwise, he stayed either at his Tusculan villa or in Atticus' company in Rome. He took refuge in his books, wrote to his friends, and even attended parties when he was in the city. All the time, he held onto the hope that Caesar might restore some form of a constitutional system. However, the test of Caesar's intentions had to wait. For the civil war was still being carried on, and Caesar was frequently called away.

In December 47 BC, after a very short spell in Rome, Caesar had left for Africa. There he defeated the republican troops at the battle of Thapsus in April 46 BC. It was an important victory, which brought an end to many notable lives (including Cato, who – obstinate as ever – committed suicide on news of the republicans' defeat). Caesar was back in Rome by July 46 BC, whereupon he embarked on a programme of reform and rehabilitation.

Many looked on in anticipation, wondering whether he planned to restore the Republic, and, for a while, it looked like there might be some signs of hope. As we have seen in the case of Cicero and his family, Caesar made 'clemency' a key virtue in his agenda: that is, he was willing to pardon former Pompeians for their part in the conflict, rather than proscribe them – as Sulla had done. And, finally, it was one such act of clemency which caused Cicero to break his silence. For Caesar made an unexpectedly generous grant of forgiveness to one of his staunchest adversaries: Marcus Claudius Marcellus.

Marcellus was a die-hard aristocrat who had violently opposed Caesar both in his career and in the civil war. And so, when Caesar decided to pardon Marcellus, Cicero was delighted: 'It was if I saw a vision of the Republic coming back to life', he later wrote to a friend.[1] Cicero could not pass over Caesar's humanity, clemency and wisdom – or so he claimed in the passage quoted above. On the spur of the moment he delivered a speech of some length, but he later wrote down and published a version of the words he spoke. It has survived under the title *For Marcellus*, although it was not a defence speech, as its title suggests. Rather, it was the first speech of its kind in Roman oratory: it was the first to *praise* a sole ruler. And it served as a model for the generations of speakers who lived under the rule of the emperors.

The credit for victories in war, however magnificent, must be shared among the armies, soldiers, allies and other factors, Cicero claimed. On the other hand, 'to conquer pride, to restrain anger and to be moderate in the face of victory' was a personal triumph – one that marked Caesar out as 'almost godlike'.[2] And as he spoke, Cicero could think back to the works of famous Greek orators who had developed the tradition behind this type of oratory. It was called a panegyric speech: a formal oration delivered as a public compliment. The specific precedent he seems to have had in mind was the Greek orator Isocrates, who had been active in the fourth century BC. Isocrates had published several speeches, as well as letters of advice that praised Philip of Macedon (Alexander the Great's father); his works provided a model for Cicero to adapt to the needs of his own speech.

Isocrates' works showed that praise could be combined with an element of persuasion – the active encouragement to behave in a way that would be beneficial to all. And so, in his speech *For Marcellus*, Cicero followed his praise of Caesar with a programme of advice – Caesar should restore the Republic, he urged:

> It falls on you alone, Gaius Caesar, to restore everything that you see knocked down and knocked flat (as was unavoidable) by the violence of war: the law courts must be

established, credit restored, extravagance curbed, the birth rate increased – everything, which has ebbed and flowed, must be bound together by tight laws. In such a civil war, when spirits and swords were raised so high, it was inevitable that the stricken state (whatever the outcome of the war) would lose many marks of her standing, and many defences in her security; inevitable too that each leader, so long as he was wearing arms and not the civilian toga, would do many things that he would not have permitted in peacetime. All these things are the wounds of war which now fall upon you to heal.[3]

The cautious handling of Caesar's autocratic power in this passage can be traced throughout the whole speech, for Cicero acknowledged that only one man could cure the present evils facing his day. Moreover, as far as Caesar's actions in restoring order were concerned, Cicero also demonstrated that he was a loyal supporter of the new regime. For all the demands for restoration that Cicero lists here – be they judicial, financial, social or demographical – had been on Caesar's programme of reform from 47 BC onwards, and in this speech Cicero publicly voiced his approval for the very first time.

Sadly, the story of Marcellus did not end well, for he was murdered on his return journey to Rome. But at the time of the speech, Cicero saw some signs that the mixed constitution, which he had praised so much in his *Republic*, might come back to fruition. Indeed, it is not impossible that Cicero saw the potential in Caesar to fill the terms of the 'ideal statesman' he had sketched in that work. And, if so, it is also extremely likely that Cicero saw a role opening for himself as Caesar's adviser. In fact, just a few months before, Cicero had already told a friend that they should both be willing, if called upon, to act 'not just as architects, but even as workmen to help build the Republic'.[4]

As the first step towards this process, Cicero devoted himself to the task of gaining Caesar's pardon for other republican-minded comrades in the months that followed. Not long after Cicero's speech *For Marcellus*, Caesar consented to the return of another man, Quintus Ligarius, whose corner Cicero had also actively defended. Buoyed on by enthusiasm, Cicero continued his work for the recall of other former Pompeians, and many of them looked to him from across the seas, calling on Cicero to help. One friend wrote to him in December 46 BC: 'All my hope lies in you. In your wisdom, you know what gives Caesar pleasure and what wins him over.'[5]

Cicero had gained some influence back – not just with Caesar, but with Caesar's whole circle. And he could use this to protect his friends and associates. It was not a wholly altruistic activity on Cicero's part – it probably helped ease his own conscience at having accepted Caesar's pardon (for men like Cato had chosen a martyr's death rather than submit to a tyrant). At the same time, Cicero wanted his former comrades back in Rome – for the Republic depended on a body of wise consulars and aristocrats for its very survival.

Yet any hopes for the future of the Republic were soon dashed within the three months separating the pardon of Marcellus and Caesar's departure for Spain. Before he left to campaign against the remaining republican forces, Caesar did not see fit to appoint the regular magistrates for the following year. Instead, he had himself appointed as the only consul for 45 BC, and he planned to hold the sole consulship in addition to his dictatorship. In his absence, Rome was to be controlled by Marcus Aemilius Lepidus, who was Caesar's 'master of the horse' (the traditional title of a dictator's deputy). And he would be helped by Oppius and Balbus, who were not even elected magistrates or senators.

The sole function of all these men was to carry out what Caesar wanted. And for as long as Rome was under their control, politics were intolerable to Cicero; oratory, too, was once more redundant. Although Cicero continued to make public appearances, he returned increasingly to his books – his 'old friends' as he liked to call them.[6]

PHILOSOPHY: A SUBSTITUTE FOR POLITICS

The years 46–44 BC witnessed a huge surge in Cicero's literary output. In 46 alone he wrote the *Stoic Paradoxes* (a series of rhetorical essays examining key tenets in Stoic philosophy), *Brutus* (a history of Roman oratory), *The Orator* (a discussion of the ideal orator) and a work on the *Classification of Oratory*. It is often said that Cicero's dedication to literature at this time marks an entire withdrawal from politics, but this is not strictly true for the first year. As he said himself, in a work published after the assassination of Caesar: 'It was in my books that I was addressing the senate, or speaking to the people. I regarded philosophy as my substitute for a role in politics.'[7]

However, his letters also make it evident that Cicero initially envisaged another role – one which was traditional for senior statesmen to take. For, just as Cicero had emulated the great men of his youth, Crassus and Scaevola, he now aspired to be a model for emulation. In this way, Cicero could still influence junior politicians through oratory. Among his 'pupils' were his estranged son-in-law Dolabella (who had now been brought back in line with Caesar, but not Tullia). Another was Aulus Hirtius, Caesar's friend and adherent. The link with political activity was there to be seen, but Cicero spelled it out explicitly in a letter written to his friend Papirius Paetus in July 46 BC:

> When I was at leisure in Tusculum – after I had sent my 'pupils' to meet Caesar, so that they could put me in the best possible light to their friend in one fell swoop – I received your most charming letter. From it I could tell that you approve of my plan: like the tyrant Dionysius, who is said to have opened up a school after he had been expelled from Syracuse, I have set up a kind of school too, now that the law courts have been abolished and I have lost my forensic kingdom.[8]

His comments remind us of a time when Cicero was taunted for being a tyrant of the courts. Admittedly, it was an insulting charge at the time, yet it goes some way towards illuminating the great disparity between Cicero's former influence and his current submissiveness. Teaching and writing now had to compensate for his public silence, but his books could be fairly outspoken when Cicero wanted them to be.

In the summer of 46 BC, Cicero composed and published a eulogy in praise of Cato. It was, of course, carefully written to cause the least possible offence to Caesar, who had been the antagonist in the particular drama of Cato's life. But it did not entirely succeed in avoiding Caesar's displeasure. For the dictator wrote an *Anti-Cato* in reply. It was full of scurrilous charges against Cato, which did little to help Caesar's cause. But Cicero and Caesar politely complimented each other's literary abilities, even if their political detachment was apparent. From this time on, their relationship revolved only around their shared intellectual pursuits.

Domestic troubles also caused Cicero to retreat further away from political activity. As we saw earlier, his personal life had taken a turn for the worse in the years 47–46 BC. Throughout this time, Cicero had been on the wrong end of his brother's vengeful temper; his nephew, too, had joined in the campaign of words against Cicero. His marriage to Terentia had ended in early 46 BC, and Tullia's marriage to Dolabella had also been terminated later that year. To add to his private problems, Cicero had since remarried a very young girl called Publilia, but this marriage was not going well either. Initially, Terentia had spread rumours that Cicero was infatuated with the teenager, but it is more likely that the match had been made for money – a commodity that had been in short supply following his return from the civil war.

Nothing, however, could have prepared him for the tragedy he experienced in early 45 BC. For Cicero's beloved daughter Tullia died as a result of childbirth; some weeks later, the baby died too. Cicero was inconsolable, and this year represents a very real departure from political life. He went to Astura, a secluded hideaway that he had recently purchased, on the coast near Antium. As he recovered, he later moved around between his various villas – at Tusculum, Arpinum, Formiae, Pompeii, and more. He avoided Rome and all social interaction. He even divorced his new wife, despite the financial difficulties this caused him. But his books and Atticus were all he wanted.

Letters of support flooded in to begin with. Later, some of his contemporaries criticized Cicero for being too grief-stricken and a recluse. Yet Cicero was being true to himself, as a man with a passion for literature and learning. He returned to philosophy. More accurately, he threw himself into philosophy – and the results were staggering.

In the short space of time between February 45 BC and September 44 BC,

Cicero tackled a whole range of philosophical problems in numerous books. It may have been the *Hortensius* that set Cicero rolling on the project, for it was a call to philosophical study dedicated to the orator Hortensius, who had died in 50 BC. He then wrote books on ethical theory (*On Ends*), three books *On the Nature of the Gods*, and a further five on topics to do with suffering, death and immortality, the *Tusculan Disputations*. There were essays, *On Fate* and *On Divination*, as well as *On Friendship* and *On Old Age*. A technical work on scepticism, called the *Academic Questions*, also survives. But we have largely lost one publication called the *Consolation*. This essay, in particular, was greatly admired in antiquity. Consolatory texts had been written before, but this was the first such work ever produced by an author trying to lessen his own grief.

Initially, Cicero had turned his attention to philosophy as a solace and as a substitute. But he continued writing even after Caesar's assassination. The final works included the *Topics* (a work on logic) and three books *On Duties*, which was written just as he was making his way back into politics. For Cicero also wanted to perform a public service for Rome. And he succeeded. In these years, Cicero provided Rome with her own philosophical literature. An undertaking of this size had never been produced in Rome, and Cicero's contribution to the history of philosophy has earned him much admiration. For us, his tremendous output is also interesting for the biographical 'commentary' it provides. For, when we consider the titles and the topics of his works, Cicero has provided us with a powerful glimpse into his mind at this time.

However, philosophy was never meant to be a permanent replacement – nor could it be for a political animal like Cicero. The death of Tullia opened up old wounds, as Cicero admitted in a letter addressed to his old friend Servius Sulpicius Rufus:

> Now, by the force of this blow, even those wounds which I thought had healed are open once more. In the past my home used to welcome and soothe me when I grieved at political affairs. But, now that I am grieving in my home affairs, I cannot take refuge in a political life or find peace in its haven. And so I stay away from home and forum alike: my private woes cannot comfort the pain I feel in my public ones, nor public woes comfort my private.[9]

Yet, the following year, something happened to help draw Cicero out of his depression and reclusion. For Caesar returned to Rome in September 45 BC – by this time he was undefeated and unstoppable. Although he did not know it, Caesar only had six months left to live, and his death provided Cicero with the ammunition he needed to return to the political stage. Before we consider Cicero's revival, however, we must briefly examine the reasons for both Caesar's growing unpopularity and his assassination.

'I AM NOT KING, I AM CAESAR'

As Cicero had predicted almost five years earlier, civil war had led to a sole ruler – a 'tyrant' or a 'king' in the Roman mind.[10] For the war was finally brought to an end on 17 March 45 BC, when the remaining Pompeians were defeated in the battle of Munda at Spain. Only Pompey's youngest son survived to fight another day; but his battle to the death with Caesar's heir happened outside of Cicero's lifetime. And now, in 45 BC, there was no one left to challenge Caesar's domination either at home or abroad.

Caesar's power had become vast in the years between the outbreak of civil war and its closure (49–45 BC). Its foundations lay in the office of dictator, which Caesar had held for long periods at a time since the year 49 BC. This office gave him unlimited control and protection against any veto. On top of this, he held the consulship in 48 BC, as he did again from 46–44 BC. His multiple political roles were supplemented by his priesthoods. Caesar had been Rome's *pontifex maximus* since 63 BC; in 47 BC he was also appointed onto the other chief religious body – the board of augurs. Rumour had it that he wanted to be adopted into a plebeian family as well, so that he could become a tribune of the plebs too. But there was no real need for it. The combination of the posts Caesar held made him supreme.

From 46–44 BC, all Cicero could do was watch as Rome underwent a huge transformation. Caesar had far-reaching plans for reform at Rome, and initially many of the changes were well judged and necessary. Indeed, to Caesar's credit, he worked with great energy and he achieved some notable results. The reform of the calendar into the twelve-month system that we still use today shows that Caesar was a practical and efficient leader. On a social level, he sought to curb licentious and extravagant expenditure. In judicial matters, he strengthened the penalties for crime and justice in the courts. He tackled the economic problems of debt and the grain dole. And he also sought to improve the administration of Rome by enrolling over three hundred new senators. But there was one thing that featured very heavily in all of Caesar's plans for the Republic – Caesar himself. While he famously declared the words 'I am not a king, I am Caesar', the fact was that he was in no rush to abandon his power – whatever title he took.[11]

It was clear that Caesar had no plans to restore the Republic, as Cicero had asked him to do in the speech *For Marcellus*. By the time Caesar returned in 45 BC, Cicero was also back at Rome, to attend meetings of the senate at the dictator's summons. But these meetings were very different to the ones Cicero had attended in the past. Caesar had increased the number of senators from six hundred to nine hundred, and it was packed with his supporters from all over the empire. The senate was no longer the place for political discussion or debate – now, it served merely as the rubber stamp on Caesar's policy.

This is not the place for a full examination of Caesar's dictatorship, or of the events leading up to his assassination. But what should be seen is this: everything Caesar did in the years of his dictatorship aroused the suspicion and hatred of men who had always distrusted and despised autocrats. Indeed, there were many instances of erratic and insulting behaviour on Caesar's part. He paraded Cleopatra as his mistress through the streets of Rome, she brought their child Caesarion with her, and she lived in one of Caesar's houses a short distance from the city. Caesar even dedicated a golden statue to her, and placed it inside a temple of Venus (the goddess of love). One can only imagine the horror this caused, not just to the general Roman sentiment but also to his wife.

Caesar had completely parted from the path of tradition. Even his whole policy of clemency marked him out as a despot, whose personal whim held sway over the lives of his fellow citizens. Cicero, too, believed that Caesar was acting like a king – this is the term (*rex*) he started to use to refer to the dictator in his private correspondence. Yet, in public, Cicero maintained a superficial relationship with Caesar.

In the December of 45 BC, he defended Deiotarus, the king of Galatia, who had helped Cicero in his Cilician command. The speech was delivered in highly unusual circumstances – in the dictator's house, behind closed doors and in front of one man, Caesar himself, acting as judge and jury. The 'trial' was a far cry from the days when Cicero had boomed his speeches out to the jury and passers-by in the forum. He felt his oratorical performance was severely hampered by these conditions, yet Cicero's speech must have retained something of his former powers. Caesar was acting both as prosecutor and judge against a man he believed had tried to kill him. However, Caesar suspended judgement on the matter, even though he did not live long enough to reconsider the case.

After this, Caesar even paid a personal visit to Cicero at his seaside villa in Puteoli. The meeting itself was amiable and polite. But, Cicero, who often fell under Caesar's charm in such circumstances, was far from spellbound this time. Indeed, Caesar's visit elicited an exasperated letter to Atticus, a flavour of which can be seen from a few extracts:

> Oh, what a guest – so weighty but not disagreeable! For it was really quite pleasant . . . But the house was so full of soldiers that there was hardly a dining room free for Caesar himself to dine in – two thousand men there were! . . .
>
> He ate and drank well, without any apprehension . . . However, he is not the kind of guest to whom you would say 'please drop in on me again, next time you are in the area.' Once is enough. There was nothing serious in our conversation, but there was much literary talk. All in all, he was pleased and it went well.[12]

This was the last time that Cicero had such an intimate conversation with Caesar, and the letter shows that he did not hate the dictator as a man. But he did hate the fact that Caesar had no desire to restore the Republic.

Caesar now treated the honoured magisterial posts both as favours he could offer to his friends and as bargaining chips in return for political support. On his return to Rome, Caesar gave up his period as sole consul and replaced himself with two senators. But his flagrant abuse of the ladder of offices reached an all-time high when one of these men died on the very last day of the year. For Caesar appointed another man in his place – to serve as consul for just one afternoon. The undistinguished consul was a man called Caninius, and the irregularity of his appointment led to a barrage of jokes from Cicero:

> And so, during the consulship of Caninius, you should know that no one had breakfast; not one crime was committed when he was consul; for he was remarkably vigilant – during his whole consulship, he never shut an eye. All this may seem very funny to you, for you are not here; but if you could see it, you would weep.[13]

By February 44 BC the situation was desperate. This was the month in which Antony three times offered a royal crown (or diadem) to Caesar. To judge from Cicero's lively account of this episode in his *Second Philippic* oration, Cicero may well have been an eyewitness. Each time Antony offered the crown, Caesar rejected it when the crowd booed. We shall never know whether he would have accepted it if they had cheered instead. But it is perhaps more important to consider what he *did* accept that month, for he took the controversial title of 'perpetual dictator'. And it was in addition to other honours and titles, both regal and divine, which were being heaped upon him.

To focus solely on the dictatorship, most modern historians agree that this step marked the final break from the tradition of the Republic. For the term 'perpetual' is ambiguous in Latin. It can be translated as 'continuous', in which case Caesar may only ever have intended to hold the dictatorship for an uninterrupted period of time. However, it can also mean 'for life'. Caesar could have planned to hold power forever, and there were many men at Rome who were not prepared to wait and find out.

Cicero was not involved in the plot against Caesar, but he was almost certainly there to witness the assassination. It took place in a hall attached to the theatre of Pompey on 15 March 44 BC (a day referred to as the 'Ides of March' by Romans). In just three days' time, Caesar was set to embark on his next great expedition – against Parthia. The praetors Gaius Cassius Longinus and Marcus Junius Brutus led the conspiracy, but they had gathered men who had fought on both sides of the civil war. More than sixty men joined them, according to Suetonius. And they acted out of fear for what might happen if Caesar won another military triumph, conquered another nation and accumulated yet more personal wealth and power.

There was also a rumour in the air: an oracle had predicted that only a *king* would be able to conquer Parthia, and there were many who now wanted to give

Caesar this title in anticipation of his campaign. The conspirators had decided that Caesar must die before he could either accept the title or set out for the East. The story has been told and embellished by many writers, but Suetonius will guide us briefly through the dictator's final moments:

> Wherever he turned, he saw that drawn daggers were attacking him, he buried his head in his toga, and at the same, using his left hand, he drew its fold down to his feet, so that he would fall more honourably, with the lower part of his body covered too. And in this way he was stabbed twenty-three times. He did not utter a word – just a groan at the first blow. Although some have reported that when Marcus Brutus rushed at him, he said in Greek: 'You too, my child?'[14]

And so Caesar fell. Cicero does not leave us a full account of the dramatic events, but he does make one brief allusion to the scene of the murder in his work *On Divination*. He adds an ironic twist to the dictator's death: that he landed at the feet of Pompey's statue. Plutarch thought that it was as if Pompey was watching this act of revenge against his former enemy. But this striking image, which portrays the figures of two men who dominated Rome between the 70s and 40s BC, also reminds us of the polarities of success and failure. The statue is reminiscent of a man who once stood tall, while the corpse – slumping low on the ground – signifies death and destruction. We can only wonder whether Cicero saw it that way.

Cicero had watched the rise and fall of each man; they, in turn, had contributed to the highs and lows of his own career. Cicero had fought hard to reach the consulship in 63 BC. And for a brief spell in 62 BC, he had enjoyed the influence that this position brought in Roman politics as a consular. Yet, within three years, the formation of the first triumvirate shattered his dreams of exercising influence in the traditional political apparatus of Rome. He was stripped of a political role, his oratory only functioned when the triumvirs wanted it to – everything he had worked for must have seemed in vain.

But then Crassus died, Caesar defeated Pompey in the civil war, and now Caesar had been assassinated. It opened the way for the republican constitution to be restored. The Republic – the political system that offered Cicero influence, standing and a platform for his oratory – was on the brink of revival, and so too was everything Cicero had devoted his life towards.

15

The Tyranny of Antony (44 BC)

LIBERTY AND TYRANNY

Antony said: 'As soon as Caesar had been killed, Brutus raised the blood-spattered dagger high into the air, and called on Cicero by name, and congratulated him on the recovery of liberty.' . . . These are Antony's words: 'Brutus, whose name I mention with respect, called out to Cicero as he held the blood-spattered dagger; this alone should make it clear that Cicero was in on the plot.'

(Cicero, *Philippic* 2.30)

Six months after the death of Julius Caesar, on 19 September 44 BC, Antony made a scathing attack on Cicero in the senate. He claimed that Cicero had been involved in the plot to kill Caesar, and that he had coerced the conspirators to commit the deed. Much had happened in between the March and September of 44 BC, as we shall see shortly. But first it is important to understand both why Caesar was killed and why Brutus congratulated Cicero within moments of the murder.

The conspirators – or the 'liberators' as they preferred to be called – had acted because they believed that Caesar's autocracy had destroyed the republican traditions. Whether they were initially prompted by genuine patriotism or by the blow that Caesar's control dealt to their own political ambitions, the result was the same: they yearned for a Republic that operated off the back of open, competitive elections rather than the favour of a dynast. Many senators did not want a master to rule over them. As Cicero explained in the *Republic*, 'the community that lives under a king is completely deprived of many advantages, in particular *liberty*, which is not the freedom of living under a just master, but of no master at all'.[1] In a world that witnessed the extremities of slavery and freedom on a daily basis, what a man considered as liberty could differ greatly from one to the next. But, for the freedom fighters who killed Caesar, what mattered was the liberty of the senate, and the ability to participate in politics.

In his lifetime, Caesar had become the symbol of anti-republicanism: some called him a king, harking back to the loathed period of monarchy that preceded the birth of the Republic. This fact alone was allegedly enough to spur on Brutus, a descendant of the celebrated Lucius Junius Brutus – the man who had expelled the last king of Rome, Tarquinius Superbus. But Rome's abhorrence of kings ran deeper than we can imagine; their attitude to kingship had long been assimilated with the Greeks' hatred of tyranny, which ran back into the mists of time.

Legend had it that in the sixth century BC two men, Harmodius and Aristogiton, had freed Athens from the yoke of tyranny by force: 'The Greeks bestow divine honours to those tyrannicides', Cicero had once recalled. 'What sights I have seen at Athens – as well as in other cities of Greece! What religious rites have been established in honour of such men! What songs! What poems!'[2] Legends and precedents provided something akin to a moral code of conduct in the Roman mind: to kill a tyrant was not just permissible; it was positively encouraged by the historical tradition. True, murder was a crime; but, to Cicero's way of thinking, tyrannicide was self-defence against a man who was killing his country.

Cicero was not, as Antony later claimed, actively involved in the plot to kill Caesar. And Plutarch was probably right to suggest that the conspirators considered him to be 'too old and too timid' to commit the deed.[3] However, they could be sure of his support after the event. In his philosophical works, speeches and private correspondence, Cicero had long perpetuated the hatred of autocracy and the legitimacy of tyrannicide. He had fashioned himself as the advocate for the Republic, and that was a fact which could now be exploited. Furthermore, his authority as an ex-consul gave weight and dignity to the conspirators' cause. That is why Brutus congratulated Cicero on the recovery of freedom – and he knew his friend well. Cicero was not just relieved to be free of tyranny, he was delighted.

EID MAR: the Ides of March, on a denarius (a silver coin) of Marcus Junius Brutus, celebrating the assassination of Caesar (© The Trustees of the British Museum).

THE RISE OF ANTONY

However, it did not take long for Cicero's exhilaration to turn into despair. For in their belief that Caesar's assassination was an act of liberation, Brutus and Cassius failed in one major respect: to create a back-up plan. They had not thought beyond the moment of the murder, envisaged any repercussions or even foreseen the hostility of the people. They thought that the Republic would restore itself, but they were wrong – as the events of the following year soon proved.

The death of Caesar created a political vacuum and set in motion a power struggle of disastrous consequences. This conflict witnessed another civil war, the death of Cicero, and eventually the collapse of the republican form of government. It is one of the most richly documented periods of Roman history, thanks almost entirely to the energy with which Cicero committed himself to the last fight he fought. Yet he did not enter the fray immediately, and to understand what lured Cicero back for this final stand, we need to review the rise of Antony, the emergence of Octavian, and Cicero's reaction to the events happening around him.

As they plotted and carried out the assassination of Caesar, Brutus and Cassius thought the crowds of Rome would be pleased to be free from tyranny; but they soon realized just how much they had miscalculated. For when they summoned a public meeting on the afternoon of the murder, they were met with a stony silence. Under the dictatorship of Caesar, Rome had seen important social changes that the senatorial government had failed, or neglected, to effect when they were in charge. For the past few years, Rome had been relatively free from crime, conflict and poverty. In addition, the banquets, games and festivals had all been lavish. And Caesar was loved by the people. When the unpopularity of their action dawned on them, the liberators quickly took refuge on the Capitoline hill. They could be safe there under the guard of some watchful gladiators who had been gathered to protect them.

Cicero visited Brutus and Cassius that same evening – on the Ides of March. He urged them to continue aggressively and to take control of the senate. However, they were determined to negotiate with Antony, for now they saw the superiority of the opposing side. Caesar's support base had been vast; plus he had the loyalty of his troops, who were eagerly awaiting him in the East to embark on the Parthian expedition. More urgently, back in Rome, Caesar's death left Antony as sole consul; and Lepidus, the master of the horse, was in command of a legion of troops just a short distance from the city.

It was a mistake for the liberators to wait, Cicero thought: Antony had taken cover in his house out of fear, and they could have struck while the iron was hot. But instead they waited and gave a dangerous advantage to the consul, for as soon as he realized that he was not a target in the assassination plot as well, Antony made every move to fortify and strengthen his own position. Lepidus was ordered to enter Rome and station his troops in the forum immediately. And that very night, Antony visited Calpurnia, Caesar's shaken widow. Calpurnia gave him all her husband's personal papers, which contained Caesar's decrees and plans relating to the state. She also gave Antony the former dictator's funds. They were both vital weapons which could be used alongside Lepidus' troops, if need be. It was still the Ides of March, but Antony had emerged to take command of the situation – and now there was a stalemate in Rome.

On 17 March, however, strife was temporarily averted. In a meeting of the senate, with Cicero acting as a mediator, the two sides reached a compromise. Cicero argued that the assassination of Caesar had been performed by patriotic citizens; he urged an amnesty and reconciliation. Antony agreed, but he wanted to make sure that all of Caesar's 'acts' – his plans for the next few years, contained in his papers – would remain valid. And so it was settled: the liberators were not to be prosecuted, and Caesar's decrees were not to be repealed. By these acts, all the magisterial and provincial appointments that Caesar had allocated for the future, were saved. This included the consulship Caesar had promised to Dolabella, who immediately became Antony's colleague. Civil war was stopped in its tracks, the people were satisfied, and that night Brutus and Cassius even dined with Antony and Lepidus.

However, the harmony was short-lived, for tensions reached boiling point when Caesar's public funeral was held just three days later. As Antony delivered an emotional oration, the people were maddened by such grief that riots broke out; they cremated Caesar's body there and then in the middle of the forum, and they attacked the homes of his assassins. Cicero later claimed Antony had purposefully used the occasion to generate hostility against the liberators. For the funeral had triggered widespread anger – and this anger was further fuelled when the contents of Caesar's will were revealed: he had left three hundred sesterces to every citizen (roughly four months' basic pay for a legionary), and made his gardens public property for the crowds to enjoy.

It was becoming increasingly impossible for the liberators to remain in Rome, and, by mid April, Brutus and Cassius had left the city. Others soon left to take up provincial commands. By this time, Cicero had already decided to leave for a tour of his Italian villas, going from one to the next, never stopping anywhere for long. He was not classed as a conspirator or foe yet, and Antony remained courteous if not friendly towards him. But Cicero did not want to get involved with politics: he wanted to visit Athens, where his son Marcus was studying. And so, from April to August, Cicero was little more than an observer of the political pendulum, which swung back and forth, sometimes offering hope, sometimes despair.

To begin with, Cicero approved of the steady course which Antony steered. The amnesty stayed in place and the senate functioned. Antony even abolished the office of dictator – an act that Cicero greatly admired. And so it should not be assumed that Antony immediately sought to replace Caesar's position of supreme power. However, Caesar's will had produced another surprise that now changed everything: the adoption of his great-nephew Gaius Octavius (known hereafter as Octavian). For with Caesar's fame and fortune behind him, Octavian set to replace Antony as the leader of the Caesarian faction.

The appearance of Octavian at Rome was enough to drive Antony from the path of moderation, for the more support Octavian gained from the plebs and the army, the more Antony had to court them too. He had to abandon his former restraint if he was to establish himself as the champion of Caesar's memory. He also needed to take drastic measures to strengthen his position and influence.

Antony's slide towards autocracy is charted in vivid detail in the speech that later became known as Cicero's *First Philippic*. It tells how Antony began to use forgeries of Caesar's papers to provide a shield of legitimacy to what were actually his own decrees. Cicero claimed he took seven hundred million sesterces from a special fund left behind by Caesar for the Parthian campaign, and he used it to buy supporters and influence. At the same time Antony also rallied Caesar's veterans, allegedly bribing them with land allotments and promises of seats on the jury-panels. He brought many of the soldiers back to Rome with him, and the rule of force once more took over the city. This is Cicero's version of events, largely tapered to stress the unconstitutional nature of Antony's actions – but it does give us a powerful glimpse into how Cicero viewed Antony at this time.

A later coin depicting Mark Antony (© The Trustees of the British Museum).

In Cicero's eyes, Antony's despotic intentions became clear in June, when he used force and an irregular procedure to secure himself a five-year command over Gaul. He was meant to go to Macedonia at the head of four legions stationed there, but that took Antony too far away from the action. Gaul, on the other hand, offered him a position of strength over the rest of Italy, just as it had done for Caesar. In the speech, Cicero was painting a picture of a man striving for personal domination, and he was helped by the fact that Antony was gathering huge troops of men around him. For, although he turned down the province of Macedonia, Antony decided to keep the Macedonian forces. But he summoned them to join him in *Italy*, and it added great manpower to his already strong army.

The description of Antony's behaviour in the *First Philippic* is a one-sided account, but it is not empty or showy rhetoric. The failure of the conspiracy and the rise of Antony plagued Cicero, and his personal correspondence enables us to witness the growing depths of his despair. Caesar was dead, but his measures (and more) continued to inhibit a free Republic. It was an impossible situation and a major political issue, as Cicero despairingly remarked to Atticus: 'The tyranny lives on, only the tyrant is dead!'[4]

The death of Caesar had created a void in the political life of Rome, and it was one which Brutus and his followers had failed to fill. The rise of Antony was alarming, yet Cicero had voiced his suspicions as early as April. In a letter to Atticus on 22 April 44 BC, Cicero referred to the assassination as 'a job half done' – for Antony too should have been killed. Almost a year later, he was even more explicit in a letter to Trebonius, one of the conspirators: 'How I wish you had invited me to that most sumptuous banquet on the Ides of March! We would have no leftovers, if you had.'[5]

With the characteristic indecision and anxiety that plagued Cicero in moments of crisis, he deliberated what to do and where to go. He saw no hope of putting up an effective political challenge to the new regime for as long as Antony remained consul. And so, when it looked as though nothing could be done to help the political situation, Cicero set out for Greece – to visit his son as he had planned. It was 6 August 44 BC.

CICERO'S RETURN TO ROME

That Cicero would re-emerge as the main protagonist in the fight for the Republic seemed unlikely at this point. Too old, too tired, and clueless as to the best course of action, all Cicero could do was say what he would or would not have done in the conspiracy and its aftermath. He could only look to 1 January 43 BC, when Aulus Hirtius and Gaius Vibius Pansa were to assume the consulship and replace Antony. But as Cicero made his journey towards Greece, something changed his mind. To begin with, the trip was not going smoothly: he had got as far as Syracuse in Sicily, but bad weather conditions had driven Cicero back to Leucopetra – on the tip of Italy's toe. However, then, before he could set sail again, some important news reached Cicero from Rome.

There was a rumour that some people were missing Cicero, and that others were criticizing him for abandoning Rome. Bad feeling was further fanned by the thought that a man of Cicero's position might be watching the Olympic games while his country was in a crisis! But, more importantly, there was a rumour too that a new compromise was to be reached between Antony and the liberators.

The competition and conflict between Antony and Octavian had been tearing the Caesarians apart, and it now seemed reasonable to hope that Antony could be induced to side with the republicans and the liberators once again. If so, there was a chance Brutus and Cassius might be able to return to resume their duties as praetors at Rome. These reports were not the kind that a man like Cicero could ignore. With a view to defending both his reputation and the Republic, Cicero hesitated no longer: he was heading straight back to the capital.

However, as he made his way back, Cicero met Brutus – and the news from Rome had taken a turn for the worse. Octavian and Antony had been forced to make a public reconciliation to appease Caesar's soldiers, who were alarmed at the rift occurring in their faction: for men who had once been united under Caesar were being torn by their loyalty to his rival successors. As a result of their reunion, any compromise between one Caesarian faction and the liberators was impossible, and Brutus and Cassius despaired for their political careers. They had decided to leave Rome and head to the East, where they hoped to recover their military strength. This was the last time Cicero and Brutus ever saw each other, although they wrote to each other frequently in the months ahead.

At the same time, Brutus also told Cicero about a disastrous meeting of the senate held on 1 August 44 BC. There was only one senator who had dared to speak up against Antony – it was Caesar's former father-in-law: Lucius Calpurnius Piso. And no one had risen to support him. Cicero's hopes for a peaceful restoration of the Republic were once more dashed. To add insult to the injury, this Piso was the same man who had traded Cicero's safety for a province back in 58 BC, when Clodius was engineering Cicero's exile. It no doubt grated Cicero that the only man left in Rome defending the Republic was his one-time enemy.

There was still nothing that could be done against Antony's domination, but now Cicero wanted to be back at Rome. On 19 August, Cicero wrote to Atticus to explain his decision: he did not intend to take part in politics again, he claimed, but he was aware that 'a man should not be too far from his grave at this time of life'.[6] However, whether he admitted it or not, he must have seen the political turmoil brewing ahead. Indeed, as Cicero made his way into the city on 1 September, he found himself in the eye of the storm.

A meeting of the senate was scheduled for the very day he returned, and Cicero heard that Antony was planning to force through another controversial resolution. Perhaps as part of his make-up to the young Octavian or, more likely, to outdo him, Antony wanted to add a day in honour of Caesar to all the festivals that were offered to the gods. It was an extravagant honour, and not one that Cicero wanted to vote on. He diplomatically decided not to attend, claiming that he was too tired from the long journey; however, this, to Antony, was an act of defiance. Whether or not Cicero had intended his absence to be read that way, the foundations for their lasting (and fatal) enmity were set.

Antony's threats in the senate that day – including one to tear Cicero's house down – set the circumstances that drew Cicero out of political retirement and onto the first phase of a determined and ruthless battle. For the next day, on 2 September, Cicero *did* attend. This time Antony was not there, yet Cicero addressed a speech to both consuls: Antony and Dolabella. This was his *First Philippic* (a nickname he later coined for the speeches he delivered against Antony), and Cicero urged the consuls to return to the path of moderation, where harmony and compromise could still be found. However, at the same time as he urged reconciliation, Cicero felt compelled to speak his mind about the political situation.

In the speech, which he published afterwards, Cicero praised Antony's initial behaviour in the aftermath of Caesar's assassination. But in his continued reliance on Caesar's acts, Cicero believed that Antony had acted counter to the spirit of the agreement: he had recalled a large number of former exiles using the legislation allegedly passed by Caesar, he had posted one of Caesar's laws that gave citizenship to the whole of Sicily, and even freed Crete from the burden of taxation on the grounds that Caesar had already done so. 'Men have been called back from exile *by a dead man*', Cicero cried out to the senate: 'Citizenship has been given not only to individuals, but to whole tribes and provinces *by a dead man*. Revenues have been abolished, through countless grants of immunity given, *by a dead man*.'[7]

Scholars are torn in their assessment of the speech. For some it suggests that Cicero was moderate and sensible; for others, it was the speech that precipitated the war. Yet either way, restrained or not, Cicero did criticize Antony for the policies he had pursued since shortly after Caesar's death. Furthermore, he was implying that Antony was forging Caesar's papers to pass his own legislation, for the repetition of *a mortuo* ('by a dead man') suggests Cicero had his suspicions about the legality of Antony's actions. This was about as fierce as the attack got. But, deep down, Cicero must have known that he was rattling a lion's cage.

Antony was furious that Cicero had opposed him, and he withdrew into a 'pit of drink and debauchery', Cicero told Cassius. There he spent days working up a scathing reply with the help of a rhetorician, and Antony delivered it at a meeting of the senate on 19 September 44 BC. Cicero did not attend that day, fearing that it might be dangerous, and the event proved he was wise.[8] Antony arrived at the senate with a gang of armed men, locked the doors, and delivered a comprehensive attack on Cicero's entire career. Sadly, we do not have a copy of the words Antony spoke, but we can gauge a fairly accurate idea from the response that Cicero wrote in the *Second Philippic*.

Antony cursed Cicero's consulship and the execution of some of the Catilinarian conspirators. He blamed Cicero for the murder of Clodius, declared that Cicero had caused the civil war between Pompey and Caesar, and even implicated him in the plot to assassinate Caesar – 'for no other reason than to incite Caesar's veterans against me', Cicero complained.[9] It was the first major gauntlet for battle on Antony's part, but Cicero was not in a position of strength from which to fight. The best he could do was to avoid Antony and to sit on the sidelines: 'What can be done against violence except by violence?' Cicero later asked.[10] For the time being, if he wanted to shout, Cicero had to shout into his books. He composed the *Second Philippic*, the speech he would like to have delivered in reply to Antony. A copy reached Atticus around 25 October – but it was not to be published *yet*, he told his friend, still hopeful that the Republic might be restored, and that it would one day be safer to circulate his denunciation of Antony.[11]

THE STIMULI TO ACTION:
INVECTIVE, PHILOSOPHY AND OCTAVIAN

Scholars generally accept that the *Second Philippic* was published as a kind of political pamphlet in December 44 BC, when Cicero embarked on his campaign to save the Republic from Antony's domination. In this way, it represents a type of writing in both the Greek and Roman worlds which had its own conventions, rules and themes. This was the slanderous abuse, or invective, which we have already seen scattered in the passages of Cicero's speeches mentioned so far. And it reminds us of the unreliability of much of our ancient 'evidence', when we consider that these routine attacks have found their way into the historical record.

Indeed, the fact that the *Second Philippic* was not delivered at all may have allowed Cicero to indulge further in his criticism of Antony than he could have done in a spoken oration. The result is an amusing caricature and scandalous attack on one of Rome's most colourful personalities; the *Second Philippic* rapidly became, and still remains, one of Cicero's most famous and popular 'speeches' – even though it was never spoken. Only a century after it was written, the Roman writer Juvenal regarded it as Cicero's 'divine *Philippic*', and it serves well to highlight the conventions that Romans had for abuse of this sort – an abuse that otherwise seems inappropriate and distasteful to a modern audience.[12]

Antony was an embarrassment to his family's name – Cicero claimed. His grandfather had been Marcus Antonius the orator. Cicero used to listen to his speeches as a boy; he used to engage with him in debate. But Antony, he mocked, had to rely on hired help to compose an oration: 'Two thousand acres of fertile Sicilian land was the price you paid to Sextus Clodius the "rhetorician" – and tax-free too. All so that, at the Roman public's expense, you could learn how to look like a fool!' This was typical of political slander – it was conventional either to criticize a man's ancestry, or claim that he was unworthy of it.[13]

Cicero complained about Antony's kingly aspirations, another favourite reserve. To make the picture more threatening, he claimed Antony bore all the marks of a tyrant: arrogance, cruelty, lust and greed. The 'speech' was a wildly exaggerated account of Antony's public and private life. Antony had squandered his inheritance, Cicero claimed, and his house was always full of whores, gamblers and drunks. He was gluttonous, eccentric, a sexual deviant, brutal, yet cowardly. His wives were mocked, and his appearance lampooned: 'What a throat, what lungs, and what a robust body – like a gladiator's!' Cicero joked.[14]

Yet behind it all there was a political agenda: an attack on Antony's personal life simultaneously highlighted his lack of political credibility – a point that Cicero never lets us forget. One of Cicero's favourite stories about Antony, recalling his public appearance with a hangover in 47 BC, sums up Antony's incompetence: 'At an assembly of the Roman people, while conducting public business as Caesar's master of the horse – when it would be disgraceful for such a man even to burp – he was sick! And he filled his own lap and the whole tribunal with scraps of undigested food reeking of wine.'[15]

It is little wonder that Cicero did not want the imaginary speech to be published yet – now was not the right time to be fighting Antony's armed forces with words. However, the date of publication is less important than what the *Second Philippic* tells us about Cicero's state of mind when he wrote it, for the abuse recalls the fire and hatred behind Cicero's attacks on his enemies in earlier orations. Whether we remember the abuse of Verres at the beginning of his career, the attack on Catiline at the peak of his consulship or the fight against Clodius in his struggles of the 50s BC – the result is the same: the old Cicero was back.

By the time that Cicero sent the *Second Philippic* to Atticus, he had withdrawn to his country villas again – retiring first to Puteoli, then Arpinum. He still saw no point in confronting Antony until after 1 January 43 BC, and so Cicero – with characteristic studiousness – retreated once more to his books. In addition to a small treatise *On Friendship*, which he fittingly dedicated to his dear friend Atticus, Cicero now embarked on the last of his major scholarly works, *On Duties*. It was a 'code of conduct' for the younger generation, in which Cicero laid out his ideals for how the responsible citizen should behave.

However, far from being a retreat from political activity, Cicero's philosophy further prepared his mind for the fight to come. For *On Duties* zealously justified the murder of tyrants – they must be removed from society, just as harmful limbs should be amputated from an otherwise healthy body: 'Suppose every limb in the body thought it could increase its own strength by taking strength from the limb next to it; the whole body would automatically become weak and die', Cicero explained. 'In the same way, if every one of us were to seize upon the advantages of others, and take what we could to satisfy our own desires, then society and community among men would automatically be overthown.'[16] It is a powerful demonstration of Cicero's thoughts: he certainly had a firm eye on justifying the death of Caesar, but Cicero was surely keeping the other on Antony.

Cicero's studies also shaped his attitude towards war. While he was a pacifist at heart, in the second book of the treatise Cicero argued that war was a justifiable course of action in one of three situations: if negotiations were impossible, if enemies needed to be repelled or if it was the only way to establish peace. In the year ahead, as we shall see, Cicero fought against Antony with a determination and lust for war that seem, at first glance, incompatible with his peace-making missions in the earlier civil war. But he had learned valuable lessons. Furthermore, Antony's character and hostile actions fulfilled these conditions for war – at least in Cicero's eyes.

Finally, Cicero's *On Duties* did not represent a 'one philosophy for all' manual. But for those who aspired to be 'good men', it offered a definition of what it meant to be a responsible citizen. In Cicero's words:

> He will devote himself entirely to the Republic, and he will seek neither wealth or power for himself, and he will protect the whole in such a way that he takes thought for every individual . . . and he will adhere so tightly to justice and integrity that – for as long as he guards them – he will endure any setback, however serious, and he will face death rather than abandon those virtues I have mentioned.[17]

Cicero's hatred and mind were now both fully engaged for battle. Antony was his personal and political enemy (the two were very rarely separate in Cicero's eyes). He believed that, if war had the potential to restore order, the good citizen should die fighting rather than submit to a dishonourable peace. However, a third stimulus – and the final call – for action came from a more unexpected source: the young Octavian. For in the time that Cicero was composing his *Second Philippic* and *On Duties*, rivalries between Antony and Octavian had resurfaced to the point that civil war was inevitable.

Back in Rome, both men were assembling troops in preparation for the fight to come. In October 44 BC, Antony had accused Octavian of planning to kill him. Octavian, of course, denied it, and the masses believed him (although there were many men, including Cicero, who were inclined to believe the rumour). However, the alleged assassination attempt was enough to remind Antony of the threat

Octavian posed, both to his popularity and to his political position. Soon afterwards, Antony left Rome to meet the four legions of soldiers who had arrived
from Macedonia. His preparations were looking ahead to his governorship in
Gaul, but also to keeping Rome under the powerful grip of his army.

However, while Antony's back was turned, Octavian went to Campania, where
his name and money helped him assemble his own army from among Caesar's
veterans. His plan was to wage a war against Antony, who was still one of Rome's
consuls. Cicero learned all this from Octavian himself, in a letter that reached him
on 1 November 44 BC. By 4 November, he was encouraged but in a quandary:

Written from Puteoli: 4 November 44 BC

Cicero to Atticus, greetings.

Two letters have reached me from Octavian in one day, asking that I make my way to
Rome at once; he says he wants to work through the senate ... In short, he presses and
I bide my time cautiously. I don't trust his age, and I am not sure what his intentions
are ... I am afraid in case Antony's strength regains, and I don't want to leave the coast.
But I am afraid Octavian will have his *aristeia* – his moment of glory – in my absence.[18]

Octavian wanted Cicero's help, advice and support; however, Octavian's age and
Caesarian ties made him an unlikely champion of the republican cause. Cicero
doubted the young man could be trusted, and he doubted Octavian was a truly
'good citizen'.

Cicero hesitated, but on 12 November 44 BC he sent his last surviving letter to
Atticus. His final words strike an ominous conclusion to the collection: *Adsum
igitur*. They mean 'I am present' – and with these words Cicero announced his
final return to the city he loved. He explained that financial worries, rather than
political developments, were bringing him back to the city. But, at the same time,
he knew that he was heading 'straight back into the fire'. Perhaps Cicero did not
know the exact nature of the role awaiting him. However, the assassination of
Caesar, the tyranny of Antony and the rise of Octavian all proved one thing –
anything could happen in politics.[19]

16

The Last Fight for Liberty (44–43 BC)

CICERO'S FINAL STAND: THE *PHILIPPIC ORATIONS*

This is the day I was waiting for when I avoided Mark Antony's barbed weapons – when he slandered my name even though I was not there; he did not realize that I was saving both myself and my strength for the right time. For had I wanted to reply to him then, when he was looking at me as the first picking in a fight, I should not now have been able to defend the Republic. But now that the time has come, senators, I shall let no moment of the day or night pass, in which I shall not also take thought – where thought must be taken – both for the liberty of the Roman people and for your dignity. Not only shall I do what needs to be done and delivered; I shall seek and demand to do and deliver more.

(Cicero, *Philippic* 3.33)

When Cicero returned to Rome on 9 December 44 BC, he found his country on the brink of yet another civil war. The pivotal moment had occurred late in November, when two of Antony's Macedonian legions defected to Octavian. It was a great blow to Antony's military superiority, and he was forced to make a hasty escape from Rome. He hoped to regain his stronghold by taking over the province of Gaul from Decimus Brutus (one of Caesar's assassins and a relative of the leading conspirator Marcus Brutus); yet Antony's opponents were determined not to let this happen.

Before this, Cicero had been intending to remain on the sidelines until 1 January 43 BC, but these new developments suddenly changed everything. From this point on, he translated his philosophical musings into political pragmatism: war, Cicero believed, was the only way to save Rome from Antony's grasp. And, if the law was broken in the process, the law had to be fixed to meet the current crisis. These two ideas, the need for all-out combat and extralegal measures, are key to understanding Cicero's political activity in the months which followed. For he now championed the illegally raised forces of the young Octavian, and he urged Decimus Brutus 'not to wait for the senate's authorization' to take a military stand against Antony.[1] This was Cicero trying to do and deliver more for his country. And his hopes rested on creating a united military and political force to challenge Antony's despotic intentions.

Cicero did not have to wait long to put his thoughts into action, for the 'right time' came on 20 December 44 BC, when a vital piece of news reached Rome: Decimus Brutus declared that he would not hand over his province to Antony without a fight. It happened that the tribunes had convened a meeting of the senate that day to discuss the security measures for the new year, but Cicero used the opportunity to speak on the exciting development. He launched a determined and ruthless attack against Antony in two speeches: one to the senate urging them to resist Antony (the *Third Philippic*) and another to the people repeating the senate's debate and decrees – presenting the information with his own selective emphasis (the *Fourth Philippic*).

Cicero wanted the senate to approve Decimus Brutus' resistance to Antony. He further called for any provincial commands pushed through by Antony to be revoked, and suggested that all current governors should remain *in situ*. This meant that Antony could not take over Gaul legally, and Decimus Brutus could not be rebuked for fighting in defence of his province. In order to bolster the republican-minded forces, Cicero also argued that everyone resisting Antony, including Octavian, should be honoured.

All these measures were intended to strip Antony of any claim to the province of Gaul, and leave him weak and exposed. At the same time, Cicero sought to legitimize the military actions of Decimus Brutus and Octavian against a consul of Rome. He was asking the senate to sanction offences which were otherwise acts of treason – and they did. Furthermore, if we can trust Cicero's version of events, the people were also delighted: 'With one mind and voice, you all shouted together that I had saved the Republic for a second time.'[2] He was referring to his last major triumph over Catiline. And now, with a confidence he had not felt for nearly two decades, Cicero prepared for his final assault on Antony.

The orations that Cicero delivered on 20 December may have been the first of the group of speeches that Cicero referred to as 'his *Philippics*',[3] for he nicknamed them after the *Philippic* orations of the Athenian orator Demosthenes, who had famously attacked the tyrannical movements of Philip II of Macedon in the fourth century BC. And, like Demosthenes' *Philippics*, from this point on, Cicero's speeches strove towards one main goal: to denounce his opponent as an enemy of freedom, and thus declare war on him. For this reason, the threats of Antony's domination and tyranny became more than standard rhetorical arguments. They were vital tools in persuading Cicero's audience, nearly always the senate, of the need for war.

On 1 January 43 BC, Hirtius and Pansa assumed their long-awaited consulships, and Cicero's fight for liberty began in earnest. By this time, Antony had blockaded Decimus Brutus and his troops at Mutina (Modena, in northern

Italy) – and he was prepared to use force to get the province he wanted. Antony's legal right to claim the province had now been rescinded, and his siege could be represented by his opponents as an aggressive and hostile attack. On the other hand, Antony had some powerful supporters in the senate who could represent the opposing side: as a consul of Rome, Antony apparently had the right to enter any province he wanted to at the time. And Antony presumably did not accept the senate's decree as valid anyway.

The legal situation was complex, but it meant that Antony's supporters managed to defer a full declaration of war until 26 April 43 BC. In the meantime, the remaining speeches in the *Philippic* collection offer a lively picture of the struggle that Cicero faced against the Antonian faction – it called for all the powers of persuasion he could muster.

Cicero's position at the beginning of 43 BC was this: he was influential from the standpoint of a wise consular – an experienced politician and statesman. He could not initiate action, but only offer his opinion when asked, and he would have to contend with the opinions expressed by the consuls and ex-consuls who spoke before him. Unfortunately for Cicero, among these powerful voices was one of Antony's supporters – Quintus Fufius Calenus. To add to Cicero's problems, Calenus was not just the current consul Pansa's father-in-law; he was also the first man of consular rank 'to be asked' for his opinion on matters of debate at every meeting – both these facts meant that Calenus was in the stronger position to influence both the consul and the senate.

The pro-Antonian faction, steered by Calenus, fought to make a peace deal with Antony for as long as they could. Yet peace on Antony's terms was 'intolerable' – or so Cicero described the unfruitful results of an embassy sent to negotiate with him in January. This theme forms a dominant backdrop to several of Cicero's orations from this period. For Cicero opposed the proposal of peace negotiations in the *Fifth Philippic*; and when Calenus convinced the senate to send an envoy anyway, Cicero addressed the people with a bold prediction in his *Sixth Philippic*: 'I bear witness, I deplore, I predict beforehand: Mark Antony will not meet any of the conditions entrusted to the envoys.' And he was right – far from meeting the senate's terms, Antony sent back his own counter-demands. These were the terms that made a settlement with Antony 'intolerable' in Cicero's eyes.[4]

Cicero seized every opportunity he could to lament the delay the self-styled 'pacifists' were causing. It could be a discussion on a completely unrelated topic, such as the trivial routine business that called the senate's attention when Cicero delivered the *Seventh Philippic*. Or the debate might somehow be connected to the crisis, as when Cicero delivered his *Ninth Philippic* on the question of what honours should be paid to his friend, Servius Sulpicius Rufus. (Sulpicius Rufus had died of natural causes while serving on the first peace embassy to Antony.) In sum, Cicero did the best he could to revert the senate's mind to the crisis at hand whenever the chance arose: 'Slowness and procrastination are detestable in the conduct of most affairs,' he warned them, 'but this war especially calls for speed.'[5]

Some scholars have seen a touch of fanaticism in Cicero's last fight – as though he had to make up for years of frustration and humiliation in his career; but this is not entirely fair.[6] Desperate times called for desperate measures: they called for a clear, persuasive, driven and decisive form of oratory – a form of oratory that pitched the battle as a fight for survival itself, rather than a fight for a political constitution. Tough-talking was the only way Cicero could hope to trigger an unwilling and uncooperative senate into urgent action, for Cicero realized he was defending the only system that ensured his own role and political career. But he needed to get the senators to realize this about their own positions too; the only way for senators to live was under a free Republic, he argued:

> We were set free from the domination of a king – or so it seemed; for a long time after that, we were oppressed more severely still by weapons at home. Even these, we have shaken off too, but they must be wrenched out. If we cannot do this – I shall speak as is right for a senator and a Roman – let us die.[7]

A stark categorization of issues – life versus death, good versus evil, slavery versus freedom, and so on – forms an essential element in Cicero's rhetorical strategy throughout the *Philippics*. And this all-or-nothing approach was central to his characterization of Antony too:

> What is being decided is this: should Mark Antony be given the opportunity to crush the state, murder her loyal citizens, divide up the city, make presents of land to his bandits, and of subjugating the Roman people into slavery; or should he be allowed to do none of them. Do you hesitate what to do?[8]

It was a grossly embellished picture, as was the one he painted of Octavian at the other extreme – a boy of 'divine wisdom and courage'.[9] But such overstatements and exaggerations were the only way Cicero could hope to break through the senate's hesitation.

At the same time, however, the situation needed to be depicted in terms that were realistic and believable. Cicero's oratory needed to be clear, if it was to be persuasive. Antony's supporters were accusing Cicero of being a warmonger. Cicero, on the other hand, had to demonstrate why he was so opposed to peace: 'Why then do I not want peace?' he asked. 'Because it is disgraceful, because it is dangerous, because it is not possible.'[10]

His answer is expressed with both rhetorical anaphora and in an ascending tricolon. Anaphora occurs in the repetition of the word 'because' at the beginning of each clause. But the ascending tricolon is the division of the sentence into three parts that lead up to a climax. Not only did the words roll from Cicero's lips but also the arguments that followed hinged on these three words. Peace was disgraceful because it would not stick to the revered political value of constancy: to back down now would be a reversal of the senate's policy to date. It was dangerous because it would give positions of power to lawless and ruthless men. And it was impossible because war would only ever be deferred, and not dispelled; it was not peace that Cicero feared, 'but war wrapped up in the name of peace.'[11]

Even after the failed embassy returned, the senate refused to acknowledge full-scale war. They described the situation by another term, a 'tumult', which meant that the senate still did not recognize Antony formally as an enemy. Throughout February and March, therefore, Antony's supporters in the senate persevered in calling for peace negotiations. There was even a proposal for a second embassy, which would include Cicero as an ambassador; however, fortunately for Cicero, this mission never happened.

Nevertheless, appeals for peace continued to come in fast and furious – not just from Antony's supporters in the senate, but also from his friends in powerful provinces. They sent letters to the senate, and on 20 March another meeting was called to discuss these new calls. This was especially urgent because one of these men, Marcus Aemilius Lepidus (whom we shall meet again), was threatening to wage a war if his advice was not followed.

Cicero delivered his *Thirteenth Philippic* this day – a vehement renewal of his attack on peace. He had made other speeches in the meantime on topics connected with the war (his *Tenth*, *Eleventh* and *Twelfth Philippics*), but this was the first occasion that brought him back to the main topic of what to do about Antony. For it happened that Hirtius had sent Cicero a copy of a letter addressed both to him and Octavian. And in the letter, Antony openly called upon Hirtius and Octavian to revive their Caesarian faction: 'What is better?' he had asked '– for us to clash and thus make it easier for the Pompeian party to grow stronger, after they have been slaughtered on so many occasions, or for us to work together, so that we are not a joke to our enemies?'[12]

Antony was trying to knock down the senatorial alliance that Cicero had worked so hard to build, but Cicero was not going to let that happen. Instead, he vividly evoked the scene of what would happen if Antony and his supporters *did* win, in order to amplify the dangers facing the senate:

> Imagine their faces, especially Antony's clan, and the way they walk, look, express themselves, and breathe; and imagine their friends, some clinging to their sides, others walking ahead. How strong the smell of wine will be! Just think about their abusive and threatening mouths![13]

This was powerful visualization at its best. Cicero was going beyond threats; he was appealing to his audience's senses to play on every emotion of indignation and revulsion he could. Quintilian – an ardent orator and rhetorician writing in the first century AD – believed that the ability to place a picture before the audience's mind was a great gift, and Cicero, he said, 'surpassed everyone in this department'.[14]

The passion behind Cicero's *Philippics*, however, responded to more than just the rhetorical occasion; it reflected the struggle of a man caught up in a very real crisis. Yet it is important to note that Cicero *had* won some important victories along the way due to his concerted and continual appeals for war. Troops had been assembled, and a period of 'tumult' declared. Even as Cicero delivered the *Thirteenth Philippic*, Pansa was on his way to join Hirtius and Octavian in the fight – and he was taking four more legions with him. For Decimus Brutus was still being besieged by Antony after several months, and swift action was needed to save him. The battle was finally about to begin, and a clash between the opposing forces was now inevitable.

By mid April, Pansa and his legions had almost reached Hirtius and Octavian, when Antony's forces intercepted and attacked them just outside of Mutina. Pansa himself was seriously wounded; however it was only an initial setback. For Hirtius had predicted Antony's tactics and, with Octavian's help, performed a counter-attack on Antony's men as they made their retreat. This event was the first battle of Mutina on 15 April 43 BC, and everything looked set for a republican victory.

Back in Rome, the slow communications and uncertainties of war were causing panic and alarm. Initial reports said that Antony had been victorious. A rumour was circulating too, probably spread by Antony's supporters, which said Cicero was planning to seize power in the city. But both reports were false. On 20 April, one of the tribunes defended Cicero before a meeting of the people. Just a few hours later, it also emerged that Antony's forces had been the ones defeated; Antony himself was still alive, but he had lost nearly all his troops.

When the news reached Rome there was great joy in the city. The delighted populace carried Cicero from his house to the Capitoline hill, almost as if he was a triumphant general. And the next day, 21 April, Cicero delivered his *Fourteenth Philippic* to the senate. He reminded the senate that the war was not over yet – Decimus Brutus was still blockaded in Mutina, and Antony had still not been declared a formal enemy. Yet he ended this speech, the last one to survive, on a note of victory and compassionate reflection. It praised the men who had fallen in battle fighting on the senate's side, proposed honours for all the republican troops and suggested high distinctions for the two consuls and Octavian.

The senate adopted Cicero's proposals after the *Fourteenth Philippic* and, for a brief spell longer, his influence guided the state of affairs. For the second battle of Mutina was taking place as Cicero delivered his speech, and it produced another decisive victory for the republican side. After several months of entrapment, Decimus Brutus at last broke free from the blockade and his troops forced

Antony to retreat. The speed and danger of all these events meant that Cicero also finally attained the goal towards which he had been striving throughout the *Philippics*: on 26 April 43 BC the senate agreed to declare Antony and his men public enemies.

Cicero had lived up to his word: from December 44 to April 43 BC, he had spent every day and night in the service of the state, just as he said he would. The speeches he delivered are only a part of his tremendous output. The letters also flew from his hands and reached men stationed all over the empire: Greece, Asia, Africa, Spain and Gaul among them. And they all wrote back to him. Nothing happened anywhere without Cicero knowing about it. But now, in his own words, he 'reaped the greatest reward' for his 'many days of work and sleepless nights'.[15] And so, it is often said of these months that Cicero led the senate, or that he was the most influential man in Rome. Yet this implies an official position of supremacy, which Cicero did not have. Rather, it should be said that he fought a long and hard campaign for military action – and he won, at least for a limited period of time, for the battle was far from over.

CICERO'S GAMBLE

The campaign Cicero led against Antony represented the last throw of the dice in his political career and the fight for liberty. However, the success of this all-or-nothing gamble was not dependent on his actions alone – for three reasons. First, he needed the senate to continue aggressively against Antony; second, this was a war that required a strong military force and the co-operation of Rome's army commanders; finally, there was Octavian. He represented the biggest risk of all; however, his armies and support were vital for Cicero to raise an effective and united coalition against Antony. The plan itself was not impossible but, as events proved, its completion was out of Cicero's control.

The twin successes at Mutina had come at a huge cost to the republican side, for the consul Hirtius was killed fighting in the second battle. Furthermore, just a few days later, the consul Pansa died from the wounds he had received in his first skirmish with Antony. Had one of these men survived to lead their joint forces against Antony immediately, Cicero's gamble might have paid off. But now, as it waited to hold a re-election, the senate lacked consuls and firm direction. The result was a political paralysis – just at the moment when prompt and rigorous action was most needed to destroy what was left of Antony's political and military power. The consequences were disastrous.

For as long as Hirtius and Pansa had been alive, the consuls, steered by Cicero, had formed a bridge between moderate Caesarians (like themselves) and the liberators. However, after the consuls' death, the fragile foundations of Cicero's coalition in the senate were rocked. Old hostilities resurfaced, competition for the vacant consulships arose, and 'party politics' between Caesarians and Pompeians divided the republican front. Just over a month after the victories of Mutina, Cicero reflected gloomily on the failure of his plans for a united force against Antony: 'The senate was my weapon, but that has now fallen apart' – he told Decimus Brutus.[16]

Yet this Brutus was having his own problems in Gaul, for the men out in the field were also forced to reassess where their loyalties lay. And immediately after Mutina, when the deceased consuls' troops were summoned to help Decimus Brutus in pursuit of Antony, the inevitable happened: men and soldiers, who had been loyal to Caesar in his lifetime, refused to fight under one of his assassins. They turned instead to Octavian, who also now declared he had no desire to help Decimus Brutus. Brutus was forced to rely on his own, depleted forces – and these were not enough to prevent Antony from escaping across the Alps. The progress against Antony was proving slow and inefficient: 'It seems that the war has not been extinguished at all, but rather it has been inflamed', Cicero remarked in despair.[17]

By the time of May, one of Antony's supporters in Italy had succeeded in leading three legions to him. Antony himself was padding out his troops with ex-slaves, and he was now recruiting a powerful fighting force again. As Cicero soon found out from Decimus Brutus, Antony was also appealing to other military commanders in the immediate area: Lepidus in Transalpine Gaul, Pollio in Spain, and Plancus in the third district of Gaul known as Long-haired Gaul. The second risk in Cicero's gamble was looking set to fail: these men were all former Caesarians, and there was more to link them with Antony than there was to the republican cause.

To give an idea of the scale of the war, there were approximately forty-five legions operating in the west after Mutina: that is, over a quarter of a million men. Eleven of these legions were under Octavian; ten under Decimus Brutus; seven under Lepidus; and thirteen under Pollio, Plancus and other generals. Antony had the remaining four, and was dramatically understaffed. That is why he needed to win over his fellow Caesarians. And it was a huge blow to the republican cause when Lepidus announced his and his army's alliance with Antony at the end of May. For it meant that Antony's hand was equipped for war again: he and Lepidus had eleven legions between them. However, they did not need to act yet, for Antony and Lepidus could watch as the republican forces turned their own hands against themselves.

The key figure was Octavian. He knew that he stood to gain more from an alliance with the senate than he did from Antony, who had never seen him as an equal. However, the senate had become distinctly cold in its attitude towards Caesar's heir – from fear that he was becoming too ambitious for his age. Cicero, at least, was aware of the need to retain Octavian's support. Despite his misgivings about Octavian in the run-up to the fight against Antony, Cicero himself had vouched for the young man's loyalty in his *Fifth Philippic*, delivered at the beginning of the year. He had since championed his name, and voted to give the young man honours after Mutina, when the rest of the senate were prepared to overlook his co-operative efforts in the fight against Antony. But not everyone approved of Cicero's strategy.

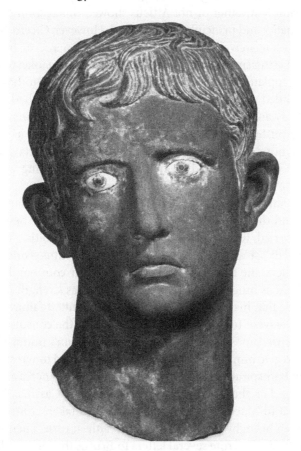

The young Octavian (later called Augustus): a boy of 'divine wisdom and courage'
(© The Trustees of the British Museum).

As early as May, there was a rumour that the nineteen-year-old wanted one of the consulships that had been made vacant by the deaths of Hirtius and Pansa. Marcus Brutus, the chief liberator, wrote to Cicero from Greece on 15 May, rebuking him in no uncertain terms: 'I am worried about the consulship, in case that Caesar of yours thinks it will be a short climb to becoming consul – seeing that he has climbed so far already off the back of your decrees.'[18] However, his criticisms struck a more personal note behind Cicero's back. Around the same time, Brutus wrote to their joint friend Atticus: 'You say that even now Cicero is afraid of the remnants of a civil war . . . but we fear death, exile and poverty too much. They seem to be the ultimate evils in Cicero's mind and – provided that he has someone to do what he wants, who worships and adores him – he does not object to servitude so long as it brings *him* honour.'[19]

We do not know whether or not Atticus showed this scathing indictment of Cicero's personality and principles to his friend. However, Cicero was aware that his support of Octavian was under negative scrutiny. It may even have been in the context of such criticism that Cicero made an unfortunate joke: Octavian ought to be 'praised, applauded and pushed' – he was rumoured to have said. There was a pun intended on the double meaning of the word 'pushed' – in the Latin *tollendum*. Octavian could be pushed further in his ambitions (i.e. elevated), or he could be pushed aside (i.e. discarded). The remark was a 'bit of silliness', Cicero replied, not denying that he had said it. But, when Octavian heard of it, the young man was not amused: he had no intention of being 'pushed' and, as the events of the next few months demonstrated, he meant it.[20]

Cicero may have been able to shrug off rumours of Octavian's detachment with himself and the senate for now; however, by mid June he was becoming increasingly worried. Referring to Octavian's ongoing ambition for the consulship, he admitted: 'We are the play-things, [Marcus] Brutus – one minute at the will of the soldiers, the next at the arrogance of their commanders. Each man demands to hold as much power in the state as he has strength in his troops.'[21] Cicero could see that his whole policy was on the brink of failure. He sent endless letters to Octavian to dissuade him from seeking the consulship. But, try as he might, there was no way of changing the young man's mind: if the senators did not agree to give him the position, Octavian intended to wrest it from them.

As affairs in Italy spiralled out of control, Cicero looked increasingly to Marcus Brutus for help. For the main liberators, Brutus and Cassius, had effected a dramatic revival in Macedonia and Syria; each had taken control of powerful provinces, which brought them armies and wealth in turn. Their legions could save Rome, and Cicero wrote several letters to Brutus throughout June and July, appealing to him desperately to come back and lead the fight in Italy – to finish what he had started. But he did not come. And, without backup, there was little the senate could do when Octavian marched his army upon Rome to obtain the consulship he desired.

On 19 Sextilis (the month which was later named August), the youngest consul in Roman history assumed his post, taking a distant relative, Quintus Pedius, as his colleague. We do not know how Cicero felt any more, for his last surviving letter was sent on 27 July 43 BC. In this letter, Cicero had still hoped he could control Octavian, but he expressed his deep nerves for the first time: he was 'in the greatest distress', he admitted to Brutus.[22] For he could not stand by the promise he had made in the *Fifth Philippic*: his guarantee to the senate that Octavian could be trusted.

This had been Cicero's greatest gamble of all. He had always been fond of nurturing protégés, and the young genuinely seemed to respect Cicero – Octavian had even referred to Cicero as a 'father' in the early days of their association.[23] Cicero may have seen Octavian as another in the line of young men to whom he had devoted his time and the resources of his wisdom; there had even been some rumour that Octavian intended to make Cicero a consul with him. However, none of this materialized. For the four months which separate Cicero's last full letter and his death, we can only guess how Cicero felt as he watched his efforts come to nothing.

THE DEATH OF CICERO

One small fragment of Cicero's voice helps us accompany him to his villa in Tusculum, where Plutarch tells us he moved, and probably stayed, after Octavian's return. All Cicero could do was to thank Octavian for the special permission he had received, allowing him to leave Rome and the senate behind him: 'I rejoice at your provision of leave for two reasons: because you both forgive what is past and offer protection for the future.'[24] Yet even in these last unheroic words, Cicero was being too optimistic in his assessment of the young consul.

About two months later, Octavian marched northwards, ostensibly to fight Antony's forces; yet it is unlikely this was ever his real intention. For Antony had recently succeeded in winning over the remaining Caesarian commanders, Pollio and Plancus; now, with Lepidus acting as a mediator, Octavian joined him too. On 27 November 43 BC, on a little island in the middle of the river Reno near Bononia (Bologna), an event out of all proportion to its humble location took place: Octavian, Antony and Lepidus became 'triumvirs for the restoration of the Republic' – a pact known to historians as the 'second triumvirate'.

However, their 'job title' was nothing more than a cover for what the triumvirs really wanted: power and revenge against their opponents. Indeed, the restoration of the Republic figured little in their plans. The three men parcelled up the empire between themselves, appointed magistrates for the next five years, and planned to lead the Caesarian faction in avenging their leader's assassination. To do this, they needed money and land so that they could pay their soldiers and settle veterans. And in one fell swoop they exacted money and retribution: they signed the largest death warrant ancient Rome had ever seen – for the first time since Sulla's reign of terror, a proscription list was published.

According to the later Greek historian Appian, the proscription lists contained the names of about two thousand equestrians and three hundred senators. Loyalty to friends and family counted for nothing, and Octavian reluctantly agreed as Antony called for the deaths of four men in particular: Marcus Tullius Cicero, Quintus Tullius Cicero and their two sons. Antony did not just want to kill his enemy; he wanted to eliminate the entire family name.[25]

Cicero was in Tusculum with his brother and nephew when they heard the news of the proscriptions – the family quarrel of the previous years evidently forgotten. And, together, they apparently set out towards one of Cicero's villas by the coast. Their plan was to set sail and join Marcus Brutus in Macedonia, where the young Marcus Cicero was now fighting too. But Quintus and his son made the fatal decision to return home – to gather more money for the long journey ahead. Plutarch tells us that the brothers parted in tears and that they hoped to be reunited again soon; however, Quintus and his son were betrayed by their servants on the way, and were killed.

As for Cicero, his own death was a moment he had seen coming for over a year: in June 44 BC, he had written a letter to Atticus in which he expressed his concerns about Antony and made his wish for a noble end.[26] But even in these last hours, to judge from Plutarch's account, Cicero's characteristic indecision and hesitation caused him to turn this way and that. Plutarch's is the fullest description to survive – complete with tales of ravens, the birds of death, and dreadful omens. But one of the barest versions, written by the Roman historian Livy, is perhaps the most poignant:

> First he fled to Tusculum, then he set out cross-country to Formiae, intending to board ship at the port of Caieta. From there he set out to sea several times, but one minute he was carried back by adverse winds, the next he was unable to endure the tossing of the ship as the dark waves swelled. Finally, tiredness of both the flight and his life overwhelmed him, and he returned inland to his villa, which was a little more than a mile from the sea. 'I shall die,' he said 'in the country I have often saved.'[27]

The stage was now set for his finest hour: the moment Cicero offered his bare neck to his assassins. He was accompanied only by his slaves, who remained loyal to the end. They even tried to rescue him, and would have fought bravely to save his life – if Cicero had let them. Their fidelity must surely stand as a testament to Cicero's own generosity as a master; for it has often been noted that his brother Quintus' slaves were not so dependable. Indeed, it was allegedly one of Quintus' freedmen, called Philologus, who betrayed Cicero's escape route as the assassins approached. And as the rest of the slaves carried their master towards the sea, Cicero's murderers chased fast behind them.

His killers were led by the centurion Herennius and a military officer called Popillius, whom he had once even defended in court. The savage pair wanted the bounty on Cicero's head and the fame for his murder, but (according to one of the stories which circulated) even these warlike men hesitated and trembled as Cicero poised still for their strike. Appian adds that it took three blows and some sawing through to sever Cicero's head from his body, but in the event the deed was done. And the gruesome parcel of his remains made their journey back to the *rostra*, for Cicero to make his final appearance on the speaker's platform at Rome.

We do not know how Terentia, the young Marcus or Atticus reacted to these events; we can only imagine that Terentia (who is said to have lived until she was over a hundred years old) grieved for her former husband and the father of her son. The younger Marcus himself was safe for now in Greece, where he continued his father's fight for the republican cause. As for Atticus, being diplomatic to the end and everyone's friend, he probably did not dare show his sorrow openly before the triumvirs. His lifelong policy of abstaining from political affairs served him well, for he survived his friend for another ten years, and he enjoyed a position of favour among the new regime until his dying day.

However, the death of Cicero allegedly caused strong reactions back in Rome. Antony and Fulvia rejoiced, for their hatred ran deep. Cicero had led the fight against Antony, he had delivered the orations that cursed his career, and then published them for all to see. But Antony's stepfather too had perished because of Cicero; he had been one of the conspirators executed for his role in the Catilinarian conspiracy – and his death must have made a heavy impression on Antony, who was only a young man at the time. As for Fulvia, she had been married to Cicero's great enemy Clodius, and she had wept before the court as Cicero defended Milo for his murder.

Popillius and Herennius also took great delight in the twin rewards they reaped – money and the favour of one of Rome's new leaders. In fact, Popillius was said to have been so proud of his role that he advertised it to the world. He later set up a statue of himself to commemorate the murder, and next to it he placed Cicero's severed head. Yet the general feeling at Rome was one of horror and indignation. Pomponia, the sister of Atticus and Quintus' ex-wife, was rumoured to have exacted a brutal revenge on the treacherous Philologus: she compelled him to cut off his own flesh piece by piece, roast it and eat it. In the forum, too, men were blinded with tears. They could scarcely lift their eyes to look upon Cicero's remains; and those who did 'saw not Cicero; but the monstrous reflection of Antony's soul'.[28]

We do not need to believe all of these stories: many are certainly exaggerated, and others may not be true. Yet the extremities of triumph and defeat, and of love and hate, which are reflected in these accounts, serve as powerful reminders – both of the emotions Cicero felt throughout his own life and of those he inspired in the men and women who knew him.

Epilogue

The Head and the Hands of Cicero

REMEMBERING CICERO

He lived sixty-three years, so that, disregarding his violent end, his death still cannot be regarded as an early one. His genius was happy both in his works and the rewards of his works, and he too was prosperous and fortunate for a long time; but time and again on that long course of happiness, great blows struck him: exile, the collapse of the political side on which he had stood, the death of his daughter, and his own sad and bitter end. Of all of these adversities, he bore none as a man should – except his death. Yet it could be argued that even this was not entirely undeserved, because his victorious enemy only made him suffer as much as he would have made his enemy suffer, had he been the victorious one. However, if anyone wanted to weigh up his virtues against his vices, they would find that he was a great and memorable man. To sing his praises, it would take Cicero to praise them.

(Livy, *The History of Rome* 120)[1]

With Livy's obituary – one of the many accounts of Cicero's death collected by the elder Seneca in the first century AD – we are reminded of the highs and lows of Cicero's life, as well as the energy and determination that drove him through these exciting and dangerous times. From the glorious days that took him swiftly to the top of Rome's political ladder, through the public and private torments of the 60s and 50s BC, to the days of civil war, the domination of Caesar and finally to his last fight for liberty, Cicero's life was documented every step of the way – and nearly always by his own hand. And so if, like Livy, we were tempted to weigh Cicero's virtues against his faults, this one observation would be important to bear in mind: Cicero the man and Cicero the writer are one and the same, and inseparable.

As recent scholarship has reminded us, we have an unrivalled access to Cicero – but 'we have access to Cicero in different ways at different points in his career'.[2] As a young man Cicero wrote poetry and works on rhetoric; as a rising politician in the 70s and early 60s, he published a vast array of the speeches he delivered in the courts; while the speeches he published during the periods of his praetorship and consulship (66–63 BC) were a blend of political and forensic orations.

In these years, Cicero tested his hand as an epic poet before he turned towards the philosophical writings of 55 BC onwards. It was only in the period from 46 to 43 BC that Cicero returned as an orator – first to flatter Caesar, and then to defend his beloved Republic against the tyranny of Antony. How we react to Cicero, then, depends very much on how we read Cicero's writings, as well as which ones we read. Taken individually, his works only allow us to see Cicero as *he* wanted us to see him at that particular moment in time, and in a way that suited that particular genre of writing. But when they are read side by side, Cicero's writings not only provide us with a detailed narrative of his life but also they enable us to see the fuller picture behind his words and actions.

Throughout these times (68–43 BC), Cicero wrote an immense number of letters, some of them extraordinarily frank and revealing, which he did not intend to be assembled and published in their entirety. It was only after Cicero's death that Tiro embarked on a programme of publications to glorify his deceased master's name: he edited some of Cicero's public works, including the speeches *Against Verres* and a treatise (now lost) *On Glory*; he also circulated Cicero's notes for some of the speeches he had delivered but not published. It is possible, too, that Tiro edited a collection of Cicero's jokes. But most important of all were his huge efforts in collecting and publishing the many volumes which contain Cicero's private correspondence.[3]

As we saw at the beginning of this study, the array of Cicero's published works have had a profound impact on how scholars, ancient and modern, have interpreted Cicero's life. Yet it was the letters that have arguably had the greatest impact on how Cicero has been remembered. It is striking indeed that Livy lists the death of Cicero's beloved daughter Tullia alongside his sufferings in exile and war, and that he passes the verdict 'he bore none as a man should'. It reminds us that we have intruded on Cicero's personal life – his 'inner world' so to speak – in a way that we rarely, if ever, can when we study an historical character. We can witness his pain and hear his despair; at the same time, we can find his whinging irritating, his emotions overbearing, and his bragging intolerable. But they do provide an insight into Cicero as a man. And if this book has gone too far in defending his motives and actions, it is because this position has been too frequently overlooked.

However, even if we have to tread carefully in using the evidence of Cicero as the benchmark for assessing his life and times, it cannot be denied that Augustus was right, years later, to remember Cicero as a master of words and a patriot. Cicero loved Rome's distinguished history and her traditions, and his pride in these was intimately connected with his literary output: the practice and history of Roman oratory, religious practices and political developments were all important areas which, in the eyes of men like Cicero, set Rome apart from every other culture.

Only the intellectual milieu of Athens could compare or compete with that of Rome, and Cicero was a self-confessed philhellene: 'Everything I have achieved,' he once told his brother, 'I owe to those studies and the disciplines which have been handed down to us in the literature and teachings of Greece.'[4] But by producing a corpus of literature to rival the pre-eminence of Greek oratory and philosophy, Cicero believed he was performing a great service for his country. Not even his contemporary Asinius Pollio, who was elsewhere highly critical of Cicero, could deny him this claim: 'his works will remain immortal for the rest of time' was his correct verdict.[5]

In this way, the new man from Arpinum had achieved what he had set out to do back in his youth, when he was advised to change his name: he had instead made the name 'Cicero' as distinguished as any in Roman history, and the word had travelled far from the humble roots of a 'chickpea'. For Quintilian, at least, the name of Cicero was to be remembered as 'the name of eloquence'.[6]

THE DEATH OF THE REPUBLIC

Cicero, however, did not just speak and think patriotically; as Livy reminds us above, the Republic was an ideal for which Cicero was willing to kill, as much as he was willing to be killed. And in this way, Livy also alerts us to a second fundamental problem that we face when we attempt to make an assessment of Cicero's life and character: he belonged to an age in which political and legal battles were literally fought to the death; there is no point judging Cicero outside the standards of his own society.

In his lifetime, Cicero had ordered the execution of men who had conspired against the constitution, triumphed at the assassination of Caesar and led the clarion call for war against the forces of Antony. But in his death, Cicero's severed head and hands stood as a powerful testament to his determination to oppose those who tried to subvert the *status quo*. He had perished, as he said he would, with his neck out-stretched in defence of liberty and the Republic. He may only have entered the fray in defence of an ideal that was past saving, but Cicero had resolved to fight to the end rather than submit to tyranny.

Sadly, however, his final fight was one which Cicero had lost; and although Cicero had declared he would be prepared to die, if it meant he might leave the Roman people free, this was a dream that could never be fulfilled. For the civil wars and bloodshed of the past century did not end with the proscriptions and the death of Cicero. Indeed, the proscriptions served mainly to provide the triumvirs with the resources they needed to exact the revenge they desired. And when they had got what they needed, the first scores to settle on their agenda were those against Caesar's assassins.

Soon afterwards, in 42 BC, Brutus and Cassius were defeated at the battle of Philippi in Macedonia. A few years later, in 39 BC, the last standing republican, Sextus Pompeius, the son of the famous general, was also pacified – only to be executed later in 35 BC. And in a chilling echo of the notorious first alliance between Caesar, Pompey and Crassus, when the triumvirs' objectives were achieved, they turned their weapons against each other. However, this time, their battle simultaneously drove the final nail into the coffin of the Republic that Cicero had known and loved.

Over a decade earlier, Cicero had held high hopes for Octavian, believing that he was the only man who could save Rome from the domination of Antony. And, in 31 BC, *this* predication finally came true, even if his hopes for the Republic never did. By this time, Lepidus had gradually been pushed into the background, leaving the two former enemies to pit their might in a great struggle for supremacy – Antony had now taken control of the eastern territories, while Octavian stood his ground in the west. Each man wanted supreme power, but the Roman Empire was not big enough for them both. The naval battle of Actium, fought just off the Greek coast, marked the end of their rivalries once and for all: Marcus Agrippa, Octavian's friend and lieutenant, routed Antony's forces and sealed a decisive victory. The result was that, less than a year later in 30 BC, both Antony and Cleopatra were dead – each killed by their own hands.

Octavian's success left him as the undisputed ruler of the Roman world, and a war-weary senate did nothing to prevent him. He claimed to have created a 'restored Republic', but it was not a constitution that Cicero would have recognized. Now there was just one statesman at the helm, and he was guiding the metaphorical ship of state into the tides of a new era: the period of Rome's emperors.[7]

However, there was one important feature that did remain the same in the new Republic: the ladder of offices still provided a career path of sorts for Rome's ambitious politicians. Moreover, in 30 BC, this senate had a very familiar name for its consul: Marcus Tullius Cicero (the Younger). Marcus had fought alongside the troops of Brutus and Cassius in Macedonia, and he had continued the fight for the Republic under Sextus Pompeius. But he had survived with his life and was pardoned by the triumvirs in 39 BC. And in the year of his consulship, it fell upon the consul Marcus Tullius Cicero to announce the death of Mark Antony, his father's assassin, to the senate of Rome.

The 'poetic justice' in this final scene has not gone unnoticed: during the younger Cicero's consulship, the senate allegedly tore down the statues of Antony, annulled all the honours that had ever been paid to him, and also voted that no member of the Antonian clan should ever be given the name Marcus. 'In this way,' Plutarch remarked, 'divine power granted Cicero's family the final fulfilment of Antony's punishment.'[8] And this remained Cicero's legacy throughout the rule of Octavian, who from 27 BC renamed himself Augustus (meaning 'majestic'): it may have been impolite to sound Cicero's achievements too loudly in Augustan Rome, but he could be remembered as the man who stood up against Antony.

FINAL VERDICTS

More, and much more, could be written about Cicero's last fight and death at the hands of Antony, as indeed it was by the schoolboys, poets and historians who studied it in the subsequent generations. Livy was one of these writers and, in the quotation at the top of this chapter, we see him grappling to come to terms with the questions that have plagued historians of all ages: was Cicero a success or a political failure? Did Cicero matter? Was he prosperous, courageous and honest? Or was he insecure, cowardly and ruthless? And, finally, did his virtues outweigh his vices, or did his faults – visible to all who knew him – detract from the qualities and achievements that had greatly facilitated his career?

These are all big questions, and the ways in which scholars of the last two millennia have interpreted Cicero's life is a topic too large in scope for the present study. Yet the fact that consensus has rarely, if ever, been achieved should perhaps alert us to the fact that there can never be any definitive answers. Indeed, it reminds us that we, in the twenty-first century, are hardly qualified to pass judgements on what a man said, or how he behaved, in ancient times. For this reason, I shall not attempt to summarize Cicero's achievements, or to evaluate his character; as Cicero himself once acutely observed when addressing Caesar on the topic of posthumous reputations: 'Among those yet unborn there will always be, as there has been among us, strong disagreement: some will sing your praises to the skies; others perhaps will find something missing – and something great at that.'[9]

On balance, Livy concluded that 'to sing his praises, it would take Cicero to praise them'. And perhaps on these grounds alone we can pass some kind of verdict on Cicero: as an orator, author and a thinker he was, indeed – as he emerges today from his speeches, letters and treatises – a 'great and memorable man'. Caesar, too, had to admit it: Cicero's achievements were worth more than any military triumph, 'for he advanced the boundaries of the Roman genius where others only extended the frontiers of her empire.'[10]

Appendix 1: Glossary

For more comprehensive information and suggestions for further reading on the items listed below, as well as on all topics connected to the classical world, see S. Hornblower and A. Spawforth (2003), *Oxford Classical Dictionary*, Oxford: Oxford University Press (3rd edn, revised). For more on the rhetorical terms and devices, see D. E. Orton and R. D. Anderson (eds, tr.) (1998), *Heinrich Lausberg: A Handbook of Literary Rhetoric*, Leiden: Brill.

Aedile	The third (and only optional) of the annual magistracies, below **consul** and **praetor**. There were four aediles elected annually in the **assembly**: two were elected by the tribal assembly (curule aediles) and two were elected in the people's assembly (plebeian aediles); all were responsible for the corn supply, putting on the public games, and for the general administration of the city. Minimum age: 36.
Allies	The *socii* or Italian communities linked to Rome by treaties of alliance. They provided Rome with men to fight in her campaigns and received certain benefits in return; they revolted in the **social war** (91–88 BC) and won their goal of citizenship as a result.
Anaphora	A rhetorical term describing the repetition of the same word at the beginning of successive clauses for emphasis.
Assembly	There were four types of assembly in ancient Rome: (1) the centuriate assembly was an assembly of Roman citizens divided into 193 centuries (military units); it met in the **campus martius** and elected **consuls, praetors** and **censors**. This assembly gave far greater authority to the rich, with birth and wealth having a dominant influence. (2) The tribal assembly was made up of 35 tribes: 4 urban and 31 rural. This was the most common type of

	assembly, which was responsible for electing the lower magistracies (two **aediles**, and **quaestors**); it was also more representative of the people than the centuriate assembly. (3) The curiate assembly: less common than the rest, it conferred **imperium** on the **magistrates**. (4) The people's assembly, which was **plebeians** only; it elected the **tribunes**, two **aediles**, and passed laws (**plebiscita**).
Augur	One of fifteen members on the board of augurs, who interpreted religious **auspices** (i.e. signs or omens that signalled the gods' approval or disapproval of an official action, such as an election or the passage of a law).
Auspices	See **augur**.
Bona Dea	The Good Goddess, worshipped only by women; the annual festival was held in December and it was hosted by the wife of either a **consul** or a **praetor**.
Boni	See '**good men**'.
Campus martius	The 'field of Mars', a floodplain to the north-west of the **forum**, beside the river Tiber. It was used for military training and for elections.
Censor	One of two **magistrates** elected every five years for a maximum duration of eighteen months. By custom, censors were ex-**consuls**, although the position was not part of the **ladder of offices**. They performed the census of all adult male citizens and reviewed the list of senators and **equestrians**.
Client	See **patron**.
Cognomen	The third part of a Roman's name, akin to an inherited nickname. Not all Romans had them; they tended to be the preserve of grander citizens (although some prominent Romans also lacked *cognomina* in Cicero's day).
Collegium/collegia	A college/colleges of men who had a common locality, trade or craft; often organized for political purposes.
Colony	An officially founded settlement, usually in Italy, inhabited by Roman citizens.
Concord of the orders (*concordia ordinum*)	Cicero's ideal of a harmony among the orders of Roman society, especially the senatorial and **equestrian** ranks.

Conference of Luca	The name given to the meeting held at Luca in April 56 BC, when Pompey, Caesar and Crassus renewed the alliance known as the '**first triumvirate**'.
Consul	The top in the **ladder of offices**; two consuls held office for the calendar year (from 1 January to 31 December). Minimum age: 42.
Consular	The term to describe an ex-**consul**: the consulars held a position of great influence in the **senate** and were asked for their opinion immediately after the consuls had spoken.
Contio	The name given to a meeting of the Roman people summoned by a **magistrate**.
Cursus honorum	See **ladder of offices**.
Curule chair	An ivory chair or stool, and a symbol of authority, which could only be used by curule **magistrates**: the **consuls, praetors** and the two curule aediles (see **aediles**).
Dictator	In the Early **Republic**, the dictator was a **magistrate** with supreme authority, appointed in times of crisis for a maximum of six months. The office was revived in the Late **Republic** by Sulla and Caesar for their own ends; Caesar was made a 'perpetual dictator' in 44 BC.
Dignitas	'Dignity' – the standing and respect that was owed to a man of good birth, wealth or high office.
Divinatio	A preliminary hearing in trials, conducted when more than one prosecutor came forward to undertake a criminal prosecution.
Equestrians	Members of the Roman middle class (the Equestrian order) who were not senators. These men were very wealthy; there was a property qualification of 400,000 **sesterces**. Unlike senators, however, they were allowed to engage in trade and some were also **tax farmers**.
Extortion court	The first permanent court of the Roman people, where citizens and provincials could recover damages suffered under oppressive **magistrates** (particularly provincial governors).
Fasces	The bundles of rods carried by a **magistrate**'s **lictors** as an emblem of his **imperium**.

'First triumvirate'	The name used by historians to describe the informal arrangement between Pompey, Caesar and Crassus, in 59 BC (renewed at the **conference of Luca** in 56 BC).
Freedman	An ex-slave. A freedman would normally remain a dependant of his former master and would become one of his **clients**.
Forum	The central area of Rome and the heart of political and legal activity.
'Good men'	The **boni**: a term used by Cicero to describe wealthy, respectable men who supported the traditional authority of the **senate** (cf. **optimates**).
Imperator	'Commander' of a Roman army; in the Late **Republic** troops hailed their general an *imperator* following a military victory and it was often the first step towards earning a **supplicatio** or a **triumph**.
Imperium	The power held by either a **consul**, **praetor** or a promagistrate (**proconsul** or **propraetor**). It entailed the right to command an army and to issue orders.
Interrex, interreges	The **magistrate**/magistrates in charge in periods when there were no regular magistrates in place.
Invective	Bold and abusive criticism of a political or legal opponent.
Ladder of office	The name given to the usual sequence of a man's progression from **quaestor, aedile, praetor** to **consul**.
Legate	An assistant to a provincial governor or military commander; also the name given to ambassadors.
Liberators	The titled adopted by Caesar's assassins in the aftermath of the Ides of March.
Lictor	An attendant upon a **magistrate** with **imperium**. A **consul** had twelve lictors and each carried **fasces**.
Magistrate	The holder of a public office (technically, however, the **tribunes** did not qualify as magistrates); **consuls, praetors, censors** and curule **aediles** were known as curule magistrates.
Master of the horse	The deputy and assistant of the **dictator**.
New man (*novus homo*)	The first man of his family to enter the **senate**, he lacked senatorial ancestors.
Nobles (*nobiles*)	A descendant of a **consul** through the male family line. Both **plebeians** and **patricians** could be nobles, as could the descendants of men who had ennobled

their family (e.g. Cicero was not noble, but his son was).

Optimates Optimate men were aristocrats (the 'best men') who held conservative opinions and favoured the authority of the **senate**; they also called themselves **boni** ('**good men**') in contrast to **populists** (*populares* in Latin), who championed the rights of the **people**.

Otium cum dignitate A Ciceronian catchphrase meaning 'peace with tranquillity'; it signified domestic peace within the state combined with the **dignitas** owed to its leaders.

Patricians Members of a very select group of Roman families: it was believed that they were descended from the first 100 senators (*patres*) chosen by Romulus, the first king of Rome.

Patron Rome's wealthier men who offered financial, legal or military protection to poorer men: their **clients**, who performed a number of services in return (e.g. clients would attend the morning greeting at their patron's house, as well as vote and canvass for him and his friends).

People The collective body of male citizens over the age of 17.

Plebeians/plebs All Romans who were not **patricians**; the term plebs is also used to describe the mass population of the city of Rome (i.e. the citizens who were not in the senatorial or **equestrian** classes).

Plebiscita Laws passed in the **people's assembly**; these laws were binding, with or without the **senate**'s approval, following a law passed in 287 BC.

Pontifex (pl. *pontifices*) A pontiff or priest of the **pontifical college**; their president was called the *pontifex maximus* (the 'chief priest').

Pontifical college Board of 15 *pontifices* (see *pontifex*) responsible for the proper performance of Roman state religion.

Populists Politicians who set out to win the favour of the **people** and used their power, often in ways considered controversial or harmful by more conservative politicians (the **optimates**), who nicknamed them *populares* ('people pleasers'). They did not form a political 'party'.

Praeteritio	A rhetorical device by which a speaker emphasizes a point by claiming that he will 'pass over it'.
Praetor	The second highest magistracy on the **ladder of offices**; eight praetors held office for the calendar year (from 1 January to 31 December). Their duties mainly involved presiding over the law-courts, both in civil and criminal suits. Minimum age: 39.
Proconsul	A **magistrate** who was not a **consul**, but who was given a consul's authority to command an army or govern a province (normally after he had served a year's term as a consul).
Propraetor	A magistrate who was not a **praetor**, but who was given a praetor's authority to command an army or govern a province (normally after he had served a year's term as a praetor).
Proscriptions	The publication of lists of names of men who automatically became outlaws (and could be killed with impunity); their property was forfeited and auctioned off. These lists are associated with Sulla in 82 BC and the **second triumvirate** in 43 BC.
Quaestor	The first rung on the **ladder of offices**; 20 quaestors held office annually and they were responsible for the financial administration of Rome and the provinces. Once a man had been a quaestor, he became a member of the **senate** for life. Minimum age: 30.
Republic	From the Latin words *res publica*, meaning the 'public matter', it generally means the state, the government; but it also represented an ideal of a mixed constitution.
Rostra	The speaker's platform in the west end of the **forum** (in front of the **senate** house), from where **magistrates** addressed the people. It was named after the prows (the *rostra*) of the captured enemy ships which adorned it.
Second triumvirate	The name used by historians to describe the appointment of Antony, Octavian and Lepidus as triumvirs (a board of three men) for the restoration of the Republic in 43 BC
Senate	The supreme council of the Roman state and the only permanent political organ. After Sulla,

it consisted of 600 men (later raised to 900 by Caesar), who automatically gained membership after serving as **quaestors**. All ex-**magistrates** were senators (except for those expelled by the **censors**). The role of the senate was to advise its magistrates; it also assigned provinces, negotiated with foreign embassies. The senate could not pass legislation but it could propose bills which would be passed as laws if they received the vote of the people. Its most famous decree was the **ultimate decree** (the *senatus consultum ultimum*), which was passed at moments of crisis. This decree stated that the consuls had 'to see to it that the state came to no harm', but it did not specify what actions a magistrate could legally condone.

Sesterces	The basic reckoning of the Roman monetary system. To qualify in the **equestrian** order, and thus be eligible for election onto the **ladder of offices**, a man needed to possess 400,000 sesterces.
Social war	See **allies**.
Supplicatio	A vote of thanksgiving by the **senate** to a **magistrate** (normally an **imperator**) for victories against the enemies of Rome.
Tax farmers	Private businessmen of **equestrian** rank whose companies leased from the state the right to collect taxes in Rome's provinces. Contracts were awarded by a process of auctioning to the highest bidder.
Treasurers	Originally the treasurers were treasury officials, but from 70 BC they were one of the three classes of jurors, below the **senators** and **equestrians** in wealth and rank.
Tribune (of the plebs)	One of ten annually elected officers whose responsibility it was to protect the interests of the **plebs**. Only plebeians could act as tribunes and, unlike other offices, their year of duty ran from 10 December to 9 December. A tribune could initiate legislation, had the authority to summon the **senate**, and could veto (ban) any proposal that they believed to be against the interests of the **people**. These powers gave them great political importance,

	even though they were not considered **magistrates** on the **ladder of offices.**
Tricolon	A rhetorical term describing the grouping of three words or phrases into a unit for emphasis.
Triumph	The ceremonial procession awarded to successful military commanders after a major victory (typically at least 5,000 enemy should have been killed).
Triumvirs	Boards of three established for varying roles and duties in the functioning of the **Republic.** The so-called '**first triumvirate**' was not a triumvirate in the normal sense, because the board was meant to be elected by the citizen-body. The **second triumvirate** was duly elected and their roles as triumvirs were officially recognized (and shown on coinage from the period).
Ultimate decree	See **senate.**

Appendix 2: Principal Greek and Roman Authors

Reliable translations of all the following works, which also reproduce the original Greek and Latin texts on the facing pages, can be found in the Loeb Classical Library, Harvard Classical Press. In addition, the principal authors can be read in either the Penguin Classics or the Oxford World's Classics series. Both are recommended as they come with good introductions to the texts they produce; although the additional explanatory notes in the Oxford texts offer valuable assistance. Nearly all the works mentioned here are now also available in translation online; in particular, see LacusCurtius (http://penelope.uchicago.edu/Thayer/E/Roman/Texts/) and the Perseus Digital Library (www.perseus.tufts.edu).

Appian	(c. AD 95–165) A Greek historian, living and writing at Rome, in the second century AD. He wrote a Roman history in 24 chapters: chapters 13–17 form the *Civil War*, which is the only surviving account that deals fully with the period from Tiberius Gracchus' death to the aftermath of Caesar's assassination (133–35 BC).
Asconius	(c. AD 3–88) Many of his works have been lost, but his commentaries on five of Cicero's speeches survive.
Cassius Dio	(c. AD 164–230) A Greek senator and historian. He wrote an 80-book history of Rome in Greek. The whole work does not survive, but we do have the portion detailing events from 69 BC to AD 46.
Caesar	(c.100–44 BC) Cicero's famous contemporary. He wrote on the *Gallic War* and the *Civil War*. These publications, together with three further works written by his unknown comrades (the *Alexandrian War*, the *African War*, and the *Spanish War*) provide a military history spanning, almost continuous, from 58–45 BC.

Cicero	(106–43 BC) See the chronology of Cicero's life for a list of his works and their dates of publication.
Cornelius Nepos	(c.110–24 BC) A Latin biographer, who wrote a series of 16 books *On Famous Men*, including the valuable *Life of Atticus*.
Pliny the Elder	(c. AD 23–79) A Roman author, best known for his 37-book encyclopaedia, *Natural History*.
Plutarch	(c. AD 50–120) A Greek biographer. He wrote the series of *Lives*, which included treatments of Marius, Sulla, Pompey, Crassus, Caesar, Cato and Brutus, alongside the highly precious record of Cicero's life.
Polybius	(c.200–118 BC) A Greek historian who lived in Rome, after first arriving as a prisoner of war. He wrote the *Histories* in 40 books (a significant amount of which survive).
Pseudo-Sallust	(unknown) Probably an Augustan rhetorician living in the first century AD. Author of the *Invective Against Cicero*.
Quintilian	(c. AD 35–100) An orator and authority on the nature of rhetoric. He wrote a 12-book treatise *On the Orator's Education*.
[Quintus Cicero]	(102–43 BC) Often cited as the author of the *Handbook for Electioneering*, although its authorship is disputed.
Sallust	(c.86–35 BC) A Roman politician and later historian. A slightly younger contemporary of Cicero, he wrote *Catiline's War*, *The Jugurthine War* and *Histories*.
Seneca (the Elder)	(c.50 BC – AD 40) A Latin writer, originally from Spain. He wrote the *Declamations* (the rhetorical exercises used for training in public speaking).
Suetonius	(c. AD 70–130) A Roman biographer, writing a century after Cicero. He wrote the *Lives of the Roman Emperors*, beginning with a *Life of Julius Caesar*.
Velleius Paterculus	(c.19 BC – AD 31) A Roman writer, and author of *History of Rome* (written in the first century AD), which was the second in a two-volume book, and the only one to survive.
Valerius Maximus	(flourished AD 30) A Roman historian and moralist who composed a handbook of historical examples for use in the schools of rhetoric: *Memorable Deeds and Sayings*.

Notes

The titles of ancient works are given in full, followed by the traditional citation (where appropriate) of book number, chapter and paragraph. For ease of reference, Cicero's letters are numbered according to the Loeb Classical Library editions of Shackleton Bailey, which are the most recent and complete translations available (see the bibliography for further details). The traditional number is given alongside to provide readers with the full information. All translations in this book are my own. I have sometimes deviated slightly from a strictly literal rendering of Greek and Latin passages to ease the flow of the English; for the same reason, I have also adapted the punctuation to the needs of a modern reader.

Notes to Prologue: A Master of Words and a Patriot

1 The opening account of Cicero's death is based on Plutarch, *Cicero* 47–9; Fulvia's attack on Cicero's head is largely paraphrased from Cassius Dio, *Roman History* 47.8.4. Tacitus, *A Dialogue on Oratory* 17, confirms the date of Cicero's death.
2 Plutarch, *Cicero* 49.5.
3 Seneca, *On the Brevity of Life* 10.5.1.
4 Cicero, *To Atticus* 25 (2.5.1).
5 Quintilian, *On the Orator's Education* 2.17.21.
6 Cicero, *On Duties* 2.51. On the morality of Cicero's advocacy and the similarities/differences between the Roman court and modern English practice, see, respectively, Powell and Paterson (2004), 19–29, 401–16.
7 Cicero, *Philippic* 2.7.
8 Petrarch, *Letters on Familiar Matters* 1.1.42.
9 Stockton (1971), 335. A representative sample of Cicero's judges and biographers include Rawson (1975), which remains the most comprehensive scholarly treatment of his entire life; the collection of essays in Dorey (1964) also provide a rounded picture of Cicero's life and his literary output. Mitchell (1991; 1979), Habicht (1990) and Stockton (1971) are largely focused on his political career. Shackleton Bailey (1971) is an excellent – although often highly critical – supplement to these; for his material is drawn chiefly from Cicero's letters, and it is focused on the last twenty years of his life. Treggiari (2007) is a biography of the women in Cicero's life and her work forms an important and very valuable complement to existing biographies. Everitt (2003) is a highly readable narrative of Cicero's life and times; it is self-consciously positive in its approach but retains many elements of Plutarch and Cassius Dio's sensationalizing. Older biographies are often outdated, but a good summary of earlier literature and attitudes towards Cicero can be found in Lacey (1978).

Notes to Chapter 1: The Senate and the People of Rome

1   Polybius, *Histories* 1.1.5; for a modern explanation of the republican constitution, see
    Lintott (1999a).
2   Cicero, *On the Republic* 1.39; for an understanding of this definition, see Schofield (1995).
    For differing views on the role of the people in Roman political life, see Millar (1998) and
    Mouritsen (2001). Millar argues that politicians regarded the people as the dominant force;
    however, Mouritsen believes that their role was far more limited.
3   Dionysius of Halicarnassus, *Roman Antiquities* 1.79.11.
4   Cicero, *In Defence of Balbus* 31; on the more general topic of Rome's relationship with her
    allies and the rest of Italy, see Keaveney (1988).
5   Cicero, *On the Republic* 5.1–2.
6   Cicero, *On the Republic* 1.31; for the importance of the Gracchi and their reforms, see
    Scullard (1988), 22–38.
7   On this period of history, see Mackay (2009) and Shotter (1994) for good general
    introductions; Wiedemann (1994) is useful for the position of Cicero within the Late
    Republic, while Patterson (2000) provides an excellent starting point for understanding
    Roman political life and culture at this time. Articles detailing the effect of expansion on
    standards of morality include Levick (1982) and Lintott (1972). The history of the Republic's
    final years has attracted a huge amount of scholarly attention. Other important studies
    include Beard and Crawford (1999), Lintott (1999a; 1999b), Brunt (1988; 1971), Gruen
    (1974), Seager (1969), and Syme (1939). One of the most comprehensive introductory
    treatments of Rome's early history, which covers the period from the Gracchi to the time of the
    emperor Nero, remains Scullard (1988), now in its fifth edition; however, the general reader
    and introductory student may find the account by Swain and Davies (2010) more accessible.
8   Cicero, *On Laws* 3.20.
9   Cicero, *Philippic* 2.118–19.

Notes to Chapter 2: The Making of the Man (106–82 BC)

1   The scholarly debate on what exactly the terms *novus homo* and *nobilis* covered in Cicero's
    time is extensive and need not be covered here in detail. For the discussion about who
    the *nobiles* were, see Badian (1990), Shackleton Bailey (1986) and Brunt (1982); although
    Flower (1996), 61–2, has convincingly suggested that the term was flexible and that the
    nobiles did not constitute a formal group in society. What is certain is that Cicero counted
    himself as a *novus homo* (a 'new man'). According to Wiseman (1971), a new man was
    simply one who lacked any senatorial ancestors; a stricter definition is given by Gelzer
    (1969), esp. 33–9, who claims that new men were those who could not point specifically
    to a consul in their family lines. Due to the uncertainty of these terms, recent scholarship,
    such as Dugan (2005), has instead emphasized simply that a *novus homo* was a 'political
    outsider'; for the challenges such a man faced in his career, see Scullard (1964).
2   Cicero, *On the Orator* 2.1. For the elder Cicero's political inactivity and health, see Cicero,
    On the Laws 2.3.

3 Cicero, *To Atticus* 32 (2.2.1). A good description of Arpinum and Cicero's early years can be found in Rawson (1975), 1–11.

4 Tacitus, *A Dialogue on Oratory* 29.1; for Cicero's discussion on the stages of infancy, see *On the Ends* 5.15.

5 Cicero, *Letter to Quintus* 25 (3.5.4); see Plutarch, *Cicero* 1–3, on Cicero's early years. For the competitive spirit of the aristocratic élite both before and during Cicero's lifetime, see Patterson (2000), 29–52. For a brief overview of Cicero's education, see Corbeill (2002a). On Greek and Roman education generally, see Too (2001) and the collection of sources by Joyal, McDougall and Yardley (2009).

6 See Horsfall (1989) for a translation and commentary of the *Life of Atticus*; on the use of Atticus' education to supplement what we know of Cicero's, I follow Clarke (1968).

7 Cicero, *For Archias* 1. The discussion presented here focuses solely on Cicero's rhetorical and oratorical training; for a full discussion of the effects of these years on his later political career, see in particular Mitchell (1979), 52–92.

8 Commentary of Asconius, *In Defence of Scaurus* 23.8C, in Lewis (2006), 47. For Cicero's expressed admiration of M. Aemilius Scaurus, see *In Defence of Murena* 16. On the more general topic of Cicero's role models, see Blom (2010).

9 For this example, see Clarke (1996), 1. For the origins of rhetoric under Tisias and Corax, see Cicero, *Brutus* 46. Other useful works on the origins of Greek rhetoric include: Usher (1999), 2–3; Cole (1991), 23–7; Kennedy (1963), 58–61.

10 Cicero, *On the Orator* 1.14. On the early development of rhetoric and oratory at Rome, see Clarke (1996), 10–49. Good general surveys of rhetoric and oratory in the ancient world include Habinek (2005) and Kennedy (1994). For a full and accessible introduction to the study of Roman oratory specifically, see Steel (2006).

11 Cicero, *On the Orator* 1.17. Cicero wrote extensively on the qualities the ideal orator should possess; for a detailed analysis of how his own practice fulfilled the requirements he detailed, see Usher (2008).

12 Cicero – following a system of rhetoric developed by Aristotle (*Rhetoric* 1.2.1356A1ff.) – repeatedly states that these are the three tasks of the orator, although often the words he uses to describe them vary, see *On the Orator* 2.115, 2.128; *Orator* 69, 128; *Brutus* 185.

13 Cicero, *Brutus* 164; for the influence of Crassus on Cicero's later orations see Kennedy (1972), 147. For Cicero's comments on the role of Crassus in his education and curriculum, see *On the Orator* 2.1–2.

14 On Antonius' delivery, see the description in Cicero, *Verrine Orations* 2.5.32; on his influence on Cicero's education, see Cicero, *Brutus* 307.

15 Cicero, *Brutus* 142; cf. Cicero, *On the Orator* 3.213; Quintilian, *The Education of the Orator* 11.3.6. On the use of gesture in oratory, see Aldrete (1999).

16 Cicero, *On Invention* 1.5.

17 Cicero, *Brutus* 306. On the war between Marius and Sulla, see Appian, *Civil Wars* 1.55–102.

Notes to Chapter 3: Climbing the Ladder of Offices (81–70 BC)

1 Cicero, *Brutus* 301–3; for another description of Hortensius' oratory, see Cicero, *Divinatio:*

Against Quintus Caecilius Niger 44–7.

2   For a fuller introduction, notes and translation of Cicero's speech *In Defence of Roscius of Ameria*, see Berry (2000), 3–58.

3   Cicero, *In Defence of Roscius of Ameria* 11.

4   Cicero, *In Defence of Roscius of Ameria* 60–1.

5   On the punishment of the sack, see *In Defence of Roscius of Ameria* 30, 71–3. According to a later writer, only patricides who confessed their guilt could be punished in the traditional way (Suetonius, *Augustus* 33), and it may be that Roscius did not have to fear this exact penalty, see Berry (2000), 5, 225.

6   Cicero, *In Defence of Roscius of Ameria* 72.

7   For the debate on the jury and their verdicts, see Riggsby (1997).

8   Cicero, *Brutus* 314; cf. Plutarch, *Cicero* 3.6. Modern scholars who dismiss the account of Plutarch include: Mitchell (1979), 93; Rawson (1975), 25–6; Stockton (1971), 12; Shackleton Bailey (1971), 12.

9   Although women did not normally travel overseas with their husbands, there is no reason to suggest that Terentia did not make part of the journey with Cicero: thus Treggiari (2007), 29.

10 Cicero, *Brutus* 316. The general period of Cicero's study in Greece and Asia Minor can be pieced together from various autobiographical references in Cicero's works, especially *Brutus* 315–16; *On Ends* 5.1–8; cf. Plutarch, *Cicero* 4.1–7. On the topic of Roman 'study abroad', see Daly (1950). I am grateful to Henriette van der Blom for discussion on this issue, as well as for allowing me to make use of an unpublished paper on the subject.

11 Plutarch, *Cicero* 5.1–2.

12 For Cicero's comments on the 'new man's industry', see *Verrines* 2.3.8; cf. Rawson (1975), 30. The evidence for Cicero's lost and fragmentary speeches, both in this period and for the rest of his career, has been collected and analysed in two separate studies by Crawford (1994; 1984).

13 Cicero often talks about the success of his election results; for the result of his election to the quaestorship, see, e.g., Cicero, *Against Piso* 2. For ancient evidence on how an election day might run, see Varro, *On Agriculture* 3.2–17, with the discussion by Patterson (2000), 15–17.

14 Cicero, *Against Verres* 2.2.5, here quoting a remark made by Cato the Elder (234–149 BC); important works for understanding the grain supply and Sicily's contribution include Rickman (1980) and Garnsey (1988).

15 For anecdotes about Cicero's quaestorship, see *Tusculum Disputations* 5.64–6 (for the discovery of Archimedes' tomb) and note 16, below (for his justice and mildness).

16 Cicero, *For Plancius* 64–6; cf. Plutarch, *Cicero* 6.1–5.

Notes to Chapter 4: Cicero on the Attack (70 BC)

1   Cicero, *Brutus* 312.

2   Cicero, *Against Quintus Caecilius* 5 (this was the speech in which Cicero actually competed for the right to prosecute Verres). For similar reservations about the act of prosecution, see

his earlier speech, *For Quinctius* 51. The typical statement concerning when it is justifiable to undertake a prosecution can be found in Cicero, *On Duties* 2.49–50; cf. the discussion of Fantham (1997).

3 Cicero, *For Cluentius* 154; for the anecdote on Julius Caesar's extensive debt, see Appian, *Civil Wars* 2.8.

4 Cicero, *To Friends* 128 (5.20.9).

5 Cicero, *On the Command of Gnaeus Pompeius* 65.

6 For the suggestion that Cicero may have stood to gain Verres' place in the senate following his conviction, see Taylor (1949), 112–16, although Alexander (1985) has offered some convincing arguments against this view of a standardized award system. It was the Remmian law which imposed penalties for a false accusation; for the brand of *kalumniator*, see Cicero, *For Roscius* 55, 57; cf. Greenidge (1901), 468–9; for the use of tattooing and branding at Rome, see Jones (1987). For a summary of the rewards and punishments for advocacy, see Powell and Paterson (2004), 12–13.

7 Cicero, *Against Quintus Caecilius* 36. For a full discussion of Cicero's challenge and his argumentative strategy in this case, see Tempest (2010).

8 For the portrayal of Caecilius as a collusive prosecutor, or 'straw man' (a *praevaricator* in Latin), see Cicero, *Against Quintus Caecilius* 30, 58. It should be noted, however, that when it suits his purpose in the subsequent trial against Verres, Cicero claimed that Caecilius genuinely wanted to see Verres convicted (see Cicero, *Against Verres* 2.1.15).

9 Cicero, *Against Caecilius* 45. On the dilemma form of argumentation, see Craig (1993a).

10 Cicero, *Against Caecilius* 58.

11 Cicero, *Against Caecilius* 45–6.

12 Cicero, *Against Caecilius* 47.

13 Cicero, *Against Caecilius* 47; for the rejection of Caecilius as a *subscriptor* in the trial, see Cicero, *Against Verres* 2.1.15.

14 Cicero, *Against Verres* 1.1.

15 Shotter (1994), 38. After Gracchus, the monopoly of the courts was restored to the senatorial order in 106 BC, only to be returned to the equestrians in 101 BC.

16 Cicero, *Against Verres* 1.40; the incident was the trial of Aulus Terentius Varro in 74 BC, who was successfully defended by his cousin Hortensius against the charge of extortion.

17 Cicero, *Against Verres* 1.40.

18 Cicero, *Against Verres* 1.20. The actual political importance of the Verres trial has been variously interpreted. Mitchell (1979), 107–49, strongly denies that the case of Verres had any political significance – either to the need for reform, or even as evidence of Cicero's political sympathies at this time; while Shackleton Bailey describes Cicero as 'not so much swimming with the tide as spurring on a horse that had already passed the winning-post' (1971), 17. Indeed, it is highly unlikely that the trial of Verres had any discernible effect on the passage of the bill – as Cicero asserts at various points in the speech (e.g. *Against Verres* 2.5.178) – but we should not discount the importance of the trial for Cicero's political self-presentation.

19 Cicero, *Against Verres* 1.5.

20 Cicero, *Against Verres* 1.19.

21 Cicero, *Against Verres* 1.33. For a good overview of how Cicero used the documentary

evidence in the trial against Verres, see Butler (2002), especially chapters 2–5; although it should be noted that Butler dramatically undervalues the role of witnesses in the case; on this point, see Griffin (2003).

22   Plutarch, *Cicero* 7.4. For a detailed overview of the procedure and strategy used in these speeches, see Lintott (2008), 81–100. It should be stated for clarity that the collection of speeches belonging to the trial – known as the *Verrine Orations* – only contains three main speeches: the *Divinatio Against Quintus Caecilius*, the introductory *First Hearing (Actio Prima) Against Gaius Verres* and the long *Second Hearing (Actio Secunda) Against Gaius Verres*. Many modern scholars further divide the *Second Hearing (Actio Secunda) Against Gaius Verres* into five smaller speeches, even though Cicero intended these five 'speeches' to be read as one; on this topic, see Tempest (2007). For a fuller introduction and partial translation of the *Verrine Orations*, see Berry (2006), 3–101. The most accessible translation of the full collection can be found in the Loeb series.

23   Quintilian, *On the Orator's Education* 6.3.98; cf. Plutarch, *Cicero* 7.8. For Cicero's production of the boy Junius in court, see Cicero, *Against Verres* 2.1.71, 151. For the story of the pirates and Verres' reaction, see Cicero, *Against Verres* 2.5.73; for the audience's reaction, see ibid. 74.

24   Cicero, *Against Verres* 2.1.9.

25   Cicero, *Against Verres* 2.3.8.

26   Cicero, *Brutus* 323.

Notes to Chapter 5: The New Man at Rome (69–67 BC)

1   Cicero, *On Duties* 2.51; cf. Prologue, note 6, above.

2   Cicero, *For Fonteius* 22; for Hortensius' general failure to cross-examine the witnesses in the trial of Verres, see Cicero, *Against Verres* 2.3.41.

3   Cicero, *For Fonteius* 21; for the role of racial attacks in this speech, see Alexander (2002), 63–4, and Vasaly (1993), 209–12.

4   Cicero, *For Fonteius* 34–5.

5   Cicero, *For Fonteius* 47. For emotional appeals in Cicero's perorations, see Winterbottom (2004), 215–30. While the result of Fonteius' trial is not known for sure, it is generally considered likely that it was successful: see Powell and Paterson (2004), 418.

6   Cicero, *For Cluentius* 126.

7   Cicero, *To Atticus* 125 (7.2.4).

8   Cicero, *To Atticus* 1 (1.5.1).

9   Cicero, *Brutus* 272; for Cicero's letter of guidance on the criteria of a suitor, see Cicero, *To Atticus* 327 (3.21a.4).

10   Cicero, *To Atticus* 2 (1.6.1).

11   Cicero, *To Atticus* 414 (16.6.2); for a list of Cicero's villas and lodgings, see Schatzman (1975), 403–9. On the importance of the aristocratic house, see Patterson (2000), 38–43.

12   Valerius Maximus, *Memorable Doings and Sayings* 6.2.8; for a good introduction to Pompey's life and career, see Seager (2002).

13   Cicero, *On Pompey's Command* 56. For the resistance of the senate towards Pompey's

acquisition of the command, see Cassius Dio, *Roman History* 36.31–36; cf. Velleius
Paterculus, *History of Rome* 2.32.1.

14   Cicero, *To Atticus* 10 (1.1.2).

15   Cicero, *To Atticus* 6 (1.10.6).

Notes to Chapter 6: The Climb to the Consulship (66–64 BC)

1   Cicero, *On the Command of Pompey* 1. For a fuller introduction, notes and translation of
     Cicero's speech see Berry (2006), 102–33. On the conventions of the *contio* (the name given
     both to the meeting itself and to the speech delivered at it), see Morstein-Marx (2004). For
     a discussion of the debate and a detailed analysis of Cicero's argument, see Steel (2001),
     114–56. For Cicero's conscious decision to speak in favour of the proposal, and the political
     implications of this decision, I follow the observation of Steel (2006), 5.

2   Cicero, *On the Command of Pompey* 19.

3   Cicero, *On the Command of Pompey* 7; for historical accounts of this incident, and the
     estimated death tolls, see Valerius Maximus, *Memorable Doings and Sayings* 9.2.3 (ext.),
     who places the total killed at 80,000 deaths; cf. Plutarch, *Sulla*, 24.4, who raises it to 150,000.

4   Cicero, *For Cluentius* 185. For the speech's popularity, even in antiquity, see Pliny the
     Younger who thought it was not only Cicero's longest oration, but also his best (*Letters*
     1.20.4).

5   Cicero, *For Cluentius* 152.

6   Cicero, *To Atticus* 9 (1.4.2).

7   For the trial of Manilius and its effect on Cicero's reputation, see [Quintus] Cicero, *Essay
     on Running for Consul* 51; for the narrative presented here, see Plutarch, *Cicero* 9.4–7 with
     the discussion by Steel (2006), 10; the events in the subsequent prosecution of Manilius
     are complex: see Seager (2002), 64, and Ramsey (1980).

8   Sallust, *Jugurthine War* 63.7.

9   [Quintus] Cicero, *Essay on Running for Consul* 5.

10   For Cicero's own, rhetorically loaded, explanation of the terms *optimates* and *populares*, see
     For Sestius 96–132, with the discussion by Kaster (2006), esp. 32, 319–30. In what follows,
     I shall use the word 'populist' to describe the political activity of the men who pandered
     to the people in opposition to the aims and objectives of the wealthy ruling class. Other
     scholars who have recently eschewed the terms, include Marin (2009), 25–6; for a full
     discussion on the problems in using Cicero's political vocabulary, see Robb (2010); I am
     very grateful to Maggie Robb both for her advice on the points raised here and for sharing
     her conclusions with me in their pre-published format.

11   Cicero, *For Cornelius* 2.5. The fragment is preserved by the ancient scholar, Asconius
     80.7–14C, in Lewis (2006), 161. For a good overview of Cicero's speech and an introduction
     to the circumstances of the trial, also see Crawford (1994), 65–70 and Lintott (2008),
     112–19.

12   Quintilian, *On the Orator's Education* 8.3.4.

13   Cicero, *To Atticus* 10 (1.1.1).

14   Plutarch, *Cicero* 7.2.

15 Asconius 86.23C, in Lewis (2006), 173.
16 Asconius 93.25, in Lewis (2006), 187.

Notes to Chapter 7: A Consulship and a Conspiracy (63 BC)

1 Plutarch, *Cicero* 12.2. For a reconstruction of the bill's contents, based on Cicero's own description, see Lintott (2008), 137–42.

2 Cicero, *On the Agrarian Law* 2.6–7; throughout the speeches against Rullus Cicero hints openly at the suggestion that Crassus and Caesar are operating behind the bill; for example, see *On the Agrarian Law* 1.1; 2.25, 44; 3.13. For the complicity of Caesar and Crassus, with references to the primary evidence, see the discussion in Mitchell (1979), especially 183–4.

3 Cicero, *On the Agrarian Law* 2.23–5; elsewhere Cicero presents the bill as an insult towards Pompey (e.g. see ibid. 2.52–5; 60–1); although for the argument that Rullus and his colleagues were actually working on Pompey's behalf, see Seager (2002), 68–9. On the more general topic of Cicero's populist language in the speeches against Rullus, see Seager (1972), esp. 334–8; Morstein-Marx (2004), 207-30 makes an interesting and valuable attempt to construct a 'plebs'-eye view' of Cicero which should also be consulted.

4 On the wording of the decree and the phrasing *senatus consultum ultimum*, see Caesar, *Civil Wars* 1.5.3; on this point, see Mackay (2009), 79.

5 Cicero, *For Gaius Rabirius* 2. On the trial of Rabirius, see Suetonius, *Caesar* 12 and Cassius Dio, *Roman History* 37.26–28. Cicero's speech *For Gaius Rabirius* is translated in the Loeb Classical Library series. For a brief introduction to the complexities surrounding the trial and her own contribution to the debate, see Rawson (1975), 87–8.

6 Cicero, *For Murena* 50.

7 Cicero, *For Murena* 51.

8 Cicero, *For Murena* 52. These elections were probably held in July as normal; see Stockton (1971), 336–7, and Benson (1986).

9 Sallust, *The War of Catiline* 23; the events described in the rest of this chapter draw largely on Sallust's account; for a full translation and introduction to this text, see Woodman (2007). My account has also been strongly supplemented by the narratives in Cicero's four *Catilinarian Orations*. Both primary sources contain an inevitable amount of bias, exaggeration and possible distortion; on the sources available to Sallust, who was writing around twenty years after the event, see the useful overview by Ramsey (2007), 8–9; another valuable companion to Sallust's work on the conspiracy is Drummond (1995). Other ancient accounts include Cassius Dio, *Roman History* 37.29–42. An old, but useful, reconstruction of events can be found in Hardy (1917). For a more thorough account of the conspiracy see, for example, Stockton (1971), 110–42, to which I am indebted here.

10 For example, Cicero remarks that Clodius had taunted him with this line in a letter, *To Atticus* 14 (1.14.5).

11 On this point I follow Stockton (1971), 114.

12 Cicero, *Against Catiline* 10; cf. Cicero, *For Sulla* 18, where he mentions the plot to kill him in his own home. A fragment of the historian Diodorus seems to corroborate Cicero's story

of such a plot; for discussion, see Treggiari (2007), 46.

13 Cicero, *Against Catiline* 1. The opening of this speech became famous. According to Suetonius, *Declamations* 7.14, over thirty years later, the younger Marcus Cicero could joke that everyone knew this speech, and especially this line.

14 For more on the significance of Cicero's decision to hold the senate meeting in the temple of Jupiter, see Vasaly (1993), 41–59.

15 Cicero, *Against Catiline* 1.4. For an overview of the debate regarding Cicero's intentions in this speech, see Craig (1993b).

16 Cicero, *Against Catiline* 2.7; for the same expression elsewhere, see *Against Catiline* 1.12.

17 Cicero, *For Murena* 22.

18 Plutarch, *Cato the Younger* 21.5.

19 Cicero, *Against Catiline* 3.12. It is commonly accepted that Cicero quotes the letter accurately; cf. Sallust, *The War of Catiline* 44.5. On the purpose of the letter, see Phillips (1976), 446–7.

20 Sallust, *The War of Catiline* 48.

21 Cicero, *Against Catiline* 4.6.

22 Caesar's speech does not survive and here we are dependent on Cicero's account (in *Against Catiline* 4.7–8). It may be – as the later historian Appian suggests – that Caesar only recommended for the conspirators to be placed under house arrest until Catiline's troops had been suppressed and they could stand trial (Appian, *Civil Wars* 2.6).

23 Cicero, *Against Catiline* 4.11–12.

24 Plutarch, *Cato the Younger* 24.2.

25 For the description of the prison and the execution of the conspirators, see Sallust, *The War of Catiline* 55. For the account of these events, also see Plutarch, *Cicero* 22.1–5.

26 Sallust, *The War of Catiline* 60–1.

27 Cicero, *For Rabirius* 35. It should be noted, however, that the speech *For Rabirius*, like the *Catilinarians*, was put on the record later by Cicero as part of a collection of consular speeches. They may well reflect the same agenda that Cicero had in 60 BC, when he published these speeches; namely, to justify his actions in executing the conspirators. However, in defending the senate's right to implement the ultimate decree in times of crisis, I believe it remains valid to claim that Cicero considered it the consul's duty to do everything he could to defend the Republic at all costs.

Notes to Chapter 8: High Hopes and Shattered Dreams (62–60 BC)

1 Cicero, *To Friends* 3 (5.7.3). For a fuller introduction, notes and translation of Cicero's *Republic*, see Rudd and Powell (1998).

2 Cicero, *To Friends* 2 (5.2.6); for further details of Nepos' actions in his tribunate and his hostility towards Cicero, see Cassius Dio, *Roman History* 37.42–4.

3 Cicero, *To Friends* 2 (5.2.7); cf. Cicero, *Against Piso* 6–7, *For Sulla* 33–4 and Plutarch, *Cicero* 23.3.

4 Scholia Bobiensia, lines 22–30, commenting on Cicero's speech *For Plancius* 85, collected by Stangl (1964), 167.

5 Cicero, *To Friends* 3 (5.7.3); for a good overview of the reasons for Pompey's coolness

towards Cicero after he received this letter, see Stockton (1971), 146–51.

6   Cicero, *On Duties* 2.29. For a fuller introduction to the trial, as well as a review of Cicero's motives for undertaking the defence, see Berry (1996), especially 26–33.

7   Cicero, *For Sulla* 72.

8   Cicero, *For Sulla* 14.

9   Cicero, *For Sulla* 22; Pseudo-Sallust, *Invective Against Cicero* 3, corroborates the hostile tradition that Cicero acted cruelly and accepted bribes in the subsequent trials of alleged conspirators. For details of the trials and further references, see Alexander (1990), item numbers 226–34.

10   Cicero, *To Friends* 4 (5.6.2); for the loan, see Gellius, *Attic Nights* 12.12.2.

11   Cicero, *To Atticus* 12 (1.12.2).

12   Cicero, *To Atticus* 12 (1.12.3). Cicero is also being fairly tongue-in-cheek at this point: he and Atticus loved a bit of scandal and gossip, as he remarks in his letter *To Atticus* 115 (6.1.26).

13   Plutarch, *Caesar* 10.9; for the general background of the *Bona Dea* scandal, also see Cassius Dio, *Roman History* 37.45–46.

14   Cicero, *To Atticus* 16 (1.16.3); for Cicero's reticence in the trial, see ibid. 16 (1.16.2). There was a rumour, too, that Cicero only gave evidence to appease Terentia, who believed he was having an affair with Clodius' sister, although this is generally believed to be little more than gossip. See Plutarch, *Cicero* 29.3, with some discussion by Treggiari (2007), 49, and Balsdon (1964), 173.

15   Cicero, *To Atticus* 16 (1.16.10).

16   Cicero, *To Atticus* 17 (1.17.8).

17   Cicero, *To Atticus* 21 (2.1.8).

18   Ancient sources detailing the formation of the triumvirate, as well as the struggles faced by Pompey, Caesar and Crassus in their dealings with the senate include Appian, *Civil Wars* 2.8–9; Cassius Dio, *Roman History* 37.49–50 (the senate's opposition to Pompey); 37.54–58 (Caesar and the formation of the triumvirate).

Notes to Chapter 9: Enemies, Exile and Return (59–57 BC)

1   Cicero, *To Atticus* 37 (2.17.1).

2   Cicero, *To Atticus* 20 (1.20.1); on Cicero's loneliness, cf. the letter, often quoted by historians, *To Atticus* 18 (1.18.1).

3   Cicero, *To Atticus* 12 (2.1.7).

4   For the comments on Pompey, Clodius and Caesar, see Cicero, *To Atticus* 21 (2.1.1); see *To Atticus* 37 (2.17.2) for Cicero's admission to being a natural optimist in previous years.

5   Cicero, *To Atticus* 21 (2.1.4).

6   Cicero, *To Atticus* 19 (1.19.1).

7   'How fortunate the state of Rome, which under my consulship was grown' is criticized for its poetic qualities at Quintilian, *On the Orator's Education* 9.4.41 (cf. Juvenal, *Satires* 10.122); Cicero refers to his opponent's mocks on the line 'Let arms to the toga cede, a soldier's laurels to glory concede' in *Philippics* 2.20 (cf. note 8, below). Fortunately, our

assessment of Cicero's poetry does not entirely depend on these two lines of verse; for a fairer view of Cicero's poetic talent, see the discussion by Townend (1964), 109–34.

8   Cicero, *Against Piso* 74.
9   Cicero, *To Atticus* 23 (2.3.3).
10 Cicero, *To Atticus* 23 (2.3.4).
11 Cicero, *To Atticus* 24 (2.4.2).
12 Cicero, *To Atticus* 38 (2.18.1).
13 Thus Appian, *Civil Wars* 2.9.
14 Cicero, *To Atticus* 38 (2.18.4).
15 Cicero, *To Atticus* 27 (2.7.4).
16 Cicero, *To Atticus* 36 (2.16.2).
17 For Bibulus' strategy, see Cassius Dio, *Roman History* 38.6; for the assault on Bibulus and his men, see Plutarch, *Life of Pompey* 48.1. Cicero remarks that Bibulus was winning great popularity in *To Atticus* 39 (2.19.2). General narratives of Caesar and Bibulus' consulship can be found at Appian, *Civil Wars* 2.10–16; Cassius Dio, *Roman History* 38.1–8; and Suetonius, *Julius Caesar* 20.
18 Cicero, *To Atticus* 39 (2.19.3); for Pompey's offer of protection over his 'dead body', see ibid. 40 (2.20.2).
19 Cicero discusses the Vettius affair at length in his letter *To Atticus* 44 (2.24.2–4); for further discussion, see Lintott (2008), 173–4; (1999b), 109, 119–20.
20 Velleius Paterculus, *History of Rome* 2.45. On Pompey's failure to help Cicero after this bill, see Plutarch, *Cicero* 31.3.
21 Plutarch, *Cicero* 30.6–31.1.
22 Cicero, *Letters to his Friends*, extracts from letter 6 (14.4).
23 Cicero, *To Atticus* 52 (3.7.2).
24 Cicero, *To Quintus* 3 (1.3.1). Hutchinson (1998), 25–48, presents a very sympathetic reading of Cicero's letters during the period of his exile and he offers convincing reasons for understanding Cicero's outbursts in these letters; in particular, he considers the disgrace and poverty inflicted by exile, as well as the generally flamboyant display of emotions among many Romans.
25 Cicero, *For Sestius* 77. The rhetorical exaggeration in Cicero's account is due to the fact that he was speaking in defence of a man who had done much to help his recall at the time.
26 On the death of Piso, see Cicero, *For Sestius* 68, 131.
27 Cicero, *To Atticus* 73 (4.1.5).

Notes to Chapter 10: Cicero and the Triumvirs (57–53 BC)

1   Cicero, *To Atticus* 73 (4.1.8).
2   For the details of the lootings and plunderings, see Cicero, *On his Return in the Senate* 18; *On His House* 60–2: it is commonly reported that Clodius was behind the destruction of Cicero's house; but this is based on Cicero's inferences and beliefs rather than any firm evidence: for the corrective to this view, see Stroh (2004).
3   Cicero, *On His Return to the Senate* 11.

4   Cicero, *On his Return in the Senate* 17.

5   Cicero, *On His Return to the People* 13; for Cicero's disappointment in Hortensius, see, for example, his letter *To Atticus* 54 (3.9.2).

6   Cicero, *To Atticus* 73 (4.1.6).

7   Cicero, *To Atticus* 74 (4.2.2). Despite Cicero's assessment of the speech here, critics of his work have not always agreed. For a full overview of the criticism the speech has received, as well as a defence of Cicero's strategy, see Stroh (2004), esp. 313–16.

8   Cicero, *To Atticus* 74 (4.2.5).

9   Cicero, *On Friendship* 64; see Balsdon (1964), esp. 179–89 on the topic of Cicero's own friendships and attitudes towards them.

10 Cicero, *To Quintus* 7 (2.3.2).

11 Cicero, *For Sestius* 97–8, 138; for the translation and meaning of the slogan, see Rawson (1975), 127. A fuller discussion can be found in Kaster (2006), 31–7.

12 In particular, see Cicero's attacks at *For Sestius* 133–6; Cicero also published a separate pamphlet detailing his attack on Vatinius, which survives under the title *The Cross-Examination of the Witness Pubius Vatinius*.

13 Cicero and Pompey seemed on friendly terms according to Cicero's letter *To Quintus* 10 (2.6.3).

14 Cicero, *To Friends* 20 (1.9.9). This letter also contains Cicero's remark that Pompey had concealed any offence he felt towards Cicero before leaving for Sardinia.

15 Cicero, *To Atticus* 80 (4.5.1).

16 Cicero, *To Atticus* 83 (4.6.2).

17 Cicero, *To Atticus* 80 (4.5.3).

18 Cicero, *To Friends* 203 (4.4.4), where, talking about a speech he delivered under Caesar's dictatorship in 46 BC – the speech *For Marcellus* – Cicero maintained that 'he [Caesar] might have thought I did not regard the present regime as constitutional if I persevered in my silence'.

19 Cicero, *To Quintus* 3 (1.3.10). For the following questions regarding the position of Cicero's family during his exile, I am heavily indebted to the work of Treggiari (2007), 56–70.

20 Cicero, *To Friends* 8 (14.1.5).

21 For Cicero's grief on hearing about Clodius' abusive treatment, see Cicero, *To Friends* 7 (14.2.2). Cicero, *For Caelius* 50 mentions Clodia's 'cruel actions against my family during my absence'. See *For Sestius* 54 on the behaviour of Clodius during Cicero's exile. The remarks he makes in the letter to Terentia – about saving others only to bring ruin upon their own family – recall the claims he also made in public orations; for example, see Cicero, *Against Catiline* 4.1–3, where he claims he is putting the country's safety ahead of his own and his family's.

22 See, for example, Cicero, *For Plancius*, 91–2.

23 Cicero, *To Atticus* 90 (4.15.4).

24 Cicero, *On the Consular Provinces* 38.

25 Cicero, *To Atticus* 90 (4.15.9).

26 Cicero, *To Friends* 24 (7.1.3).

27 Tacitus, *The Annals* 14.20; for the Romans' attitude towards the games and theatre, see Edwards (1993), 121–6.

28 Cicero, *To Atticus* 89 (4.16.8).
29 Cicero, *To Quintus* 25 (3.5.4).
30 Cicero, *To Atticus* 92 (4.18.2).
31 Pseudo-Sallust, *Invective Against Cicero* 7.
32 In 59 BC, when Caesar was trying to persuade Cicero to enter the alliance he forged with Pompey and Crassus, Cicero had told Atticus (in perhaps mock-serious tone) that a position on the board of augurs may have tempted him; see *To Atticus* 25 (2.5.2). For the fact that Hortensius now sponsored his admission, see Cicero, *Brutus* 1.
33 Habicht (1990), 57.

Notes to Chapter 11: Cicero, Clodius and Milo (52 BC)

1 Cicero, *For Milo* 73.
2 Thus Tatum (1999); paraphrased by Connerty in (2000), 514 .
3 Cicero, *To Atticus* 73 (4.1.8); Cassius Dio also mentions Clodius' continued attacks on Cicero in *Roman History* 39.20.
4 Cicero, *For Caelius* 34.
5 For the account of events in this section, I draw chiefly on Asconius, *On Behalf of Milo* 30C–42C in Lewis (2006), 61–85; other treatments of the death of Clodius and the trial of Milo include: Appian, *Civil Wars* 2.20–24; Cassius Dio, *Roman History* 40.48–55; Plutarch, *Cicero* 35.1–5.
6 Cicero, *To Atticus* 106 (5.13.1).
7 For Cato's reaction to the appointment of Pompey as sole consul, see Plutarch, *Life of Pompey* 54.
8 Cicero, *For Milo* 105.
9 Cicero, *For Milo* 23; for further discussion of Cicero's argumentative strategy and its relationship to the rhetorical theory, see Wisse (2007).
10 Fotheringham (2007), 69.
11 Asconius 41–2C, in Lewis (2006), 85; cf. Plutarch, *Cicero* 35.5 and Cassius Dio, *Roman History* 40.54.2 (cf. 46.7.2–3). A useful and fuller overview of the trial and its importance, upon which I have drawn, can be found in Lintott (1974).
12 Cassius Dio, *Roman History* 40.54.3.
13 For the anecdote about Cato, see Plutarch, *Pompey* 55.5.
14 Plutarch, *Pompey* 54.1.

Notes to Chapter 12: Away from Rome: Governor of Cilicia (51–50 BC)

1 Cicero, *To Atticus* 100 (5.7.1).
2 Cicero, *To Atticus* 103 (5.10.3).
3 Cicero, *To Atticus* 108 (5.15.2).
4 Cicero, *To Atticus* 109 (5.16.2).
5 Cicero, *To Atticus* 115 (6.1.16); for Cicero's summaries of his measures and achievements,

see ibid. 114 (5.21.7) and 116 (6.2.4).

6 Cicero, *To Atticus* 121 (6.6.1); for Appius' mixed reactions towards Cicero, see *To Atticus* 115 (6.1.2); for Cicero's letters to Appius, see *To Friends* 64–76 (3.1–3.13).

7 For Cicero's acknowledgement as *imperator*, as well as Bibulus' defeat, see Cicero, *To Atticus* 113 (5.20.2–4).

8 Cicero, *To Atticus* 113 (5.20.1).

9 Cato to Cicero, in Cicero *To Friends* 111 (15.5.2); other letters were exchanged between the two men on this point: see Cicero, *To Friends* 110–12 (15.4–15.6).

10 Both quotations are from Cicero, *To Atticus* 125 (7.2.7).

11 Cicero, *To Atticus* 121 (6.6.3).

12 Cicero, *To Friends* 97 (8.14.2). For later historical accounts of events at Rome, see Appian, *Civil Wars* 2.25–31 and Cassius Dio, *Roman History* 40.59–66.

13 Cicero, *To Atticus* 124 (7.1.2–5).

Notes to Chapter 13: Away from Rome Again: Civil War (49–47 BC)

1 Appian, *Civil Wars* 2.30.

2 Cicero, *To Atticus* 128 (7.5.4).

3 Cicero, *To Friends* 143 (16.11.2); cf. other accounts of the letter and subsequent events in Caesar, *Civil War* 1.5, and Appian, *Civil Wars* 2.32.

4 Appian, *Civil Wars* 2.34.

5 Cicero, *To Atticus* 134 (7.11.1).

6 Cicero, *To Atticus* 161 (8.11.2).

7 Cicero, *To Atticus* 155 (8.7.2).

8 Cicero, *To Atticus* 135 (7.12.2).

9 Cicero sent Atticus a copy of Caesar's letter, which is preserved in Cicero, *To Atticus* 172A (9.6.A).

10 Cicero, *To Atticus* 177 (9.10.1).

11 Cicero, *To Friends* 151 (4.2.2).

12 Cicero, *To Atticus* 187 (9.18.1).

13 Cicero, *To Atticus* 197 (10.6.1); for further expressions of anxiety and the mounting pressure from Caesar's men, who were urging Cicero to stay in Italy, see ibid. 199 and 199B (10.8 and 10.8B).

14 Plutarch, *Cicero* 38.7.

15 Cicero, *To Atticus* 216 (11.5.4).

16 Cicero, *To Friends* 156 (8.17.1).

17 For the death tolls, see Caesar, *Civil War* 3.99.

18 Cicero, *To Atticus* 217 (11.6.2).

19 Cicero, *To Atticus* 217 (11.6.5).

20 Cicero, *To Atticus* 222 (11.11.1).

21 Cicero, *To Atticus* 219 (11.8.2).

22 Plutarch, *Cicero* 39.5

Notes to Chapter 14: Cicero and Caesar (46–44 BC)

1   Cicero, *To Friends* 203 (4.4.3–4). A fuller introduction to the events behind Cicero's speech *For Marcellus*, as well as a translation and notes, can be found in Berry (2006), 204–21.

2   Cicero, *For Marcellus* 8; for the Isocratean precedent for this line of thought, see Isocrates, *Letter 2 to Philip I* 121.

3   Cicero, *For Marcellus* 23–4; on the place of Cicero's speech within the development of the panegyric tradition, see Braund (1998), 53–76.

4   Cicero, *To Friends* 177 (9.2.5). Cicero's sincerity in this speech has often been questioned; but Winterbottom (2002) has argued convincingly that the position Cicero adopts in this speech corresponds to what we know of his thoughts and feelings about the Republic at the time.

5   Cicero, *To Friends* 237 (6.7.5).

6   Cicero, *To Friends* 175 (9.1.2).

7   Cicero, *On Divination* 2.7.

8   Cicero, *To Friends* 191 (9.18.1–2).

9   Cicero, *To Friends* 249 (4.6.2); cf. Cicero, *To Atticus* 12.14.3: 'I can confirm that no consolation is as effective as this. I write for days on end; not to make a full recovery, but for the time being it distracts me – not enough, it has to be said (for the strength of my grief bears heavy upon me), but still it brings respite.'

10   See Chapter 13, note 2, above.

11   For the event and Caesar's reaction, see Suetonius, *Julius Caesar* 79; cf. Taylor (1973), 78.

12   Cicero, *To Atticus* 353 (13.52.1–2).

13   Cicero, *To Friends* 265 (7.30.2).

14   Suetonius, *Julius Caesar* 80; for other descriptions see: Cicero, *On Divination* 2.23; Plutarch, *Life of Caesar* 66; Appian, *Civil Wars* 2.117.

Notes to Chapter 15: The Tyranny of Antony (44 BC)

1   Cicero, *Republic* 2.43; for a fuller analysis of what republican writers meant by 'liberty', see Wirszubski (1950).

2   Cicero, *For Milo* 80.

3   Plutarch, *Cicero* 42.2.

4   Cicero, *To Atticus* 363 (14.9.2).

5   Cicero, *To Friends* 364 (10.28.1); cf. Cicero's letter to Cassius for the same expression in *To Friends* 363 (12.4.1).

6   Cicero, *To Atticus* 415 (16.7.7). This letter includes the report of Cicero's journey and meeting with Brutus; cf. Cicero, *Philippic* 1.7–10.

7   Cicero, *Philippic* 1.24. See Ramsey (2003), 132–3, for further references and explanations of Antony's reliance on Caesar's papers. As regards the tone of the speech, Cicero later admitted that he spoke 'rather freely', yet he adds that he was 'less liberal than normal' (*Philippic* 5.19). Modern scholars are torn in their assessment: those who see it as an attack on Antony and consequently blame Cicero for the hostility that developed include Habicht (1990), 78–9, and Syme (1939), 140; on the other hand, Mitchell (1991), 301, and

Stockton (1971), 293, are inclined to see it as more moderate; while Fuhrmann (1990), 179, and Rawson (1975), 275, view its tone as 'mild'. More recently, Blom (2003), 301, has stressed a middle ground between the opposing views: Cicero's *First Philippic* was not a 'declaration of war', but it was still a 'systematic and persuasive condemnation of Antony's policies'.

8 Cicero, *To Friends* 344 (12.2.1); for Cicero's decision that it was too dangerous to attend the senate that day, see *To Friends* 341 (10.2.1); for the description of the armed men around the senate and Antony's actions that day, see Cicero, *Philippic* 5.20.

9 Cicero, *To Friends* 344 (12.2.1).

10 Cicero, *To Friends* 345 (12.3.1).

11 Cicero, *To Atticus* 416 (15.13.1).

12 Juvenal, *Satires* 10.125.

13 Cicero, *Philippic* 2.43.

14 On the general conventions of invective, I follow Nisbet (1987), 192–7, as well as the summary of their use in the *Philippics* by Craig (2004), 191–2; Corbeill (2002b) presents a useful introduction to the general topic of invective; see also the essays collected in Booth (2007).

15 Cicero, *Philippic* 2.63. Cicero tells this story either directly or implicitly elsewhere: cf. *Philippic* 2.50, 75, 84, 104; and at *To Friends* 344 (12.2.1); 373 (12.25.4). Plutarch, *Antony* 9.6, also tells the story adding (possibly by way of his own invention) that one of Antony's friends caught the vomit in his toga. Of course, as Ramsey (2003), 252, has noted, Antony may just have been sick because of an illness; by way of comparison, Ramsey adds that the US president George Bush senior was struck by one such illness on a state visit to Japan in 1992.

16 Cicero, *On Duties* 3.22; cf. 3.32.

17 Cicero, *On Duties* 1.86; on Cicero's definition of a 'good citizen', as well as the more general question of how Cicero's philosophical musings entered the 'real world of politics' in the period of the *Philippics*, see Arena (2007).

18 Cicero, *To Atticus* 419 (16.9.1).

19 Cicero, *To Atticus* 426 (6.15.6). Scholars have detected a hint of irony in these last words; this irony is perhaps best expressed by Shackleton Bailey (1971), 254: 'For *adsum* also meant "present!", the self-announcement of a Roman, soldier or civilian, reporting for duty.' Cf. Stockton (1971), 300, followed by Habicht (1990), 80, who noted that these were the words used by senators to answer the roll of names – as if, by using them, Cicero was announcing his return to the political stage (even though he explicitly tells Atticus he is not returning for this reason).

Notes to Chapter 16: The Last Fight for Liberty (44–43 BC)

1 Cicero, *To Friends* 354 (11.7.2).

2 Cicero, *Philippic* 6.2. It is important to note that Cicero may well have been exaggerating the extent of the people's happiness over Antony's expulsion, in order to emphasize the support he had for his efforts against Antony in the published versions. On this point, see

Manuwald (2007), vol. 2, 750.

3   Cicero called them *his Phillipics* when he sent copies of the speeches to Marcus Brutus in
    Greece. Brutus approved and replied: 'I am now willing to let them be called the *Phillipics*,
    as you jokingly suggested in one of your letters.' Brutus' letter to Cicero survives in the
    collection of letters *To Brutus* 2 (2.3.4). On the more general topic of Cicero's debt to
    Demosthenes in the *Philippics*, see Wooten (1983).

4   Cicero, *Philippic* 6.5.

5   Cicero, *Philippic* 6.7.

6   For Cicero's 'frustrations and humiliations', see Syme (1939) followed by Everitt (2003),
    296. The essays in Stevenson and Wilson (2008) do much to elucidate the ideology behind
    Cicero's rhetoric in the *Philippics*, as well as the nature of his oratory in these speeches.

7   Cicero, *Philippic* 7.14; for a similar argument, see *Philippic* 3.36: 'It is to glory and to liberty
    we were born; let us either hold fast to these or die with dignity.'

8   Cicero, *Philippic* 5.6.

9   Cicero, *Philippic* 3.3.

10 Cicero, *Philippic* 7.9.

11 Cicero, *Philippic* 7.19.

12 Cicero, *Philippic* 13.38.

13 Cicero, *Philippic* 13.4.

14 Quintilian, *On the Orator's Education* 8.3.64.

15 Cicero, *To Brutus* 7 (1.3.2).

16 Cicero, *To Friends* 413 (11.14.1).

17 Cicero, *To Friends* 394 (11.12.1).

18 Cicero, *To Brutus* 11 (1.4a.2).

19 Cicero, *To Brutus* 26 (1.17.4).

20 Cicero, *To Friends* 401 (11.20.1).

21 Cicero, *To Brutus* 17 (1.10.3).

22 Cicero, *To Brutus* 24 (1.18.3).

23 Plutarch, *Cicero* 45.2; on the pleasure Cicero generally took from mentoring the young,
    see Cicero, *On Old Age* 26, 28–9.

24 Cicero, *Letter Fragments* 23B.

25 Appian, *Civil Wars* 4.5; cf Plutarch, *Cicero* 46 for the suggestion that Octavian fought to
    save Cicero.

26 Cicero, *To Atticus* 397 (15.20.2).

27 Livy, *The History of Rome* Book 120; the fragment is preserved in Seneca the Elder,
    Declamations 6.17; the versions of other historians – Aufidius Bassus and Cremutius
    Cordus – are also assembled by the elder Seneca in ibid. 6.18–19. For the accounts of
    Cicero's death, see Prologue, note 1, above.

28 Plutarch, *Cicero* 49 contains the details both of the people's general reaction and of
    Pomponia's alleged torture of Philologus.

Notes to Epilogue: The Head and the Hands of Cicero

1 Fragment preserved by Seneca the Elder, *Declamations* 6.22.

2 For these observations, I follow Steel (2005), 15, which is a crucial work for understanding the more general question of the relationship between Cicero's writings and his political persona.

3 The idea to publish *some* of Cicero's letter had been raised, and agreed by Cicero as early as 46/45 BC: see Cicero, *To Atticus* 410 (16.5.5); *To Friends* 186 (16.17.1); Cornelius Nepos, *Life of Atticus* 16.3. For the publication of the speeches *Against Verres* and the treatise *On Glory*, see Gellius, *Attic Nights* 1.7.1; 15.6.2. For Tiro's other publications, including the *commentarii* and the joke collection, see, respectively, Quintilian, *On the Orator's Education* 10.7.30–31 and 6.3.5. On the process of the publication and the dissemination of Cicero's letters, see Beard (2002), esp. 116–19.

4 Cicero, *To Quintus* 1 (1.1.28).

5 Fragment preserved by Seneca the Elder, *Declamations* 6.24; this is not the place for a detailed examination of Cicero's posthumous fame either as an orator or as a philosopher. The classic study for readers of German remains the work of T. Zielinski (1929), *Cicero im Wandel der Jahrhunderte (Cicero through the ages)*, Leipzig: Teubner (4th edn); other useful starting points include Clarke (1964) and Rawson (1975), 299–308.

6 Quintilian, *On the Orator's Education* 10.1.112.

7 For Octavian's later claim (made when he was called Augustus) to have restored the Republic in 28/27 BC, see Augustus' *Res Gestae* (an inscription recording his lifetime achievements) 34.1; cf. Suetonius, *Augustus* 28. Scholars have debated the extent to which this restored government contained the ideals which Cicero had expounded years before in his speeches and political works – ideals such as a concord of the orders, united under and guided by the policy of an ideal statesman. A positive assessment can be found in Shotter (1994), 99–101, whereas Syme (1939), 321, argued that 'only a robust faith can discover authentic relics of Cicero in the Republic of Augustus'. Augustus, for his part, certainly never made any explicit connection between his political agenda and Cicero's works.

8 Plutarch, *Cicero* 49.4; on the 'poetic justice', see also Rawson (1975), 296.

9 Cicero, *For Marcellus* 29.

10 Quotation preserved by Pliny the Elder, *Natural History*, 7.117.

Bibliography

The material available for studying all aspects of Cicero's life, times and oratory is vast, and a select bibliography cannot do justice to the number of fundamental works that stand behind most of what I say. The following list is only an illustrative selection of what is available in English, but one should not neglect to mention the hugely important contributions to Ciceronian studies that have been made by German, French and Italian scholars in particular. The recent boom in companion editions will point the way to further study for anyone wanting to read more about the topics covered in this book. The most in-depth and accessible introductions to all aspects of the Roman Republic, complete with suggestions for further reading, are (i) the companion edited by Rosenstein and Morstein-Marx (2006); (ii) the collection of essays in Crook, Lintott and Rawson (1994). Flower (2004) also contains a number of essays on the Roman Republic which are useful for the introductory student. On topics connected to Cicero's rhetorical works and oratory, see May (2002), which includes an excellent survey by Christopher Craig (pp. 503–31) providing a critical bibliography for the individual speeches.

Aldrete, G. S. (1999), *Gestures and Acclamations in Ancient Rome*. Baltimore: Johns Hopkins University Press.

Alexander, M. C. (2002), *The Case for the Prosecution in the Ciceronian Era*. Ann Arbor: University of Michigan Press.

—(1990), *Trials in the Late Roman Republic, 149 BC to 50 BC*. Toronto: University of Toronto Press.

—(1985), '*Praemia* in the Quaestiones of the Late Republic', *Classical Philology* 80: 20–32.

Arena, V. (2007), 'Invocation to liberty and invective of dominatus at the end of the Roman Republic', *Bulletin of the Institute of Classical Studies* 50: 49–73.

Badian, E. (1990), 'The consuls, 179–49 BC', *Chiron* 20: 371–413.

Balsdon, J. P. V. D. (1964), 'Cicero the man', in T. A. Dorey (ed.), *Cicero*. London: Routledge & Kegan Paul, pp. 171–214.

Beard, M. (2002), 'Ciceronian correspondences: making a book out of letters', in T. P. Wiseman (ed.), *Classics in Progress: Essays on Ancient Greece and Rome*. Oxford: Oxford University Press, pp. 103–44.

Beard, M. and M. Crawford (1999), *Rome in the Late Republic: Problems and Interpretations*. London: Duckworth.

Benson, J. M. (1986), 'Catiline and the date of the consular elections of 63 BC', in C. Deroux (ed.), *Studies in Latin literature and Roman History IV*, Collection Latomus. Brussels: Latomus, pp. 234–46.

Berry, D. H. (2006), *Cicero: Political Speeches*. Oxford: Oxford University Press.

—(2000), *Cicero: Defence Speeches*. Oxford: Oxford University Press.

—(1996), *Cicero Pro P. Sulla Oratio*. Cambridge: Cambridge University Press.

Blom, H. van der (2010), *Cicero's Role Models*. Oxford: Oxford University Press.

—(2003), '*Officium and res publica*: Cicero's political role after the Ides of March', *Classica et Mediaevalia* 54: 289–319.

Booth, J. (ed.) (2007), *Cicero on the Attack: Invective and Subversion in the Orations and Beyond*. Swansea: Classical Press of Wales.

Braund, S. (1998), 'Praise and protreptic in early imperial panegyric: Cicero, Seneca, Pliny', in M. Whitby (ed.), *The Propaganda of Power: The Role of Panegyric in Late Antiquity*. Leiden: Brill, pp. 53–76.

Brunt, P. (1988), *The Fall of the Republic and Related Essays*. Oxford: Oxford University Press.

—(1982), '*Nobilitas* and *novitas*', *Journal of Roman Studies* 72: 1–17.

—(1971), *Social Conflicts in the Roman Republic*. London: Chatto & Windus.

Butler, S. (2002), *The Hand of Cicero*. London and New York: Routledge.

Clarke, M. L (1996), *Rhetoric at Rome: A Historical Survey*. London and New York: Routledge (3rd edn; revised and with a new introduction by D. H. Berry).

—(1968), 'Cicero at school', *Greece and Rome* 15: 18–22.

—(1964), '*Non hominis nomen, sed eloquentiae*', in T. A. Dorey (ed.), *Cicero*. London: Routledge & Kegan Paul, pp. 81–107.

Cole, T. (1991), *The Origins of Rhetoric in Ancient Greece*. Baltimore: John Hopkins University Press.

Connerty, V. (2000), 'Review of Tatum: the patrician tribune Publius Clodius Pulcher', *Classical Review* 50: 514–16.

Corbeill, A. (2002a), 'Rhetorical education in Cicero's youth', in J. M. May (ed.), *Brill's Companion to Cicero: Oratory and Rhetoric*. Leiden: Brill, pp. 23–48.

—(2002b), 'Ciceronian invective', in J. M. May (ed.), *Brill's Companion to Cicero: Oratory and Rhetoric*. Leiden: Brill, pp. 197–217.

Craig, C. (2004), 'Audience expectations, invective and proof', in J. G. F. Powell and J. J. Paterson (eds), *Cicero the Advocate*. Oxford: Oxford University Press, pp. 187–214.

—(1993a), *Form as Argument in Cicero's Speeches: A Study of Dilemma*. Atlanta: Scholars Press.

—(1993b), 'Three simple questions for teaching Cicero's *First Catilinarian*', *Classical Journal* 88: 255–67.

Crawford, J. W. (1994), *M. Tullius Cicero. The Fragmentary Speeches: an edition with commentary*. Atlanta: Scholars Press.

—(1984), *M. Tullius Cicero: The Lost and Unpublished Orations*. Göttingen: Vandenhoeck & Ruprecht.

Crook, J. A., A. Lintott, and E. Rawson (eds) (1994), *The Cambridge Ancient History*, Vol. 9. Cambridge: Cambridge University Press (2nd edn).

Daly, L. W. (1950), 'Roman study abroad', *American Journal of Philology* 71: 40–58.

Deroux, C. (ed.) (1986), *Studies in Latin literature and Roman History IV*, Collection Latomus. Brussels: Latomus.

Dominik, W. J. (1997), *Roman Eloquence: Rhetoric in Society and Literature*. London and New York: Routledge.

Dorey, T. A. (ed.) (1964), *Cicero*. London: Routledge & Kegan Paul.

Drummond, A. (1995), *Law, Politics and Power: Sallust and the Execution of the Catilinarian*

Conspirators, Historia Einzelschrift 93. Stuttgart: Steiner.

Dugan, J. (2005), *Making a New Man: Ciceronian Self-fashioning in the Rhetorical Works*. Oxford: Oxford University Press.

Edwards, C. (1993), *The Politics of Immorality in Ancient Rome*. Cambridge: Cambridge University Press.

Everitt, A. (2003), *Cicero: The Life and Times of Rome's Greatest Politician*. New York: Random House.

Fantham (1997), 'The contexts and occasions of Roman public rhetoric', in W. J. Dominik (ed.), *Roman Eloquence: Rhetoric in Society and Literature*. London and New York: Routledge, pp. 111–28.

Flower, H. I. (ed.) (2004), *The Cambridge Companion to the Roman Republic*. Cambridge: Cambridge University Press.

—(1996), *Ancestor Masks and Aristocratic Power in Roman Culture*. Oxford: Oxford University Press.

Fotheringham, L. (2007), 'Having your cake and eating it: how Cicero combines arguments', in J. G. F. Powell (ed.), *Logos: Rational Argument in Classical Rhetoric*, BICS Supplement 96. London: Institute of Classical Studies, pp. 69–90.

Fuhrmann, M. (1990), *Cicero and the Roman Republic* (trans. W. E. Yuill). Oxford: Blackwell.

Garnsey, P. (1988), *Famine and Food Supply in the Graeco-Roman World*. Cambridge: Cambridge University Press.

Gelzer, M. (1969), *Roman Nobility* (trans. R. Seager). Oxford: Blackwell.

Gotoff, H. C. (1993), *Cicero's Caesarian Speeches: A Stylistic Commentary*. Chapel Hill: University of North Carolina Press.

Greenidge, A. H. J. (1901), *The Legal Procedure of Cicero's Time*. Oxford: Clarendon Press.

Griffin, M. (2003), 'Review of Butler: the hand of Cicero', *Journal of Roman Studies* 93: 364–5.

Gruen, E. (1974), *The Last Generation of the Roman Republic*. Berkeley: University of California Press.

Habicht, C. (1990), *Cicero the Politician*. Baltimore: Johns Hopkins University Press.

Habinek, T. (2005), *Ancient Rhetoric and Oratory*. Oxford: Blackwell.

Hardy, E. G. (1917), 'The Catilinarian conspiracy in its context: a re-study of the evidence', *Journal of Roman Studies* 7: 153–228.

Horsfall, N. (1989), *Cornelius Nepos: A Selection, Including the Lives of Cato and Atticus*. Oxford: Clarendon Press.

Hutchinson, G. O. (1998), *Cicero's Correspondence: A Literary Study*. Oxford: Clarendon Press.

Jones, C. P. (1987), 'Tattooing and branding in the Graeco-Roman antiquity', *Journal of Roman Studies* 77: 39–55.

Joyal, M., I. McDougall and J. Yardley (2009), *Greek and Roman Education: A Sourcebook*. London and New York: Routledge.

Kaster, R. A. (2006), *Marcus Tullius Cicero: 'Speech on behalf of Publius Sestius'*. Oxford: Clarendon Press.

Keaveney, A. (1988), *Rome and the Unification of Italy*. London and New York: Routledge.

Kennedy, G. (1994), *A New History of Classical Rhetoric*. Princeton, NJ: Princeton University Press.

—(1972), *The Art of Rhetoric in the Roman World*. Princeton, NJ: Princeton University Press.

—(1963), *The Art of Persuasion in Greece*. London: Routledge & Kegan Paul.

Lacey, W. K. (1978), *Cicero and the End of the Roman Republic*. London: Hodder & Stoughton.

Levick, B. (1982), 'Morals, politics, and the fall of the Roman Republic', *Greece and Rome* 29: 53–62.

Lewis, R. G. (2006), *Asconius: Commentaries on Speeches of Cicero*. Oxford: Clarendon Press.

Lintott, A. W. (2008), *Cicero as Evidence*. Oxford: Oxford University Press.

—(1999a), *The Constitution of the Roman Republic*. Oxford: Oxford University Press.

—(1999b), *Violence in Republican Rome*. Oxford: Oxford University Press (2nd edn; first published 1968).

—(1974), 'Cicero and Milo', *Journal of Roman Studies* 64: 62–78.

—(1972), 'Imperial expansion and moral decline in the Roman Republic', *Historia* 21: 626–38.

Mackay, C. S. (2009), *The Breakdown of the Roman Republic*. Cambridge: Cambridge University Press.

Manuwald, G. (2007), *Cicero, Philippics 3–9* (2 vols). Berlin and New York: Walter de Gruyter.

Marin, P. (2009), *Blood in the Forum: The Struggle for the Roman Republic*. London and New York: Continuum.

May, J. M. (ed.) (2002), *Brill's Companion to Cicero: Oratory and Rhetoric*. Leiden: Brill.

Millar, F. (1998), *The Crowd in Rome in the Late Republic*. Ann Arbor: University of Michigan Press.

Miller, J. F, C. Damon and K. S. Myers (eds) (2002), *Vertis in usum: Studies in Honor of E. Courtney*. Munich: Saur.

Mitchell, T. N. (1991), *Cicero: The Senior Statesman*. New Haven: Yale University Press.

—(1979), *Cicero: The Ascending Years*. New Haven: Yale University Press.

Morstein-Marx, R. (2004), *Mass Oratory and Political Power in the Late Roman Republic*. Cambridge: Cambridge University Press.

Mouritsen, H. (2001), *Plebs and Politics in the Late Roman Republic*. Cambridge: Cambridge University Press.

Nisbet, R. G. M. (1987), *Cicero: In L. Calpurnium Pisonem Oratio*. Oxford: Clarendon Press.

Patterson, J. R. (2000), *Political Life in the City of Rome*. Bristol: Bristol University Press.

Phillips, E. J. (1976), 'Catiline's conspiracy', *Historia* 25: 441–8.

Powell, J. G. F. (ed.) (2007), *Logos: Rational Argument in Classical Rhetoric*, BICS Supplement 96. London: Institute of Classical Studies.

—(ed.) (1995), *Cicero the Philosopher*. Oxford: Oxford University Press.

Powell, J. G. F. and J. J. Paterson (eds) (2004), *Cicero the Advocate*. Oxford: Oxford University Press.

Ramsey, J. T. (2007), *Sallust's Bellum Catilinae*. Oxford: Oxford University Press.

—(2003), *Cicero, Philippics I-II*. Cambridge: Cambridge University Press.

—(1980), 'The prosecution of C. Manilius in 66 BC and Cicero's pro Manilio', *Phoenix* 34: 323–36.

Rawson, E. (1975), *Cicero: A Portrait*. London: Allen Lane.

Rickman, G. (1980), *The Corn Supply of Ancient Rome*. Oxford: Clarendon Press.

Riggsby, A. M. (1997), 'Did the Romans believe in their verdicts?', *Rhetorica* 15(3): 235–52.

Robb, M. A. (2010), *Beyond* Populares *and* Optimates: *Political Language in the Late Republic*, Historia Einzelschriften 213. Stuttgart: Steiner.

Rosenstein, N. and R. Morstein-Marx (eds) (2006), *A Companion to the Roman Republic*. Oxford: Blackwell.

Rudd, N. and J. G. F. Powell (1998), *Cicero: The Republic, The Laws*. Oxford: Oxford University Press.

Schofield, M. (1995), 'Cicero's definition of *res publica*', in J. G. F. Powell (ed.), *Cicero the Philosopher*. Oxford: Oxford University Press, pp. 63–83.

Scullard, H. H. (1988), *From the Gracchi to Nero: A History of Rome from 133 BC to AD 68*. London and New York: Routledge (5th edn; first published 1959).

—(1964), 'The political career of a *novus homo*', in T. A. Dorey (ed.), *Cicero*. London: Routledge & Kegan Paul, pp. 1–25.

Seager, R. (2002), *Pompey the Great: A Political Biography*. Oxford: Blackwell (2nd edn; first published 1979).

—(1972), 'Cicero and the word *popularis*', *Classical Quarterly* 22: 328–38.

—(ed.) (1969), *The Crisis of the Roman Republic*. Cambridge: Cambridge University Press.

Shackleton Bailey, D. R. (2002), *Cicero: Letters to Quintus and Brutus. Letter Fragments. Letter to Octavian. Invectives. Handbook of Electioneering*. Cambridge, MA: Harvard University Press, Loeb Classical Library.

—(2001), *Cicero: Letters to Friends*, 3 vols. Cambridge, MA: Harvard University Press, Loeb Classical Library.

—(1999), *Cicero: Letters to Atticus*, 4 vols. Cambridge, MA: Harvard University Press, Loeb Classical Library.

—(1986), '*Nobiles* and *novi* reconsidered', *American Journal of Philology* 107: 255–60.

—(1971), *Cicero*. London: Duckworth.

Shatzman, I. (1975), *Senatorial Wealth and Roman Politics*, Collection Latomus 142. Brussels: Latomus.

Shotter, D. (1994), *Fall of the Roman Republic*. London and New York: Routledge.

Smith, C. J. and R. J. Covino (eds) (forthcoming, 2010), *Praise and Blame in Roman Oratory*. Swansea: Classical Press of Wales.

Stangl, T. (1964), *Ciceronis orationum scholiastae*. Hildesheim: G. Olms (photographic reprint of 1912 edn).

Steel, C. (2006), *Roman Oratory*, Greece & Rome, New Surveys in the Classics 36. Cambridge: Cambridge University Press.

—(2005), *Reading Cicero: Genre and Performance in Late Republican Rome*. London: Duckworth.

—(2001), *Cicero, Rhetoric and Empire*. Oxford: Oxford University Press.

Stevenson, T. and M. Wilson (eds) (2008), *Cicero's Philippics: History, Rhetoric and Ideology*, Prudentia 37–8. Auckland, NZ: Dept. of Classics and Ancient History, University of Auckland.

Stockton, D. (1971), *Cicero: A Political Biography*. Oxford: Oxford University Press.

Stroh, W. (2004), '*De Domo Sua*: legal problem and structure', in J. G. F. Powell and J. J. Paterson (eds), *Cicero the Advocate*. Oxford: Oxford University Press, pp. 313–70.

Swain, H. and M. E. Davies (2010), *Aspects of Roman History 82 BC–AD 14: A Source-Based Approach*. London and New York: Routledge.

Syme, R. (1939), *The Roman Revolution*. Oxford: Oxford University Press.

Tatum, J. (1999), *The Patrician Tribune Publius Clodius Pulcher*. Chapel Hill and London: University of North Carolina Press.

Taylor, D. (1973), *Cicero and Rome*. Basingstoke and London: Macmillan Education.

Taylor, L. R. (1949), *Party Politics in the Age of Caesar*. Berkeley and Los Angeles: University of California Press.

Tempest, K. L. (2010), 'Combating the odium of self-praise: Cicero's *Divinatio in Caecilium*', in C. J. Smith and R. J. Covino (eds), *Praise and Blame in Roman Republican Rhetoric*. Swansea: Classical Press of Wales, pp. 145–63.

—(2007), 'Cicero and the art of *dispositio*: the structure of the *Verrines*', *Leeds International Classical Studies* 6.02. Available at: http://www.leeds.ac.uk/classics/lics/2007/200702.pdf (accessed 21 September 2010)

Too, Y. L. (2001), *Education in Greek and Roman Antiquity*. Leiden: Brill.

Townend, G. B. (1964), 'The poems', in T. A. Dorey (ed.), *Cicero*. London: Routledge & Kegan Paul, pp. 109–34.

Treggiari, S. (2007), *Terentia, Tullia and Publilia: The Women of Cicero's Family*. London and New York: Routledge.

Usher, S. (2008), *Cicero's Speeches: The Critic in Action*. Oxford: Aris & Phillips.

—(1999), *Greek Oratory: Tradition and Originality*. Oxford: Oxford University Press.

Vasaly, A. (1993), *Representations: Images of the World in Ciceronian Oratory*. Berkeley: University of California Press.

Walsh, P. G. (2008), *Cicero: Selected Letters*. Oxford: Oxford University Press.

Whitby, M. (ed.) (1998), *The Propaganda of Power: The Role of Panegyric in Late Antiquity*. Leiden: Brill.

Wiedemann, T. (1994), *Cicero and the End of the Roman Republic*. Bristol: Bristol Classical Press.

Winterbottom, M. (2004), 'Perorations', in J. G. F. Powell and J. J. Paterson (eds), *Cicero the Advocate*. Oxford: Oxford University Press, pp. 215–30.

—(2002), 'Believing the *Pro Marcello*', in J. F. Miller, C. Damon and K. S. Myers (eds), *Vertis in usum: Studies in Honor of E. Courtney*. Munich: Saur, pp. 24–38.

Wirszubski, C. (1950), *Libertas as a Political Idea at Rome*. Cambridge: Cambridge University Press.

Wiseman, T. P. (ed.) (2002), *Classics in Progress: Essays on Ancient Greece and Rome*. Oxford: Oxford University Press.

—(1994), 'The senate and the *populares*: 69–60 BCE', in J. A. Crook, A. Lintott and E. Rawson (eds), *Cambridge Ancient History*, Vol. 9. Cambridge: Cambridge University Press (2nd edn), pp. 327–67.

—(1971), *New Men in the Roman Senate, 139 BC–AD 14*. Oxford: Oxford University Press.

Wisse, J. (2007), 'The riddle of the *Pro Milone*: the rhetoric of rational argument', in J. G. F. Powell (ed.), *Logos: Rational Argument in Classical Rhetoric*, BICS Supplement 96. London: Institute of Classical Studies, pp. 35–68.

Woodman, A. J. (2007), *Sallust: Catiline's War, the Jugurthine War and Histories*. Harmondsworth: Penguin.

Wooten, C. (1983), *Cicero's Philippics and their Demosthenic Model: The Rhetoric of Crisis*. Chapel Hill and London: University of North Carolina Press.

Index

The names of prominent figures are listed according to the form generally used in the text. Names are followed, where appropriate, by details of their most important political offices e.g. Cicero, Marcus Tullius (consul 63 BC). Numbers in italics indicate pages with illustrations.